THE PORTUGUESE IN WEST AFRICA, 1415–1670

The Portuguese in West Africa, 1415–1670, brings together a collection of documents – the majority in new English translation – that illustrate aspects of the encounters between the Portuguese and the peoples of north and west Africa. This period witnessed the diaspora of the Sephardic Jews, the emigration of Portuguese to west Africa and the islands, and the beginnings of the black diaspora associated with the slave trade. The documents show how the Portuguese tried to understand the societies with which they came into contact, and to reconcile their experience with the myths and legends inherited from classical and medieval learning. They also show how Africans reacted to the coming of Europeans, adapting Christian ideas to local beliefs and making use of exotic imports and European technologies. The documents also describe the evolution of the black Portuguese communities in Guinea and the islands, as well as the slave trade and the way that it was organized, understood and justified.

Malyn Newitt is Emeritus Professor in the Department of Portuguese and Brazilian Studies at King's College London. He is the author or editor of twelve books on Portuguese colonial history, including *History of Portuguese Overseas Expansion*, as well as multiple journal articles.

THE PORTUGUESE IN WEST AFRICA, 1415–1670

A Documentary History

Edited by

MALYN NEWITT
King's College London

CAMBRIDGE
UNIVERSITY PRESS

CAMBRIDGE UNIVERSITY PRESS
Cambridge, New York, Melbourne, Madrid, Cape Town, Singapore,
São Paulo, Delhi, Dubai, Tokyo, Mexico City

Cambridge University Press
32 Avenue of the Americas, New York, NY 10013-2473, USA

www.cambridge.org
Information on this title: www.cambridge.org/9780521159142

First published 2010

Printed in the United States of America

A catalog record for this publication is available from the British Library.

Library of Congress Cataloging in Publication data
The Portuguese in West Africa, 1415–1670 : a documentary history / [edited by]
Malyn Newitt.
p.   cm.
Includes bibliographical references and index.
ISBN 978-0-521-76894-8 (hardback)
1. Africa, West–Discovery and exploration–Portuguese–Sources.   2. Portuguese–Africa,
West–History–Sources.   3. Africa, West–History–To 1884–Sources.   4. Slave
trade–Africa, West–History–Sources.   I. Newitt, M. D. D.   II. Title.
DT472.P67 2010
303.48′2469060903–dc22   2010018052

ISBN 978-0-521-76894-8 Hardback
ISBN 978-0-521-15914-2 Paperback

CONTENTS

MAPS

PREFACE

This book was originally designed to be part of a series of publications (since discontinued) entitled Portuguese Encounters with the World in the Age of the Discoveries, and was to be the companion volume to the one on east Africa that was published by Ashgate in 2002. The general editor of the series laid down the format to which all the volumes were to conform. The object of the series was to provide a selection of original sources in English translation that would illustrate the interaction of the Portuguese with the peoples of Africa, Asia and America in the period from 1400 to 1700. The emphasis would be on the way Europeans and non-Europeans reacted to these first contacts, and how their mentalities and cultures were changed by the experience. This volume follows closely the original conception of the Portuguese Encounters series.

Anyone approaching the history of the Portuguese in northern and western Africa soon becomes dependent on the great collections of documents edited by Pierre de Cenival, António Brásio and Louis Jadin, which have never been translated into English. English readers have had to rely on the publications of the Hakluyt Society and the scholarly volumes edited by Paul Hair and Avelino Teixeira da Mota. These are the main sources from which the documents in this collection have been drawn, supplemented with extracts from von Ehingen, Pigafetta, Cadornega, Carletti, the Anonymous Pilot who wrote about São Tomé and the manuscript of Valentim Fernandes.

I am immensely grateful for the scholarly insights and editorial skills of John Villiers, the General Editor of the original Portuguese Encounters series. His vision and persistence are responsible for the appearance of the volumes, which have contributed substantially to widening the understanding of Portuguese expansion in the English-speaking world.

I would especially like to acknowledge help with translation received from Alexander Keese and Maria Eduarda Pinheiro.

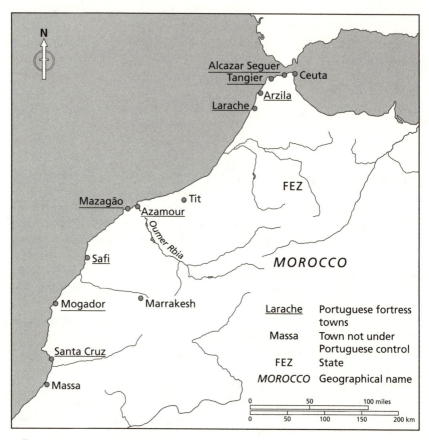

N

Alcazar Seguer
Tangier ● Ceuta
Arzila
Larache

FEZ

Mazagão ● Tit
Azamour
Oumer Rbia

Safi
MOROCCO

Mogador ● Marrakesh

Santa Cruz

Massa

Larache	Portuguese fortress towns
Massa	Town not under Portuguese control
FEZ	State
MOROCCO	Geographical name

0   50   100 miles

0   50   100   150   200 km

Portuguese possessions in Morocco.

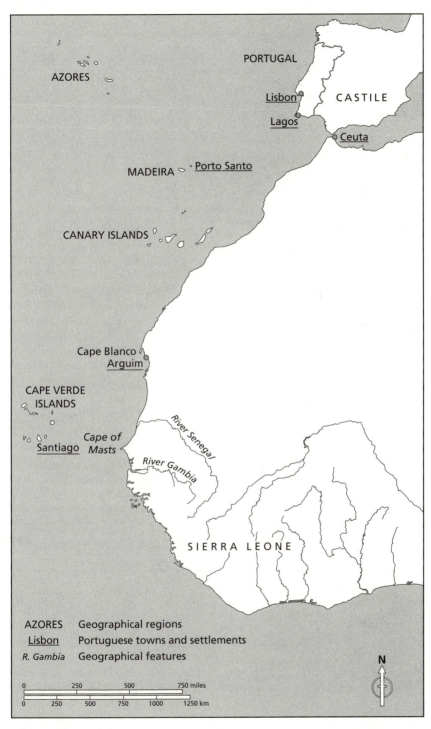

PORTUGAL

AZORES

Lisbon

CASTILE

Lagos

Ceuta

MADEIRA Porto Santo

CANARY ISLANDS

Cape Blanco
Arguim

CAPE VERDE
ISLANDS

River Senegal

Cape of
Masts

Santiago

River Gambia

SIERRA LEONE

AZORES   Geographical regions
Lisbon   Portuguese towns and settlements
R. Gambia Geographical features

0   250   500   750 miles
0   250   500   750   1000   1250 km

N

The north-east Atlantic.

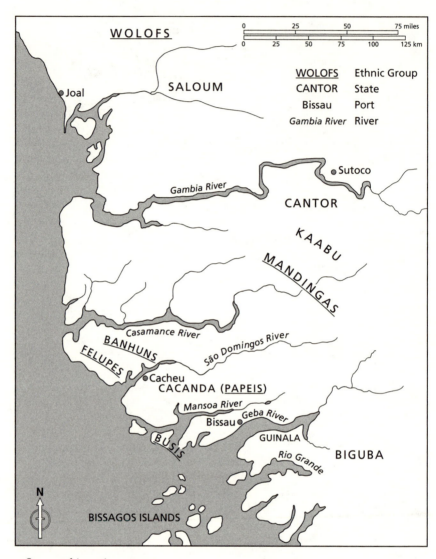

Senegambia region.

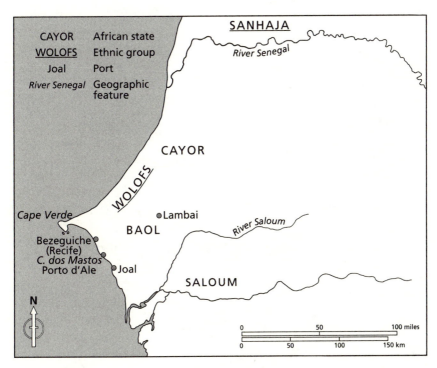

Upper Guinea.

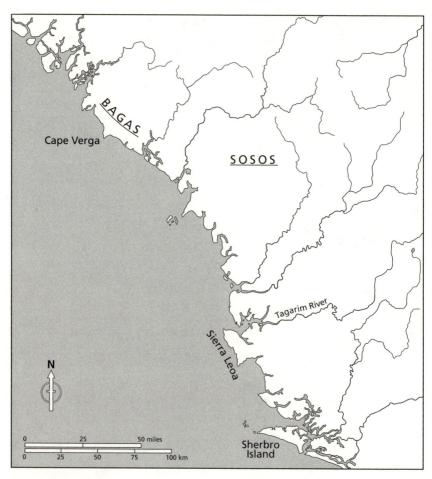

Sierra Leone region.

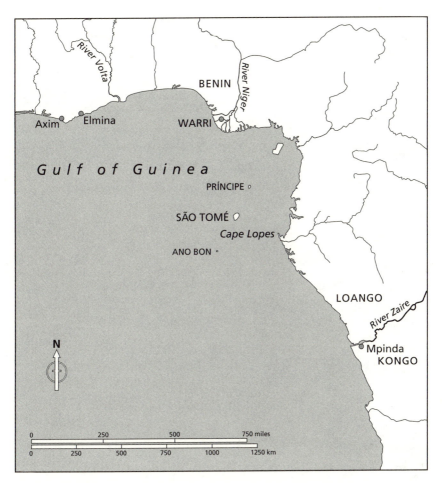

Gulf of Guinea.

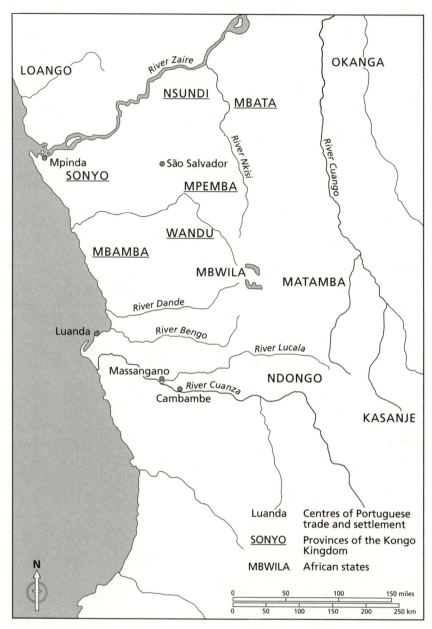

Kongo and Angola.

INTRODUCTION

The Creation of the Atlantic World

In the fifteenth and early sixteenth centuries, Portugal and Spain developed two economic and political systems in the Atlantic, comparable in many respects with the Mediterranean world which had dominated the culture and economy of Europe, north Africa and the Middle East since the days of the Greek and Persian empires. These Atlantic worlds linked western Africa, the eastern coasts of North and South America and the Atlantic coastline of Europe and north Africa, and included wholly new societies brought into being in the Atlantic islands. The Spanish Atlantic system eventually extended to the Pacific, the Philippines and China, while the Portuguese system was linked to the empire that Portugal created in the Indian Ocean. These systems were built up through constantly expanding and increasingly interdependent economic activity, and by migrations of population and the cultural interplay of religions and ideas from all four continents. One of the first consequences of this interdependence was that diseases that were endemic in one continent, and plant and animal species from hitherto ecologically distinct areas, now spread throughout the Atlantic basin. Moreover, although these imperial systems were based on old and established practices, their novelty and very size demanded new concepts of law and sovereignty.

The northern parts of the Atlantic, including North and Central America and the Caribbean basin, for some time remained a Spanish world, with the Canary Islands as an outlying fragment; the southern part of the ocean, in turn, was almost exclusively Portuguese. This 'Portuguese South Atlantic' originated as an enterprise sponsored, and controlled, by the Portuguese Crown through official expeditions and embassies, the appointment of royal governors and the operation of royal trade monopolies. However, this was only a part of the story, and by the seventeenth century much of this south Atlantic system

1

had evolved beyond the effective control of Lisbon. There were many people other than the Crown's immediate servants who embarked on economic enterprises and territorial expansion, or who were uprooted from their homelands to people this new world. The Portuguese Crown also enlisted many client groups to aid its enterprises. These included soldiers of fortune of many different nationalities, merchants, sugar growers and financiers from Italy, and later Africans and native Brazilians. Entrepreneurs, some of them Italians, were awarded captaincies in the uninhabited Atlantic islands, which they undertook to settle and which they developed in ways that sometimes ran counter to the interests of Lisbon, while the royal governors of the Moroccan fortresses and of the colony based at Luanda carried out their campaigns in search of booty and slaves with scant regard to any policy objectives laid down in Portugal. Other agencies were also at work. The missions sent out by the Church were, at first, instruments of royal policy, but by the end of the sixteenth century were acting largely independently of Lisbon. The Jesuits and the authorities of the Inquisition operated according to their own perceived objectives, while the direct intervention of Rome in the final years of the sixteenth century, and papal encouragement of non-Portuguese missionary orders, such as the Italian Capucins, challenged the control of the African Church by the Portuguese Crown.

Similarly, following the establishment of forts and factories in South America, Brazilian interests also became an agency in west African affairs and operated with little reference to the policies of Lisbon. By the seventeenth century, Brazilians traded directly with western Africa, supplying ships and trade goods and, in the years following the Dutch seizure of Luanda in 1641 when the Portuguese Crown was hard pressed in Europe, even providing governors and soldiers to reconquer and defend the Portuguese possessions in Angola.

Portuguese overseas expansion can also be understood as three separate but interconnected diasporas – three streams of migrants who mingled to form the new communities of the Atlantic world. One migrant stream was provided by ordinary people leaving the poverty-stricken rural communities of Portugal to make their living at sea or to search for new land in the islands on which to settle. Many of these eventually moved on from the islands to the mainlands of Africa and America as traders and settlers, carrying with them their language, religion, technical skills and networks of contacts.

These Christian Portuguese migrants met and mingled with the diaspora of the Sephardic Jews. The expulsion of the Iberian Jews who would not convert to Christianity took place in the final decade of the fifteenth century. Although many moved away from the territories of the

Iberian rulers altogether, others found that the Portuguese communities that were being formed in the Atlantic were more tolerant of religious difference. Many Jews went either to north Africa and settled in the fortified Portuguese port towns, or to the islands and the mainland trading posts, from where they could put down roots in the coastal African societies. Most of the Portuguese communities in west Africa had numbers of so-called New Christians (*cristãos novos*), who practised their ancestral Judaism more or less openly (Docs. 4, 15 and 56). Others moved to Brazil and played a large part in the development of the sugar industry, enjoying official toleration during the period of the Dutch occupation (1630–54) and spreading from there to the non-Portuguese world of the Caribbean and the north Atlantic.

The third diaspora was that of Africans, sold as slaves by their compatriots on the mainland and taken to Portugal, the islands and the Americas. These forced emigrants contributed substantially to the peopling of the Portuguese Atlantic, supplementing the limited numbers of settlers that mainland Portugal was able to provide. To a large extent, the Portuguese South Atlantic of the sixteenth and seventeenth centuries was a creole world – peopled by the mixed descendants of Portuguese and Africans, speaking creole dialects of the Portuguese language, practising religions heavily coloured by African as well as European ideas and developing a texture of culture that owed its richness to European, Judaic and African traditions.

Medieval Portugal's Interaction with the Non-European World

Portugal, like Castile and Aragon, had a long tradition of contacts with the non-European world. Until the reconquest of the Algarve in 1249, southern Portugal had been part of the Islamic world of north Africa, and thereafter an Islamic and Jewish population continued to inhabit the south under Christian overlords. Commercial contacts with north Africa continued, and Christian Portuguese soldiers were often to be found fighting in the wars in Morocco. Portugal remained a country where Islamic, Judaic and Christian cultural influences met one another and merged, the mixture being constantly enriched by the import of slaves. The Portuguese obtained slaves from Muslim north Africa and, in the fourteenth century, took part in raids on the Canary Islands to capture slaves from among the native Guanches. Meanwhile, the Portuguese themselves were liable to be carried away as slaves to north Africa whenever the Moroccans raided the southern coasts of Portugal.

While medieval Portugal interacted constantly with the northwest Atlantic seaboard of Africa, it was also increasingly involved in the political struggles of northern Europe and the commercial expansion of the Italian cities. The struggle for power between the Plantagenet rulers of England and the Capetian dynasty of France overflowed into the Iberian peninsula, and English, French and Castilian armies operated in northern Spain and Portugal, interfering in Portuguese politics and threatening the independence of the Portuguese kingdom. In 1385, one of the decisive battles of the Hundred Years War was fought at Aljubarrota north of Lisbon, where an Anglo-Portuguese force defeated an army made up of French and Castilians and installed a new dynasty under João, the Master of Avis and bastard son of the former king Dom Pedro.

These wars saw the growth of a military class, which depended for its status and its fortune upon plunder, ransoms, patronage, the seizure of land and the spoils of war in general. In 1411 Portugal was eventually able to make peace with Castile, but the military class of nobles and knights continued to demand opportunities for advancement and an outlet for their energies. So, in 1415, ten days after Henry V of England opened a new phase of the Hundred Years War with his invasion of Normandy, his uncle by marriage, Dom João I of Portugal, launched an invasion of Morocco. The attack on the north African port-city of Ceuta was an official enterprise, planned and carried out by the king's sons, the Royal Council and the agents of the Crown. The intention was to establish a bridgehead for the conquest of Morocco, and this aspect of the plan was supported by most of the leading nobility. The propaganda of the time represented this attack as a crusade against Islam, and Zurara, the chronicler who recorded the events thirty years later, shaped his narrative to reflect the ideals of chivalry in the same way that Jean Froissart, on whom he modelled his chronicles, had dignified the massacres and plundering raids of the Hundred Years War (Doc. 1).

Throughout the fifteenth century, the conquest of Morocco remained a royal project. An unsuccessful attack on Tangier in 1437 was followed – once the young king, Afonso 'O Africano', came of age – by the capture of Alcazar Seguer (the modern Ksar es Sghir) in 1458 and the surrender of Arzila and Tangier in 1471. This gave Portugal control of a strip of the northern coastline of Morocco. Dom João II (1481–95) attempted only one ill-considered campaign in Morocco, but his successor, Dom Manuel, encouraged the renewal of attempts to conquer territory. Between 1504 and 1514, the Portuguese captured and occupied most of the port-towns on the Atlantic coast of Morocco, including Safi, Mazagão, Mogador, Azamour and Agadir (called at that time Santa Cruz). It was only after the defeat of the Portuguese army at Mamora in 1514 that the conquest of

Morocco was recognized to be impractical, though none of the garrison towns was evacuated until the 1540s.

The capture of these Moroccan towns and the need to garrison them against the constant threat of attack meant that the Portuguese had to maintain an army at great expense. The Moroccan fortresses became a military frontier where generations of Portuguese soldiers were trained and saw their first active service. It was in these fortresses that outdated religious and military values were cultivated and became entrenched. Portuguese and Moroccans squared up to each other on the battlefield, re-enacting archaic rituals of single combat (Doc. 2), while the Portuguese commanders in the fortresses looked for opportunities to mount raids on the countryside to carry off prisoners, cattle and moveable goods (Docs. 5 and 6), as had been customary in the Iberian peninsula before the completion of the *Reconquista*.

Alongside the raids, however, a more peaceful interaction was taking place. Many Moroccans sought protection against plundering raids by recognizing Portuguese overlordship, and the Portuguese reciprocated by developing a thriving trade in horses, textiles and foodstuffs (Doc. 3). Jews expelled from mainland Portugal also settled in the Portuguese towns in north Africa and negotiated protection for themselves, the traditional tolerance of the Portuguese reasserting itself outside the borders of the kingdom of Portugal (Doc. 4). In these documents, one can see an informal empire of trade, religious toleration and cultural assimilation coming into existence alongside, and often in opposition to, the military purposes of the Crown and the aristocracy.

West African Trade

While the Crown and the military aristocracy took the lead in attempting to make conquests in Morocco, settlements were being made in the Atlantic islands. Although peace had been signed with Castile in 1411, adventurers from the two countries continued to compete for land and slaves in the Canary Islands. Slavers from both Portugal and Castile had regularly raided these islands in the fourteenth century, and various claims to seigneurial rights had been registered. The raiding continued in the fifteenth century with the difference that both Castilians and Portuguese now tried to establish permanent settlements, and frequently clashed with each other as well as with the native inhabitants. The attempt to control the islands should be seen in the same context as the warfare in Morocco. Like the Moroccan expeditions, the Portuguese fleets that attacked the Canaries were organized by members of the military aristocracy and were strongly backed by the Infante Dom Henrique

('Henry the Navigator'). Major expeditions were sent in 1425 and again during the 1440s and 1450s. In this war of raid and counter-raid, the Castilians gradually gained the upper hand, and eventually, in 1479, the Portuguese recognized Castilian sovereignty over the islands. Their subsequent conquest and division into *encomiendas* took place in the 1490s at exactly the time that Columbus was establishing the first Castilian settlements in the Caribbean.

It was this rivalry with Castile that prompted the Portuguese to advance their claims to the other island groups. Madeira and the Azores were uninhabited and had only occasionally been visited by sailors looking for a convenient landfall. However, in 1419 the Portuguese formally took possession of Madeira, and after 1431 began to establish themselves in the Azores. Once again, the nobility and the Crown became involved, eager to secure seigneurial rights to these new settlements. The islands were distributed as 'captaincies', a form of feudal overlordship that promoted the entrepreneurial settlement of the islands while preserving the essential rights of the Crown. The Infantes Henrique and Pedro secured titles to the islands and placed their own followers as hereditary captains. Henry also secured the ecclesiastical rights for the Order of Christ of which he was governor, having previously obtained similar privileges in Morocco.

However, the peopling of the islands was not entirely a royal enterprise. Once the first island settlements had been planted, considerable numbers of peasant farmers and fishermen migrated from Portugal. During the fourteenth century, the Portuguese countryside had become increasingly deserted. The Black Death had taken its toll while the poverty of the land and the custom of establishing *morgados* (entailed estates) discouraged peasant agriculture. The *Lei das Sesmarias* of 1375, which created a legal framework for bringing wasteland back into cultivation, was a sign that the Crown was aware of a serious social and economic malaise. More and more people moved to the coastal towns to seek employment in commerce and maritime activities. Madeira and the Azores offered attractive opportunities for farmers, as their soils and climate were extremely favourable, and they provided bases for commercial enterprise and deep-sea fishing.

Also involved in the island settlements were Italian entrepreneurs. Ever since the thirteenth century, the Italian city states had been increasing their trade with north Africa and northern Europe, and an Italian colony grew up in Lisbon as the city became an important port of call for ships bound from the Mediterranean to the north. There was also a Genoese factory in Ceuta at the time of the Portuguese conquest. The Italian presence in Portugal led to the spread of Mediterranean expertise in ship design, map making and navigation, and to the Italians becoming partners in the entrepreneurial activities of the Portuguese kings. It was Genoese sugar growers looking for new land who became involved in the settlement of Madeira and the Azores, providing capital and setting up the first sugar industry in the islands. Italians were also to be prominent among the ship owners and traders who began to exploit the new commercial outlets in Africa. The Perestrello family were involved in the settlement of Madeira, Antonio di Noli was the first captain of Santiago in the Cape Verde Islands and a Venetian, Alvise da Cadamosto, not only traded to Senegambia but wrote the first detailed account of the island settlements and the trading activities on the African coast, giving a vivid picture of Europe's first encounters with sub-Saharan Africa (Docs. 11, 16 and 17).

The same combination of official enterprise and the activity of clients under contract to the Crown was to be followed when other island groups were discovered. The Cape Verde Islands were discovered and explored in the 1450s and 1460s, and once again Italians were foremost in their exploration and settlement, the institutional device of captaincies being used to secure their development. Here the Portuguese again faced Castilian competition, and during the war of 1474–79, the Castilians briefly occupied Santiago and claimed possession of the archipelago. Then, when the Guinea Islands were discovered in the 1470s, entrepreneurial captains were once again appointed to try to secure their settlement and commercial development.

Meanwhile, the traditional Portuguese practices of privateering and slaving were leading to the growth of commercial links with the African mainland. Ships would be sent to sea, either by their owners or sponsored by noblemen, to secure prizes and slaves to sell or important prisoners to ransom. If all else failed, the boats could return with a stinking cargo of seal pelts and oil. It was these privateers who first discovered the commercial potential of what appeared to be a barren Sahara coastline. In the 1430s, seamen began to raid the undefended villages of the coast, carrying off women and children and ransoming men of importance. Such raids put the local population on their guard, so that each year the raiders had to travel further to find undefended coastal villages (Docs. 8 and 9). In this way the raiders became explorers, seeking out ever more remote stretches of coastline. On one of these raids, contact was made with desert traders, who offered gold in exchange for foodstuffs and metal ware. The availability of gold attracted a lot of attention, and in 1443 it was decided to establish a permanent trading post on the island of Arguim off the coast of modern Mauretania, which the Crown leased to a consortium of merchants.

Gold whetted the appetite of men of all classes, but the profitability of such speculative voyages remained in doubt until the return of a raiding expedition commanded by Lançerote in 1444. The excitement caused by the arrival at Lagos of a large consignment of slaves was graphically described by the chronicler Zurara, who gave it a central place in his narrative of the discovery and conquest of Guinea (Doc. 35).

By the 1450s, the trade in gold and slaves was attracting a lot of interest from Portuguese nobles and merchants, and also from non-Portuguese, principally Castilians and Italians. The Portuguese royal family was involved to the extent that it took care to secure the Crown's fiscal and juridical interests. All ecclesiastical rights were vested in the Order of Christ, while the Crown declared the trade of Africa to be a royal preserve, which meant that all merchants had to receive a royal licence and a 'fifth' had to be paid on trading profits. These royal prerogatives were granted to the Infante Dom Henrique who secured papal Bulls, which recognized the exclusive rights of the Portuguese Crown. However, such extensive privileges had to be effectively enforced against interlopers, especially during Portugal's war with Castile from 1474 to 1479 when the Castilians made a concerted attempt to breach the Portuguese monopoly.

Meanwhile, new communities with a distinct creole identity were emerging in the islands. Migrants from Portugal were ready enough to settle Madeira, which was relatively close to Portugal. However, fewer people went to the Azores and fewer still to Cape Verde and distant Guinea. Some of the captains tried to recruit settlers from the Netherlands and Italy, and it seems that one of the captains of São Tomé in the Gulf of Guinea arranged for Jewish children, taken from parents who refused to convert, to be consigned as colonists to the tropics. However, it was the importation of slaves from Africa that eventually secured the demographic success of the island colonies. Although considerable numbers of slaves were brought to Madeira to work the sugar plantations, the Portuguese element in the population always predominated. In Cape Verde and São Tomé, however, imported slaves soon became the most important element in the population. Portuguese settlers took African wives and their descendants formed a free black population, which retained strong cultural links with mainland Africa and had correspondingly fewer direct ties with Portugal.

These Afro-Portuguese creole communities established commercial relations with the African mainland, operating largely independently of the Portuguese Crown and its representatives. A new 'Portuguese' diaspora now began. Not only were people leaving Portugal to settle the islands and to man the trading and slaving ships, but the islands themselves were becoming the springboard for onward migration and further expansion. One of the captains of Madeira mounted his own slaving expeditions (Doc. 9), while ship owners based in the Azores began exploratory voyages westwards in search of new islands to settle. Meanwhile, the creole inhabitants of the Cape Verde and Guinea islands were themselves moving to the African mainland to trade, settle and make their fortunes. The interests of these islanders were soon to clash with those of the Crown.

The Crown Tries to Recover the Initiative

The Infante Dom Henrique had held the right to licence and tax traders going to west Africa but, after his death in 1460, the Crown's interest in Africa and the islands declined. The Cape Verde and Guinea islands were granted to captains and the right to trade in west Africa was leased to Fernão Gomes, a Lisbon merchant. The interests of Afonso V were clearly and explicitly focused on Morocco and latterly in trying to secure the throne of Castile. It was his bid for the Castilian throne that led to the war from 1474 to 1479. During that war, the Castilians organized fleets to trade in west African waters and to challenge the Portuguese occupation of the Cape Verde islands. The danger was perceived to be so great that the king appointed his son, the Infante Dom João, to take control of all the west African enterprises. João not only proved effective in fighting off the Castilian challenge, but devised a coherent strategy for a more direct exploitation of the economic opportunities in western Africa. So successful was he in the first of these that, when the peace of Alcáçovas was negotiated with Castile in 1479, Portugal was able to write into the agreement clauses recognizing its sovereignty in four of the five island groups so-far discovered, as well as its exclusive right to control west African trade. Only in the Canary Islands did Portugal have to abandon its claims in favour of Castile.

Having secured for Portugal exclusive rights to trade in west African waters, Dom João, who became king in 1481, decided to build a fortified settlement in the centre of the gold trading region and to make the gold trade a royal monopoly. The fortress of Elmina, which was established by Diogo de Azambuja in 1482, was not like the Moroccan fortresses in that it was not intended to be a base for raiding the surrounding country or a launching pad for conquest (Doc. 22). It was a trading factory, whose fortifications were aimed primarily at discouraging other Europeans, or even other subjects of the Portuguese Crown, from breaching the trading monopoly. It was to be the blueprint for many such fortified factories that were later to be built in the Indian Ocean.

Dom João also pursued a policy of making alliances with important African rulers. These would be cemented where possible by the conversion of the ruler to Christianity, thereby enabling Portuguese trade to expand and rivals to be kept at bay. The king's third objective was to find a sea passage to India and to ensure that such a vital strategic discovery would be made by Portugal and not by any of its rivals.

A number of traders had already made direct contact with African rulers, and Cadamosto's friendly and inquisitive account of his dealings with the rulers of Senegambia feature in Docs. 16 and 17. Dom João, however, wanted such contacts to be made whenever possible between two rulers. So, when he heard that Diogo Cão, a captain in his service, had established relations with a powerful king who controlled the land on the southern bank of the Zaire estuary, it became one of his priorities to turn this discovery into a firm alliance. The embassy of 1491 (Docs. 25, 26 and 27) had consequences that must have been as unexpected as they were gratifying. The ruler of the coastal province of Sonyo, and later the king himself, eagerly embraced Christianity and allowed a group of Portuguese, who included priests among their number, to establish themselves in his country.

João's third objective was less easily achieved. The king believed that a sea route to the East was within his grasp, and was determined that it would be a royal initiative that would secure it for Portugal. When Diogo Cão returned to Portugal to report on his visit to the Kongo region, Dom João informed the Papacy that the route to India was open. It seems that the same year he rejected the approaches of Columbus – which was not surprising as Columbus was seeking extensive control for himself over anything that he might discover. Cão was dispatched on another expedition, and after his death Bartolomeu Dias was sent to continue his work, while two spies went in disguise overland to report on the commercial centres of the East and to establish contact with the Christian ruler of Ethiopia. Dias returned in 1489, having found the sea route around the end of Africa, but the king did not immediately follow up this discovery. His more immediate concern was to send an embassy to Kongo, a clear indication that, at that time, developing royal trade in western Africa took precedence over establishing trade with India.

Cultural Interaction

The fifty years that culminated in the conversion of the Kongolese aristocracy in 1491 had seen numerous encounters between Europeans and Africans, while the streams of emigrants emanating from Portugal and Africa had met in the islands and had begun the creation of a creole culture. The records of these early encounters were collected by the chroniclers, Zurara, Rui de Pina and João de Barros, and turned into elegant and scholarly narratives. As few of those who had been to west Africa wrote about their experiences, it is not surprising that most contemporaries described and sought to understand the newly observed cultures of black Africa within a matrix of received ideas. Classical learning and medieval legend formed the basis for the world view of educated fifteenth-century Europeans, which it was the perceived task of the Renaissance scholar to reconcile with the reported experiences of seamen and the scientific observations of ships' pilots. So Ptolemy's geography continued to influence cartographers, even as they received the reports and charts of contemporary navigators, and the accounts of Africa contained in Herodotus and the classical ideas of the natural world as described by Pliny continued to appear alongside live reports from returning adventurers. The best example of legend becoming reconciled with experience is the case of Prester John, the medieval story of a priest-king eventually being squared with the existence of a Christian ruler in Ethiopia. In this collection, Duarte Pacheco Pereira examines various theories that explain differences of skin colour while trying to fit the medieval tales of dog-headed people into what he knows of Africa from his own experience. Both he and Cadamosto report on silent trade, as did Herodotus, another convenient coming together of classical and contemporary knowledge (Doc. 10).

If Cadamosto's open-minded and cosmopolitan Venetian upbringing allowed him to observe and understand what he saw in Africa without being too concerned to make it fit into received knowledge, the royal chroniclers of Portugal had a more difficult task. Their works were part history and part propaganda and public relations. Events had to be recorded and interpreted to match the professed ideals and values of the ruling elites of the time. This could generate singular tensions, as when Zurara questioned whether the Azaneghi could really be cannibals (Doc. 8) and whether the selling of people into slavery could be reconciled with Christian ethics, even when carried out by the Infante Dom Henrique, the Christian hero of the chronicle (Doc. 35).

Where misinterpretation and misunderstanding seem to become almost wilful is in the case of the conversion of the Kongo. The contemporary chronicler Rui de Pina, and his successors Damião de Gois and João de Barros writing a generation later, record the conversion of this African kingdom as a miraculous Christian narrative that could almost have come from the lives of one of the saints. However, while the story of the conversion and the subsequent triumph of the Christian prince, Afonso, is being told, the chroniclers are also recording in some detail the political struggles and the social tensions that accompanied the introduction of a new cult into a major African kingdom. Christianity, once introduced, becomes a royal burial cult controlled from the centre by the king, while Christian ideas of marriage and inheritance compete with traditional practices in which rival lineages contest the succession (Doc. 39). Africa and Europe are meeting not in confrontation, but with the creative tensions that create a unique creole culture (Docs. 26, 27 and 29).

However, cultural exchange was not always one way. It was not only Africa that received and absorbed new ideas and material culture, for the sixteenth century witnessed numerous instances of Portuguese leaving their own communities and settling among the Africans of the mainland, marrying local women and modifying their religion and way of life to fit in with the customs and practices of their hosts. These were the *tangomaos* and *lançados* who were the founding fathers of Atlantic creole culture, but who were so often denounced by visiting priests for their dubious morals and heretical beliefs. They were also deeply distrusted by the king, as they undermined the Crown's trade monopolies and commercial agreements with African sovereigns (Docs. 21, 51 and 57).

The Official and Unofficial Empires in the Sixteenth Century

In 1494, Portugal and Castile signed the Treaty of Tordesillas, which divided the Atlantic along a line of longitude running 370 leagues west of Cape Verde. This treaty dividing oceanic space, when placed alongside the papal Bulls that had granted spiritual rights to the Order of Christ, created the juridical basis for Portugal's south Atlantic empire. In 1499, Vasco da Gama returned to Lisbon having opened up the sea route to India, and the following year Cabral announced the discovery of the mainland of Brazil. Da Gama's voyage seemed to offer Portugal an immense opportunity to expand its riches and power and led to the creation of the *Estado da Índia* five years later. Cabral's landfall in Brazil, which seemed much less immediately promising, nevertheless completed the boundaries of the Portuguese Atlantic. Soon the Portuguese would be creating a south Atlantic system of trade, migration and social interaction that would bring America, the islands and Africa into close and continuing contact with each other. The south Atlantic would become an economic and cultural system every bit as coherent and interactive as the Indian Ocean or the Mediterranean.

During the first thirty years of the sixteenth century the Portuguese Crown, while claiming sovereignty over the seas and control of the Catholic Church in the whole south Atlantic region, limited its direct activity to two areas. The first was the gold trade centred on Elmina castle and its outlying port of Axim. This remained a very profitable undertaking for the Crown, whose monopoly was not seriously challenged until the last years of the century. The second area of direct Crown activity was the kingdom of Kongo, where a royal trading factory was established and where the king of Portugal in alliance with the Manikongo claimed a monopoly of trade and direct control over the Kongolese Church.

The alliance between Portugal and the Kongo had many strands to it, but the adoption of a Christian cult by the ruling elites of the Kongo remains an exceptional example of the creolization of an African ruling class taking place without prior conquest by a European power. The Kongolese aristocracy adopted Portuguese names, titles, coats of arms and styles of dress, and imported material goods from Portugal. The king of Kongo sent youths from the elite families to Europe for education (Doc. 42) and had one of his sons consecrated in Rome as a bishop. Many of the Kongo elite became literate and were ordained as priests in the local church, while the kings sent embassies to Rome and maintained correspondence with the popes (Doc. 45). Christian festivals were observed, churches and chapels were erected and local craftsmen made Christian religious artefacts. Religious brotherhoods were founded and orders of 'knighthood' instituted in imitation of Portuguese practice (Docs. 46, 52 and 53). The king of Kongo received regular gifts from Portugal of prestige goods and was able to import European manufactures.

Portuguese priests took charge of the royal Christian cult, which was controlled by the Crown and undoubtedly strengthened the king of Kongo's authority. However, this cult also caused opposition from 'traditionalists', and the kings remained very dependent on the continued support of Lisbon. This can be seen in many plaintive letters written by King Afonso, in which he tries to strengthen his alliance with a Portuguese Crown that was increasingly preoccupied with the affairs of India, and whose interest in the Kongo was largely confined to securing the continuation of the slave trade (Doc. 41).

Although the conversion of the king to Christianity was gratifying and played well to the religious ideologies of the Portuguese monarchy, the real reward was the access it gave Portugal to the Kongo markets. The Portuguese bought items important in local trade such as fine quality bark cloths, *cori* beads and *nzimbu* shells, but their chief interest was to purchase slaves. Many of these slaves were exported to other markets in Africa or to the island of São Tomé to supply labour for the sugar plantations, but it was the growth of the American market that made the trade of Kongo especially important. The Tordesillas Treaty had left the whole of Africa in the Portuguese half of the world, and the Portuguese were anxious to continue to exclude the Castilians. However, this could only be achieved if the Portuguese themselves met the Castilian demand for slave labour. As the slave trade grew, relations between the Portuguese and the Kongo king became ever more strained (Doc. 36).

While the affairs of Elmina and the Kongo were directly under the authority of the Crown, the rest of western Africa was treated in a different way. The trade with the Niger delta and Arguim, for example, continued to be leased to contractors, while the islands developed under the rule of their captains with a minimum of direct Crown interference. It was the captaincy of São Tomé that caused the greatest problem. As this island was situated close to Kongo, the captain and the islanders were determined to participate in the commerce of the kingdom. This was in direct contravention to royal policy, and Doc. 30 shows the extent to which the captain was able to interfere with the smooth operation of relations between the king of Kongo and Portugal.

The king of Portugal reacted to this direct challenge to his authority by abolishing the captaincy and bringing São Tomé directly under the control of a royal governor. At the same time, the king used his right of patronage over the Church to establish a bishopric in São Tomé in 1534, which had responsibility for ordering Church affairs in the whole of western Africa from Elmina southwards, a see that included the Kongo kingdom. However, direct royal government in São Tomé was easier to decree than to implement. The disease environment in the island was so hostile (Doc. 12) that many governors died and others refused to take up their appointment. Bishops were similarly either absentees or short-lived. Local power passed into the hands of the *Senado da Câmara* and the cathedral Chapter, both of which were made up of representatives of the local Afro-Portuguese families. Creole São Tomé had a certain dynamism and expanded its commercial activity in all directions. Traders from São Tomé were active along the African seaboard from Elmina to the coast of modern Angola. They bought spoiled trade goods from the factor at Elmina (Doc. 23) to trade in the Niger delta, where an informal Portuguese community grew up in Benin and Itsekiri, supplemented from time to time with Christian missionaries. Men from São Tomé were also actively running contraband into Kongo, and it was they who first settled on the coast near Luanda Island to exploit the *nzimbu* shell fishery and the trade opportunities in the interior. At the same time, the tiny island became increasingly torn by civil strife. The settlers were faced with periodic slave revolts and with communities of escaped slaves (maroons) living in the interior (Doc. 14). There were also frequent disputes with the bishops who accused the islanders of being New Christians or crypto-Jews (Doc. 15).

Until the last quarter of the century, the islands remained prosperous and produced large annual cargoes of sugar for the European market (Doc. 13). However, in the 1590s, São Tomé was attacked by the Dutch, and this, together with the frequent maroon wars, caused most of the sugar planters to relocate to Brazil, taking with them their expertise and accumulated capital, and in this way weaving one more strand into the web of interdependency between Africa, Europe and America.

The other centre of the Portuguese informal empire was in the Cape Verde Islands where the main item of trade was slaves. These were obtained by the Afro-Portuguese from African brokers, and brought to Cape Verde where they were taught some rudiments of the Portuguese language, and it was to Cape Verde that buyers for the American market came in search of cargoes. The islanders also developed a cloth-weaving industry and Cape Verdian cotton fabrics established an important position in the African market.

The close commercial ties with the mainland resulted in Afro-Portuguese towns growing up on the tidal rivers of upper Guinea, where the communities of traders developed complex relations with the local African kingdoms. Although the Portuguese built some fortified settlements, like the one at Cacheu constructed in the 1580s, these only existed with the consent of the local kings (Doc. 51). Some rulers were scrupulous in their dealings with the motley Portuguese community of traders, exiles and priests, but it was always possible for some incident to sour relations. The roads to the interior would then be closed and Afro-Portuguese traders robbed or even murdered. Moreover, African politics were a shifting kaleidoscope and the Portuguese found that they were dealing with an endlessly changing structure of political power and ethnic relations, which they struggled to understand. Although writing in the early seventeenth century, the Jesuit Manuel Álvares's attempt to assemble the knowledge which the Portuguese had gained of the African peoples of Senegambia anticipates the 'scientific' approach adopted by writers of the Enlightenment. The different African nations are described and to each is assigned a certain character – an early example of the attempt to classify human societies in the same way as scientists were later to classify plants and animals (Doc. 54).

The creole culture of Cape Verde derived partly from the increasingly complex relations with the peoples of the mainland. Cape Verde islanders supplied coastal rulers with luxury commodities (Doc. 21), and in return were able to lease land to grow food when the islands were afflicted by drought. Meanwhile the islanders offered refuge to exiles from the wars in the interior, notably during the so-called Mane invasions. In this way African religious beliefs were implanted in Santiago

(Doc. 44), while Christianity made converts on the African mainland. Cementing it all together were the creole dialects spoken in the islands and along the Guinea coast. However, creole culture also drew sustenance from the central position of the islands on the world's shipping routes. The Cape Verde Islands were the only regular port of call used by *naus* on their way to the Indian Ocean or to Brazil, and they thus became a great imperial crossroads, a kind of hinge on which swung the two empires of the *Estado da Índia* and of the South Atlantic.

Angola and the Angolan Wars

By 1560 Portugal's relations with its overseas settlements were undergoing an important change. In the East, although pepper was still shipped on the Crown's account, most of the other restricted commodities, along with the official trading voyages, were being leased out. Consortia consisting of Portuguese *fidalgos* with Crown appointments, private merchants and Indian financiers now operated the voyages from Mozambique to Goa, from Coromandel to Melaka and, most profitably, from Goa to Macau and Nagasaki. However, although the Crown was withdrawing from its direct commercial activities, it was becoming increasingly interested in acquiring direct control over territory where it could reward its followers with offices and lands, where there would be large native populations to provide taxes and manpower, and where the resources needed by the empire could be obtained. Moreover, the missionary orders encouraged the idea that direct political control provided the most effective means of achieving mass conversions. So, during the last forty years of the century, the Portuguese began to establish formal control over territory in eastern Africa, Sri Lanka and along the western coast of India.

These events were echoed in the south Atlantic. In 1530, it had been decided to begin the settlement of the Brazilian coast, using the device of the captaincy, which had been largely successful in the islands. However, by 1549 relatively little progress had been made and the Crown superimposed a royal governor to oversee the rule of the captains. By 1560, the governors had expelled the French from the coast, and the expansion of the mainland settlements and the incorporation of the Indian population into mission villages was well under way. Immigrants began to arrive from Portugal and the islands, and by the last quarter of the century sugar plantations were flourishing and with them the demand for slaves.

The 1560s also saw major changes in the Kongo region. Around 1567 the kingdom of Kongo was invaded by warrior bands, called by contemporaries the Jaga. No one knows exactly where they came from, but they were clearly bands of warriors who lived off the land and practised cannibalism, probably as part of their initiation and war rituals. In the face of this invasion, the kingdom of Kongo came near to collapse and the capital, São Salvador, was abandoned to the invaders (Doc. 40). In response to an appeal from the king of Kongo, the Portuguese sent an armed force under Francisco Gouveia de Sottomayor, whose firearms were able to defeat the Jaga and clear them out of the kingdom. This campaign not only restored the king of Kongo but led to a great increase of Portuguese influence in the kingdom as numbers of demobilized Portuguese soldiers settled in the country as traders. The Portuguese also claimed subsequently that, as a *quid pro quo* for their military support, the king had agreed to hand over the gold and silver mines in his kingdom (Doc. 49). Such mines did not exist, but the Portuguese had heard of the mines discovered by the Castilians in Peru and Mexico and were convinced that Africa had mines as rich if only they could be discovered. It was a delusion that was to dominate their thinking in both east and west Africa until the end of the seventeenth century.

Along the southern borders of the Kongo kingdom were states that owed a kind of distant allegiance to the king of Kongo, whose authority traditionally extended through the Dembos Mountains to the Cuanza River and Luanda Island. The rulers of this southern region had wanted direct commercial links with the Portuguese and had encouraged the contraband trade of the São Tomé islanders. The Jesuits had also identified this region as a possible mission field. Informal contacts had begun at least as early as the 1520s and culminated in the sending of an official diplomatic mission to the Ngola, ruler of the kingdom of Ndongo, led by Paulo Dias de Novais, grandson of Bartolomeu Dias, and a Jesuit priest (also confusingly called Francisco Gouveia). The embassy was detained in Ndongo for the best part of five years. Eventually, however, Paulo Dias returned to Portugal in circumstances that provided a colourful foundation myth for the kingdom (*reino*) of Angola (Doc. 34). He sent reports to the queen regent, Catarina, and the Royal Council, which were substantiated by letters written by Father Gouveia, all of which emphasized the wealth of the Angolan hinterland, the dense population and the commercial and religious opportunities (Doc. 31).

In 1571 the Crown decided on a grandiose project for the conquest and settlement of this region, which, controversially, it deemed to be separate from the kingdom of Kongo. The plan was to place part of the coast under a royal governor and to make the rest an hereditary captaincy to be conquered and settled by the captain. Captaincies had already proved a disappointment in Brazil, and it is strange that the

Crown should once again have used this device to achieve its aims in western Africa. However, by this time Lisbon had become disillusioned with the alliance with the king of Kongo. In the eyes of the clerics of the Counter Reformation the Kongo church had deviated a long way from Catholic orthodoxy, while the Kongo king was increasingly unable and unwilling to supply the numbers of slaves that the Atlantic economy was now demanding. On the other hand, the Portuguese army, which had gone to the aid of the king of Kongo against the Jaga, had achieved notable success, and this must have encouraged the belief that the conquest of land in Africa would be swift and relatively easy. The Crown was very concerned that any conquests should remain firmly under its control, but at the same time it did not want to bear the costs of the operation. It all added up to the package that was eventually negotiated between Paulo Dias and the Crown's lawyers in 1571 (Doc. 32).

In spite of its legal terminology, the donation Charter granted to Paulo Dias de Novais provides a window into the finely balanced relationship between the Crown and the great landowners and office-holders of Portugal. It also throws light on the official mind of Portuguese imperialism and the way that the Portuguese conceptualized their African ambitions. On the one side, it demonstrates a concern to secure the Crown's fiscal rights and its ability to intervene wherever and whenever necessary to safeguard itself against treason and rebellion. On the other side, one can see the concerns of the great landowners for the family and hereditary rights on which their position as a separate caste in society depended. This document is also a charter that sets out the juridical aspects of colonial rule. Like the Spanish, the Portuguese represented their overseas settlements as new kingdoms. The *Estado da Índia* had been a new kingdom to add to that of Portugal and the Algarve. Angola was also to be a kingdom of the Crown of Portugal. As such, the laws of Portugal with regard to landholding, justice and hereditary succession were to apply. There is no reference at all to the rights of the indigenous population or to their juridical position. Once conquered, it was assumed that they would become subjects of the king.

Paulo Dias duly arrived to begin the conquest of his captaincy in 1575. He made Luanda his capital and organized expeditions to try to secure the Cuanza valley as a highway to the interior. At first he worked in cooperation with the king of Kongo, who saw his arrival as an opportunity to punish rebellious vassals in the south of his kingdom and to reassert his power following the disasters of the Jaga invasions. However, Paulo Dias had not come like Gouveia to re-establish the authority of the king of Kongo but to found a separate Portuguese state. His campaigns on the

Cuanza were difficult and prolonged, but he succeeded in occupying the strategic position at the confluence of the Lucalla and the Cuanza, where he built the fortress and town of Massangano (Doc. 33). This was to be the base for future wars of conquest in the interior.

The founding of Luanda and the occupation of the lower Cuanza as far as Massangano were dramatic departures for the Portuguese in their relations with western Africa. In upper Guinea, Benin and Kongo, the Portuguese had settled and traded within the dominions of African sovereigns. Now they were creating their own sovereign territory. Luanda was the capital of a Portuguese state under the sovereignty of the Portuguese king, who was also king in São Tomé, the Cape Verde Islands and Brazil.

Although Portuguese soldiers and settlers had come out with Paulo Dias, and provision had been made in the charter for a colony of European settlement, in the event the population of Luanda was largely made up of Afro-Portuguese creoles from São Tomé and the Kongo and from locally born offspring of the soldiery and African clients who attached themselves to Portuguese landowners and slave traders. The Afro-Portuguese, together with their slaves and clients, soon became a distinct ethnic group. For the most part black like the local Africans and speaking the Kimbundu language as well as Portuguese, they began to compete for land, slaves and resources with the rulers of the interior. In Luanda the Afro-Portuguese were linked with the wider Portuguese world. Soldiers, priests and governors came either from Portugal or from Brazil, and the institutions typical of the Portuguese colonial world were established – the *Misericórdia*, the Christian brotherhoods and the *Senado da Câmara*. Luanda began slowly to eclipse the kingdom of Kongo. Although the latter retained its Afro-Portuguese population and institutions, Luanda gradually replaced Mpinda as the main port of the region and became the principal link between central Africa and the growing Atlantic economy.

Luanda also established its dominance over the Kongolese Church. This was the unexpected result of the attempt by the king of Kongo to free himself from the control of the absentee bishop of São Tomé. Towards the end of the sixteenth century, the king of Kongo approached the Holy See to appoint a bishop for the Kongo. Reports were called for and in 1596 a separate see was created (Docs. 43 and 55). However, the jurisdiction of the new bishopric covered Luanda as well as Kongo and the bishops preferred to reside in Luanda, thereby making it the centre of Christian power in the region.

With the rise of the Afro-Portuguese of Luanda, relations with the kingdom of Kongo deteriorated. The main problem was the difficulty of determining where the boundaries of the two states lay. Luanda itself was disputed territory as the king of Kongo claimed that it was traditionally part of his kingdom, while many of the states on the southern borders of the Kongo kingdom only owed a loose and sketchy allegiance to São Salvador. The Portuguese saw this as a kind of no-man's-land and gradually expanded their own control by incorporating these people into the Angolan state. It was one such shift of allegiance, when the ruler of Mbwila recognized the overlordship of the Luanda Portuguese rather than the king of Kongo, that precipitated the war that ended in the decisive battle of Mbwila in 1665.

At first the objectives of the Portuguese wars of conquest were to find the legendary silver mines of Cambambe and to control the sources of salt and copper in the region (Docs. 33 and 47), but by the early seventeenth century, the wars had become a broader struggle for regional supremacy between the Luanda Portuguese, the king of Kongo and the independent Mbundu kings (Doc. 45). The Afro-Portuguese of Luanda only began to make real inroads into the lands on the Kongo borders after 1618, when they struck up an alliance with the Imbangala warlords. The Imbangala (called Jaga by the Portuguese) were bands of warriors who lived in fortified settlements known as Kilombos where young male captives were initiated into the group – initiation ceremonies that involved ritual cannibalism. The Imbangala did not allow any children to be born to the group, and instead raided neighbours for women and male children. They were formidable fighters, and the Portuguese found that with their assistance, the smaller Mbundu and Kongo states were easy game. The raids provided the Imbangala with the recruits they required and the Portuguese with a regular supply of slaves for the ever-expanding Atlantic trade.

Descriptions of warfare in Angola show the realities of these military encounters between Africa and Europe. For their numbers, the Portuguese armies relied on their Imbangala allies, on their own clients (known as *guerra preta*) and on the soldiers provided by vassal *sobas*, but there were also contingents of Portuguese musketeers and frequently small units of cavalry and artillery. These might consist of soldiers sent from Portugal and Brazil, but more often they were contingents raised from the local Portuguese community. It was the muskets, artillery and cavalry that, when they could be deployed, gave the Portuguese an advantage, but in the press of a battle or a rout, Portuguese troops could easily be outnumbered and overwhelmed. Moreover, many Afro-Portuguese were to be found fighting for the African kings, and at the battle of Mbwila, the Kongo king had in his army a large contingent of Portuguese under their captain to confront the official Portuguese army from Luanda (Doc. 49). The enemies of the Portuguese would also try to fight during rainstorms in order to prevent the firearms being used. For both the Africans and Portuguese, warfare was largely about plunder, and Portuguese armies on the march would frequently be encumbered with booty, slaves and cattle.

For the Dutch also, the south Atlantic had become, by the mid-seventeenth century, a single economic and strategic zone. In 1641 a Dutch fleet captured Luanda and São Tomé in an attempt to control the slave trade to the sugar-growing regions of Brazil, which since 1630 had also been in Dutch hands. Many Angolan rulers, not least the kings of Kongo, collaborated with the Dutch in the hope of expelling the Portuguese entirely, so when the Dutch were themselves expelled by an expedition sent from southern Brazil, the Portuguese launched a series of punitive wars to regain their ascendancy (Docs. 48, 49 and 50). These culminated in 1665 with the famous battle of Mbwila, in which the Kongo king was defeated and killed, and his head taken to Luanda for ceremonial burial. After the battle, the Kongo kingdom slid into a morass of civil conflict that, by the 1680s, led to the abandonment of the capital and the falling apart of the kingdom into its component provinces. The Portuguese, however, also suffered in these wars and their defeat in Sonyo in 1670 (Doc. 50) led to their abandoning any hope of permanently conquering and incorporating the kingdom of Kongo into their Angolan territories.

The Slave Trade

It has been estimated that in the whole history of the Atlantic slave trade, a third of all slaves exported from Africa were carried by the Portuguese to their colonies, principally to Brazil. The slave trade remained the single most important economic activity pursued in western Africa by Portuguese and Afro-Portuguese, and, together with gold and sugar, it provided the most profitable commercial activity of the whole south Atlantic complex. The slave trade drew the upper classes of Portugal to become involved in west African island settlements and commercial enterprise; it attracted the Church, which financed its operations from the ownership of slaves; it was the mainstay of the commercial activities of the New Christians and small traders who settled along the west African coast and formed the nucleus of the Afro-Portuguese communities of *tangomaos*; and it came to form the principal source of commercial wealth for African rulers and middlemen who were increasingly becoming participants in the south Atlantic economy. The slave trade provided the wives and mothers who enabled the island groups of São Tomé and

Cape Verde to be peopled, and it gave rise to the communities of free black 'Portuguese' who controlled the affairs of these coastal towns. Finally, it was the slave trade that led to the development of the distinctive creole dialects and creole culture of the islands and the Guinea rivers.

Early in the fifteenth century, Portuguese expeditions to the African coast raided for slaves, but from the late 1440s trade replaced raid, the Portuguese becoming buyers in a market that was supplied by African rulers and slave agents. During the lifetime of the Infante Dom Henrique, most slaves were brought to Portugal for sale, the prince himself taking a fifth of all those brought in. After Henrique's death, the Crown leased out the trade of west Africa to entrepreneurs and to the settlers in the islands. The Cape Verde and later the Guinea islands proved convenient bases from which to pursue the trade and provided the islanders with a lucrative form of commerce. Slaves brought to the islands were either retained locally to provide labour or were kept for resale. The trade in slaves between Cape Verde and the kingdoms of upper Guinea persisted throughout the seventeenth century, but it was only one in a wide variety of commercial activities that made Portuguese relations with the Wolofs and Mandinga of the region more complex than their relations with the peoples of Angola. It was here that, in one of the ironies of the slave trade, Portuguese themselves were sometimes seized, stripped and sold as slaves in the interior (Doc. 54). In the second decade of the sixteenth century, the demand for slaves in the Spanish colonies began to grow, and captives were collected in the islands to meet the demands of the Spanish market (Docs. 37 and 38). By the end of the century, formal contracts, known as *asientos*, were in existence to supply the Spanish Indies, the *asientistas* making huge profits and paying the Crown a lump sum in advance for the privilege.

African reaction to the trade was mixed. Although many African rulers were active participants, Afonso, the first Christian king of Kongo, expressed strong misgivings at the growth of the trade (Doc. 36). Although slaves continued to be exported from Mpinda, the Kongo kingdom gradually ceased to be a major source of slaves for the Atlantic trade. Instead the Portuguese turned to Angola. As the conquest of the Cuanza valley and its hinterland slowly proceeded, the slaving frontier moved inland. Although other factors, such as the search for mines and claims to territorial sovereignty were often the ostensible reason for the constant fighting, it was the slave trade that remorselessly fed the flames of war. Every successful campaign resulted in a renewed flow of captives, who provided the cargoes for Brazil. Early in the seventeenth century, the Crown ceded its rights over the trade to the governors of Angola. As these held office for only three years, they had every incentive to press forward with campaigns or to initiate violence if they found the country at peace. To improve access to the interior south of Luanda, a slaving port was founded at Benguela in 1617, and this gradually became the nucleus of a second Afro-Portuguese settlement. In the interior, new African kingdoms emerged, chief among them Matamba and Kassange, the strength of which lay in their ability to supply the trade. The same thing happened in the *planalto* inland from Benguela, where stronger kingdoms grew up among the Ovimbundu, often centred around fortified mountain strongholds, the power of which also rested on the ability of the kings to reward followers with booty and imported goods obtained by trading slaves with the Portuguese.

More than any other factor, it was the slave trade that turned the south Atlantic into a Portuguese lake. Soldiers for the Angolan wars were increasingly recruited in Brazil (some of them apparently Brazilian Indians), and Brazilians were appointed as governors, especially after the Dutch occupation when the reconquest of Angola had been the work of the Brazilians. It was also the Brazilians who brought American food crops to Africa. The slaves who were sent across the Atlantic took with them their cultures, religions, languages and skills and refounded or reinvented African societies in the New World. In between, the creole societies in the islands and the mainland settlements flourished with their cultural flexibility and their syncretic religious practices.

In the sixteenth and seventeenth centuries, there were no serious challenges to the growth of the slave trade, but the documents in this collection show that those involved in slaving constantly felt the need to justify what they were doing. In the fifteenth century, Zurara's rhetorical imagination allowed him, in a number of passages, to recognize the trauma experienced by slaves separated from their families and uprooted from their own homelands. However, for him this suffering was mitigated by the benefits of conversion to the True Faith (Docs. 9 and 35). This remained the constant justification that the Portuguese advanced for their activities, and the term *resgatar* (to ransom or redeem) was frequently used for the purchase of slaves, to denote that they were being rescued from heathendom. The soldier chronicler Cadornega claimed that many African victims of the wars in Angola were saved from the fate of being eaten by cannibal 'Jaga', and wrote that 'by this trade they avoid having so many slaughterhouses for human flesh'. Moreover the slaves were 'instructed in the faith of our Lord Jesus Christ and, baptized and catechized, they sail for Brazil or other places where the Catholic faith is practised. They are thus taken away from their heathen ways and are redeemed to live lives which serve God and are good for commerce' (Doc. 34).

However, other arguments were sometimes employed. The anonymous Portuguese Pilot, who wrote about São Tomé in the middle of the sixteenth century, claimed that Africans sold their children into slavery because this guaranteed them better prospects in life (Doc. 37), while Dom João III, in a letter to king Afonso of Kongo, pointed to the wider commercial and political benefits that the Kongo derived from its trade with Portugal (Doc. 36). The Jesuit Father Álvares thought that the argument often advanced. ' "But if I don't buy them, their own people will kill them, because they are witches!" is a poor argument, for as long as witches are sold they will be uncovered daily' (Doc. 21). The Italian merchant Francesco Carletti (Doc. 38) provided a more complex discourse. On the one hand, his narrative makes it clear that in many respects he thought the Africans were merely animals, which justified his treating them as such. On the other hand, he recognizes the evil of the trade on the grounds that Africans are human beings and have souls. He justifies himself to his patron, the grand duke of Tuscany, by saying the trade never pleased him and that he had had to pay penance for it when disaster overtook his commercial operations on the way back to Europe.

Conclusion

The texts included in this collection describe only the eastern side of this south Atlantic world – north Africa, the islands and western Africa. They reflect the interaction of the official agents of the Crown with the unofficial entrepreneurs, and the merging streams of ideas and influences stemming from medieval and Renaissance Portugal, from the Jewish diaspora and from the strong Islamic and animist influences of Africa. This is a story not just of Portuguese encounters with Africa but of Africa's encounters with the Christian and Judaic world of Europe and the cultural syncretism that was the result.

1

THE PORTUGUESE IN MOROCCO

---

1   THE PORTUGUESE CELEBRATE MASS IN THE MOSQUE IN CEUTA, 1415

From Gomes Eanes de Zurara, *Crónica da Tomada de Ceuta*, Reis Brasil ed. (Lisbon, 1992), pp. 271–6. Translated by Malyn Newitt.

Zurara succeeded Fernão Lopes as Portuguese royal chronicler. He was a member of the household of Prince Henry 'the Navigator' (the Infante Dom Henrique) and was a knight of the Order of Christ. He was the author of four chronicles, all probably written after 1448, including the famous Crónica da Guiné *(see Docs. 8, 9 and 35). This chronicle and the* Crónica da Tomada de Ceuta *are the most important sources on the life of Prince Henry, and it is on the evidence contained in them that the iconic reputation of the Prince has been built. Ceuta was a port city on the northern coast of Morocco, more or less opposite Gibraltar. On 21 August 1415, a large Portuguese army captured the town, which was subsequently incorporated into the possessions of the Portuguese Crown. This was not the first Portuguese overseas enterprise, as there previously had been a number of slaving voyages to the Canary Islands, but it was the first major expedition organized by the Crown. The reasons for this costly expedition, which had taken years to organize, are still hotly debated. It seems clear that the Portuguese saw the capture of this port as a bridgehead which would enable them to undertake further conquests in Morocco, opening up opportunities for the military aristocracy and the Church to acquire lordships, lands and subject populations as they had during the long years of the* Reconquista. *It is also clear that some people hoped that such conquests would open up rich opportunities for Portuguese commerce and would give Portuguese merchants a share in the trade in grain, cloth and gold in which the Genoese already participated.*

The Crónica da Tomada de Ceuta *was written more than thirty years after the events it describes. As a chronicler, Zurara was heir to the consummate artistry of Fernão Lopes, for whom history was a literary art form, and to Jean Froissart, whose chronicles were designed to record the chivalrous deeds of the knightly class of fourteenth-century Europe. Like Fernão Lopes, one of Zurara's main concerns was to establish the legitimacy of the new dynasty of Avis, and the story of the conquest of Ceuta was designed to demonstrate the wisdom of the king, Dom João I, as well as the knightly virtues of the royal princes, the sanctity of their mother Philippa (the niece of Edward, the Black Prince) and the vindication of the crusading ideal. The rededication of the mosque in Ceuta and the knighting of the princes were events central to Zurara's account of Prince Henry's life, while for later generations they were acts of dedication which justified Portugal's overseas expansion. In their encounters with the peoples of west Africa, the Portuguese were always ready to interpret their activities in the light of a crusading mission, even when they were directed most overtly towards material gain.*

On the Wednesday following, the twenty-third day of the month, the king[1] sent for Master Fra João Xira and for Afonso Eanes, his principal chaplain,[2] and said to them: 'This next Sunday, if it please God, I intend to go to hear a solemn Mass with a sermon in the great mosque. So you must assemble all my sons' chaplains and all the other priests who have come with my fleet, and make all the preparations in the chapel which are necessary for the performance of this public ceremony.' Early the next day the chaplain went to look at the mosque and busied himself in getting it cleaned, for although the floor was very well tiled, it was covered with a great deal of filth. And this was because of the large number of old and rotten mats which were laid there by the Moors, who place themselves on the ground when saying their prayers and go without their shoes and so put the mats there because of the cold. And it seems that, when the first mat that has been placed there becomes rotten, they do not trouble to remove it but throw others on top of it, and they continue to do this until such time as the first mats are gone and all the others are destroyed and turned into filth. For this reason, on the Saturday, a great number of hoes and baskets were assembled with which they threw all the filth outside. After this the whole building was cleaned very thoroughly, and in the same way they made all the other preparations pertaining to that office for the following day.

On the following day, all the priests who had come on the campaign assembled in the mosque, and together they constituted a very fine college. And it happened that, at that time, no bishop was to be found there because, when the opportunity presented by the armada arose, some bishops were dead, others were busy with their studies, and yet others were at the Court of Rome. As a result, no bishops were to be found, and in fact they were not needed as there were enough priests to celebrate that office. Many of those clergy wore their finest priestly vestments, and the priest with his deacon and subdeacon prepared a cauldron with water and salt to celebrate the office.

The king arrived accompanied by his sons, by the Constable,[3] the Master of the Order of Christ and the Prior of the Hospital, joining all the other barons and nobles[4] and great lords who were assembled there, all clothed with great magnificence in honour of so important a festival.

The priest began his exorcism with salt and water, saying over it a prayer which is said in the Holy Mother Church, with the following words: 'All Mighty God, we piously ask you that with your infinite mercy you will bless and sanctify this salt, which by your holy grace you have given for the health and benefit of the human race.' The same was done with the water, which was in a silver cauldron, and meanwhile the priests sang an antiphon with the words, 'The Lord's house is built on the highest mountains to which all the peoples come singing "Glory be to you Our Lord".' When this ceremony ended, they took the curtains and began to arrange them, and they set an altar in place, and it was a beautiful thing to see how the tasks were shared and everything was done by the priests in such good order; here one brought some cloth, another the twine and the nails from which to hang it. And all the other things were done in an orderly fashion until the altar was set up and the sign of the Cross had been made over it with holy water. ... When all was completed, the clerics sang *Te Deum Laudamus* with a loud voice in good counterpoint, and at the end the trumpets sounded. Imagine the noise that 200 trumpets made.

... The Infante Dom Henrique recalled that in former times the Moors had carried away two church bells from Lagos. He ordered that a diligent search be made for them and that they be brought there, and it pleased God that they were found and set up in such a manner that they were rung during that Mass.... Immediately after Mass, the Infantes withdrew to their apartments and armed themselves, and in this manner they came together to the church, which was a splendid thing to see, for they were all large and well formed and were dressed in clean and decorated harnesses and were wearing their swords, which had been blessed,[5] by their sides and their coats of arms. Before them went trumpets and shawms, and it was a sight that no one could see without great pleasure, and the greatest pleasure was for him to whom they owed the most, the king their father.

When they came before the king, first the Infante Dom Duarte[6] fell to his knees and, drawing his sword from the scabbard, kissed it and gave it to him, and from the hand of his father he was made a knight. And his brothers did the same, and when this was over they kissed the hand of the king, and then each went his own way, and in their turn they made knights of those in their retinue. ...

Notes

1 Dom João I (1385–1433).
2 In Portuguese *capelão-mor*.
3 The celebrated Nun'Alvares Pereira.
4 High ranking Portuguese were still known in the fifteenth century as *ricos homens*.
5 The swords had been blessed by their mother, Queen Philippa, as she lay dying – a scene described in great detail by Zurara.
6 He was heir to the throne and eventually reigned from 1433 to 1438.

---

2 CHRISTIANS AND MOORS – SINGLE COMBAT IN THE STRUGGLE TO CONTROL CEUTA DURING THE MOROCCAN WARS

From Georg von Ehingen, *Reisen nach der Ritterschaft*, Gabriele Ehrmann ed., Göppinger Arbeiten zur Germanistik Nr 262 II Kummerle Verlag (Göppingen, 1979), pp. 51–61.
Translated by Malyn Newitt.

Georg von Ehingen was born in 1428, and he was a member of the minor German nobility. He served in the retinues of different princes and, in 1454, undertook a pilgrimage to Jerusalem. On his return he set out as a soldier of fortune to France and Navarre but, finding no employment, took service with Afonso V of Portugal and was sent with an army to reinforce Ceuta, which was threatened by a large Moorish force. He subsequently campaigned in Spain and then entered the service of the Duke of Württemberg, dying in 1508 at the age of eighty. The Reisen *were first printed in 1600, and the only surviving manuscript is in the Landesbibliothek at Stuttgart.*

This extract shows how insecure Portugal's hold on Ceuta had become by the 1450s. The Portuguese had not been able to break out and begin the conquest of Morocco, and the defence of the town had already proved extremely costly. The account shows the Portuguese recruiting foreign troops to assist with its defence – not only von Ehingen himself but other soldiers who spoke 'the low German tongue'. Von Ehingen mentions the large force of cavalry which the Portuguese kept in the city and which was used to raid the surrounding countryside. There is no reason to doubt the story of the single combat between the champions of both sides; it well illustrates the way in which archaic military values continued to be cultivated in the Moroccan fortresses, along with the belief that Muslims were the perpetual, sworn enemies of the Christians.

We all embarked and immediately crossed over from Portugal to Africa, for at this point the sea is narrow. The night we arrived in the great city of Ceuta,[1] everyone assembled with their arms and armour in a great square and that same night a number of messages arrived that the Moors[2] were approaching with a large force. Although throughout the day and the following night we could see and hear detachments passing in front of the city, the most powerful part of the main force had not arrived. On the fourth day, when the governor and captain-general had put the fortifications in a state of defence and had divided the soldiers among the different quarters and sectors, I was ordered by him to be the commander of one of these sectors or quarters, and many capable men were placed under my command, many of whom could speak or understand the low German[3] dialect. ...

Ceuta is a great and broad city, three parts of which face the land while the fourth faces the sea, and to me it appeared larger than Cologne.[4] On the landward side are dry ditches, and within it a high citadel with towers has been erected with embrasures low down and the upper parts covered with tin,[5] and a wall built around it facing the city. The citadel with its towers was well defended and was divided into different sectors because it was very spacious. The captain with a good detachment of light cavalry and a number of specially selected infantry went out to clear the area between the citadel and the surrounding walls, and when necessary to ride and walk there, which subsequently he did satisfactorily. ...

When the king of Portugal had news of the seriousness of this siege, he decided to come over to Ceuta with all his forces with the intention of attacking the Moors in their trenches outside the city, because otherwise it would not be possible to bring them to battle. When the enemy realised this, they attacked us without ceasing for three days, fighting continuously beginning early in the morning until night. Both sides fought strenuously, and many of the Moors were shot and lay in piles in the ditches around the city and around the walls. They attacked so many times that the Christians were driven back from their defences, and if the captain had not come with soldiers on horseback and on foot, as previously mentioned, who knows what would have become of us. Because the Moors had attacked us so strongly for three days and had lost a great many men, a foul smell rose from the dead bodies, and the Moors gave up and retreated.

Then we decided to pursue them with 400 horsemen and 1,000 foot soldiers, the best we had. Many times they turned back on us and fought us, until eventually we took possession of one of the mountains while the Moors took possession of another. In between was a beautiful level valley. When it was evening some of our people came and said that one of the mightiest of the Moors had challenged any of the Christian knights to fight with him at some place between the two camps. I then requested of the captain that I might go out to meet him because I was well prepared and quite agile in my chain mail. I also had a very strong horse,[6] which had been given to me by the king. The captain acceded to my request and ordered the skirmishers[7] to retire so that they returned to their positions.

Then I made the sign of the cross with my lance in front of me and advanced from our position and rode towards the Moors in the valley. When the Moors saw me approaching, they returned to their positions. Then our captain sent a trumpeter to the positions of the Moors who sounded [their trumpets] and gave the signal. At once a Moor mounted on a beautiful Barbary horse rapidly advanced into the valley. I did not long delay and advanced towards him. The Moor raised his shield in front of him and resting his lance on his arm with a shout rode with determination towards me. On my part I did the same, resting my lance on my thigh, and when I was near him placed my lance at rest and struck at his shield. And although his lance struck me in the flank and sleeve of my armour, on meeting him I gave him such a blow that horse and rider fell to the ground. However, his lance was caught in my armour in such a manner that I could not easily free myself and dismount from my horse. He was already dismounted. I had my sword in my hand and he had also taken hold of his. Then we approached each other, and each gave the other a mighty blow. The Moor had good armour, and although I struck him on the shield I was not able to injure him and his blows also did me no harm. We then seized each other by the arms and wrestled so that we both fell to the ground next to each other. But the Moor was very strong and broke away from me, so that we both faced each other upright but on our knees. I then kept him away with my left hand so that I might give him a blow with my sword, which I was able to do. I pushed him so far from me with my left hand that I was able to give him a blow in the face. Although the blow was not fully effective, I wounded him, so that he swayed backwards and was partly blinded. I then struck him again in the face and felled him to the ground. Then leaning forward, I stabbed him in the neck. After that I stood up, took his sword and went over to my horse. Both horses stood next to each other. The whole day they had worked hard and were quite quiet.

When the Moors saw that I had triumphed, they retreated towards their positions, but the Christians and the Portuguese came and cut off the head of the Moor, took his lance and stuck [the head] on it, and removed his armour. It was costly and masterfully fashioned in the Moorish manner, well made and richly decorated. They also took his shield and his horse, and led me to the captain. He was delighted with me and embraced me, and there was great celebration in the whole army for on that day many men and horses had been shot, stabbed and wounded. The captain ordered that the head of the Moor and his shield, sword and horse should be carried before me and he ordered the most distinguished lords, knights and squires to attend. And I had to ride next to him with a trumpeter going before me, and in this way I was led in great triumph through the streets of the city of Ceuta. And the Christian population expressed great joy at this event and treated me more magnificently than I deserved. God almighty had fought for me in my hour of need, for I had never been in greater danger as the Moor was an outstandingly strong man and I knew that his strength was far greater than mine.

Notes

1   Ceuta is called Sept in the German text.
2   Von Ehingen uses the term *heiden*, which literally means heathen. It seems appropriate, in this context, to translate this as Moors.
3   The word in the German is *niderlandisch*.
4   Köllen.
5   The German text has *zinnen*.
6   The word in German is *jennetten*.
7   *Scharmitzen* in the German text.

---

3   THE MOORS OF MASSA RECOGNIZE PORTUGUESE OVERLORDSHIP

Letter of Dom Manuel I to the Inhabitants of Massa

From Pierre de Cenival ed., *Les Sources Inédites de l'Histoire du Maroc: Archives et Bibliothèques de Portugal, Tome 1 (1486–1516)* (Paris, 1934), pp. 31–5.

The original document is in Arquivo Nacional de Torre de Tombo, *Livro das Ilhas*, fol. 50.

Translated by Malyn Newitt.

When Dom Afonso V came of age and took over the government of Portugal in 1448, the Portuguese renewed their attempts to conquer territory in Morocco.

In 1458 a Portuguese expedition, led by the king, captured Alcazar Seguer, and a subsequent campaign in 1471 led to the capture of Arzila and Tangier. Portugal now controlled a significant amount of Moroccan territory, including a growing Moorish population. There were no further expeditions, however, because Afonso became betrothed to the putative heiress to the throne of Castile and was embroiled in a war with Ferdinand and Isabella which lasted from 1474 to 1479. When Dom João II became king in 1481, the Portuguese sought to expand their influence in a more peaceful manner, particularly in the south. Moorish populations were encouraged to seek Portuguese protection and to acknowledge Portuguese overlordship, and the numbers of these so-called mouros de paz *increased in the hinterland of the Portuguese forts. Massa, situated at the mouth of the river of that name, had been an important centre for Genoese trade with Morocco, and together with Azamour and Safi, two other port towns in western Morocco, it came peacefully under Portuguese influence after 1488, partly to escape Castilian raids and partly to gain access to the markets of Lisbon. By these agreements the Moors would be under 'our protection and [would] be treated, guarded and defended as our natural subjects and vassals'. These agreements with the* mouros de paz *enabled Portuguese commerce and political influence to expand, but it was a policy that did not accord with the crusading mentality that was still very much alive among the Portuguese nobility and which came to dominate Portuguese policy once again after the death of Dom João II. This agreement with the inhabitants of Massa points to a tradition of toleration and co-existence between Christians and Muslims that was too often overlaid by the concurrent, if increasingly outdated, traditions of the crusade.*

Dom Manuel, by the grace of God, king of Portugal and of the Algarves on this side and beyond the sea in Africa, Lord of Guiné,[1] make known to you, honourable men among the Moors, elders and chiefs and heads of towns and places in the land of Massa, and also to all the other residents and peoples present there or in its neighbourhood that the honourable Velavizize, your sheikh, and Mafamede Bembarca and Cide Aya, your messengers, came to us in their own name and the names of the rest of you, and by virtue of your letter of credence and with the full power of attorney that they brought and presented to us. They spoke with us and we listened to all that they said on their own and on your behalf. They told us how everyone among you had agreed to take us as your Lord, and that you would always, generously and with good will, serve us as our good and loyal servants and vassals, for which, as a sign and acknowledgement, you will give us each year two horses which will be embarked on our ships free of all duties. You further agreed that none of our ships which bring merchandise to the markets of Massa shall pay tribute of any kind, nor will those which bring from there merchandise or things of any kind by our order and that they may carry them throughout our kingdoms and dominions. However, all other ships, whether belonging to our subjects or to foreigners, shall pay the dues which should be paid, and you will be obliged to allow safe entry and departure to both kinds. And likewise you will be obliged to welcome and receive within the said towns our factors and agents and their servants whom we send there, and you will respect, pay heed to and do all that they tell you and order you to do on my behalf; and in the same way it shall please you to enable our factors to buy horses[2] and despatch them, acting according to the signed and sealed orders that we will send you.

Also you will allow us to build a fortress there wherever we shall ordain and desire, and of a size that seems good to us, for the building of which we will send artisans and lime and you will supply assistance to carry the stone, sand and water, and will help the artisans with the work until it is finished; and you will give and cause to be given to the artisans and other persons who are there the provisions and all the other necessary things which they will buy from you; and also, after the said fortress is built, you will not allow anyone who is among you, whether from our kingdoms or from any other, to enter it without my permission, which will be contained in a letter that they will bring. Nor will you trade in our ports with any ship belonging to our subjects or to any other person except with the permission of our factor, who shall be in the fort. All these things you will generally be obliged to keep, to carry out and entirely to observe.

All this has been seen by us and heard by the above-mentioned people, so that we know the good will which they and you have to serve us and which you have demonstrated by accepting and raising our flags. And we will protect you and consider everything concerning which you have sent word to us as being our service, by which you have offered and are obliged to serve and recognize us. And we accept everything in the manner and form in which you have said it.

So that our factor may be well and safely lodged and may be able to trade and do business with our merchandise and the above-mentioned things, you will be obliged, while the fortress is not yet built, to give him a good and secure building in which he can house his people and servants, and store our merchandise. And if you do everything that is mentioned above, we will receive you and treat you as our own, and from now on we will command that you be under our protection and be treated, guarded and defended as our natural subjects and vassals.

And by this present letter we hereby notify all the captains of our kingdoms and our admirals, *sotaalmirante*,[3] and sea captains, and all our vassals and subjects and captains and masters of ships, whether of the armada or merchant ships, that if they come across any citizens or people of the said towns or villages, they will not do them any harm or damage, either to their persons or to their merchandise, and will permit them freely to conduct their journeys, not impeding them in any way, but rather favouring and treating them as ours and as if they were our vassals and subjects. In the same way, it pleases us to let them come and go with their merchandise to any place or places in our kingdoms and lordships that they please. And we order that they shall be well treated, and that no innovation shall be introduced into the tribute that they pay, but that they shall pay just the same as our other vassals and subjects and in every respect shall be treated and favoured like them.

Whatever misfortune you shall suffer at sea or on land, we promise that we shall strive to find a remedy for it to each and everyone of you, and to do all that we can for you, as we do and are obliged to do for any of our native vassals or subjects. And when you wish to go to sea, it shall only be in our ships or those of our subjects and nationals, because they can carry you more securely and you will go aboard them by the order of our factors and not in any other way, so that, when they receive them from the hands of our factors, the captains of our ships that will carry them may take better care of them. And we order our factors and the masters and captains of the said ships that, whenever any of you desire to come to our kingdoms, they carry you up to the number of six persons, without the payment of any freight charge on your persons, and in the same way that they feed you at our cost while at sea.

And by this we entreat and recommend to the captains, vassals and subjects of the kings of Castile, our very dear and much-loved cousins, and also to any other kingdoms with which we have peace and friendship that, out of respect for us, and in order to please and serve us in this, should you meet with the above-mentioned people they should do no harm to you without reason nor start any quarrel, either with regard to your persons or your goods, and that they treat you well and allow you to go freely as if you were our servants and as being under our lordship and protection and of the singular charge that we have, which we will receive and esteem as a great service. And anyone who will do this for us will have honour and reward.

And in witness of our truth and good faith, we order this letter patent to be issued, signed by us and sealed with our lead seal in the town of Estremoz on 11 January. Made by Gil Alvarez in the year of Our Lord 1497.

And, moreover, in addition your above-mentioned representatives tell us that, as we have ordered them to build the fortress, and while they are building it and before it is finished, you will give us fifteen of the children of your principal people as hostages for the security of our people who will be there, with which we agree with pleasure, for it seems that you will do this in order to serve us.[4] And with this condition and with the others mentioned above, we accept you in the abovementioned manner and we order the hostages to be welcomed and well treated in our kingdoms while they are there.

Notes

1 Dom Manuel I (1495–1521). This older version of the royal title perpetuated the tradition, going back to Roman times, that the kingdom of Algarve extended beyond the straits into Morocco. The royal title was to be fundamentally altered following Vasco da Gama's voyage to India.
2 It is clear from this document that the horse trade was of particular importance to the Portuguese, as horses fetched a very high price on the Guinea coast and were the principal commodity for which slaves were exchanged.
3 A *sotaalmirante* might be translated as vice-admiral. It referred to a subaltern admiral.
4 The taking and receiving of hostages (by both Moors and Portuguese) was a routine way of ensuring that the conditions agreed in any negotiations would be observed. The best-known example is that of the prince, the Infante Dom Fernando (the Infante Santo), who, after the Portuguese defeat at Tangier in 1437, was to be held as a hostage until the Portuguese fulfilled the terms of the ceasefire that had been agreed.

4 LETTER PATENT OF DOM MANUEL TO THE JEWS OF SAFI, 1509

From Pierre de Cenival ed., *Les Sources Inédites de l'Histoire du Maroc: Archives et Bibliothèques de Portugal, Tome 1 (1486–1516)* (Paris, 1934), pp. 174–6.
The original document is in Arquivo Nacional de Torre de Tombo, *Livro das Ilhas*, fols 179–179v.
Translated by Malyn Newitt.

The town of Safi had come under Portuguese control in 1488 as part of the policy of peaceful expansion pursued by Dom João II, and had become a centre of cloth production with a thriving Jewish community. In 1495 Dom Manuel I had ordered the Jews of Portugal to convert to Christianity or leave the country. Many of them had crossed over to Morocco to escape the subsequent persecution, beginning the diaspora of Sephardic Jews which was to play such an important part in the subsequent history of the Atlantic. Then, early in the sixteenth century, the Portuguese began again to expand their territory in Morocco, occupying Agadir in 1505 (which they called Santa Cruz do Cabo de Gué) and Mogador in 1506. This was followed by the occupation of Azamour in 1513. In these years, the spirit of crusading warfare revived, with annual raids mounted into Moroccan territory. Dom Manuel tried to reassure the Jewish mercantile population, and it is significant that this grant of privileges followed soon after the massacres of New Christians in Lisbon in 1506. This grant made it clear that the policy of forced conversion would not be extended to the north African fortress towns (praças) though, having granted immunity, the patent goes on to envisage a time when these privileges might have to be withdrawn. Once again, this letter enshrines a tradition of toleration and flexibility which was stifled in Portugal itself by the influence of the Castilians, and later by the Portuguese Inquisition, but which was to mark many of the Portuguese overseas settlements where the influence of the Inquisition was not so strong.

To the city of Safi, the privilege is granted to the Jews who live there that at no time can they be expelled from the said city against their will, nor shall they be made Christians by force.

Dom Manuel etc. to whomsoever my letter shall come: We make it known by this present letter that, having in mind what is necessary for our service and for the welfare and prosperity of the affairs of our city of Safi, it pleases us to grant to the Jews who now live and reside in our city, and who in future will live and reside there, that at no time will we order them to be expelled, nor in any manner will they be expelled from the said city contrary to their will, nor will we order them to become Christian by force or by any other means against their will; and if any of them of their own wish desire to be converted and to turn to the faith of Our Lord Jesus Christ, we desire and order to be observed what is laid down about the number of days that have to pass before they be given the water of Holy Baptism.

And if by any chance it should happen to suit our service that they be expelled from the city and no longer reside there, in that case we order that they be notified so that they can prepare themselves for their departure and be allowed to go to whatever place seems good to them; and they shall be given the space of two years from the day on which they are so notified, and will be able to remain in the said city as safely as they could before the notification of their departure. And at the end of those two years, they can depart with all their merchandise and belongings, without any harm or wrong being done to them because such is our grant.

However, for their protection and to make sure that this is remembered, we order that this letter with our seal shall be given to them and also to Diogo de Azambuja,[1] a member of our Council and captain of the said city, and to all the captains we shall appoint there in the future, and also to the sea captains, the *corregedores*,[2] justices and judges so that they shall fulfill, carry out and secure its terms and make sure that its contents are carried out without any diminution or hesitation whatsoever, and this is because we consider that it is our will and very much for the good of our service.

Given in our city of Évora on the fourth of May in the year of Our Lord Jesus Christ 1509.

Notes

1   Diogo de Azambuja was one of the most distinguished servants of the Portuguese Crown. He had been selected by Dom João II to establish the fort of Elmina in 1482 (see Doc. 22). In 1506 he built the fort of Mogador on the Moroccan coast and was appointed governor of Safi.

2   A *corregedor* was a royal official who had authority to enter any town or jurisdiction to safeguard the Crown's interests.

---

5 LETTER OF JOÃO DE MENESES TO DOM MANUEL ON THE STATE OF AZAMOUR, 1514

From Pierre de Cenival ed., *Les Sources Inédites de l'Histoire du Maroc: Archives et Bibliothèques de Portugal, Tome 1 (1486–1516)* (Paris, 1934), pp. 545–8.

The original document is in Arquivo Nacional de Torre de Tombo, Gaveta 15, maço 1, n° 52.

Translated by Malyn Newitt.

By 1514, warfare was raging along the southern coast of Morocco. The Portuguese mounted armed raids into the interior to carry off cattle and captives for ransom, while Moroccan warlords placed the Portuguese towns in an almost constant state of siege. Azamour, which had informally recognized Portuguese overlordship for the previous thirty years, was attacked and captured in 1513 by the Duke of Bragança, and in 1514 its governor, Nuno Fernandes de Ataíde, led a raid as far as the walls of Marrakesh. However, this letter shows eloquently the precarious nature of the Portuguese coastal strongholds. They could communicate with each other only by sea and were dependant on help being constantly sent from the Algarve. The soldiers, particularly the noblemen from Portugal, were not used to garrison duty and were ill-disciplined and resentful. There were few permanent residents, and everyone desired to leave at the earliest opportunity. With the rise of the new Saadian dynasty in Marrakesh after 1524, the hopes of a permanent Portuguese presence in north Africa and of peaceful and profitable relations with the inhabitants, which appear in the earlier letters (Docs. 3 and 4), had almost entirely disappeared. Safi and Azamour were eventually abandoned in 1541 after the fall of Santa Cruz (Agadir).

Azamour, 6 May 1514

Sire,

After having written that other letter to Your Highness, no message has come from Safi either by land or by sea until today, Saturday 6 May, and the caravel in which Nuno Gato came, which was to have returned at once with the message, has not returned. And the Moors of Tit[1] wrote to me that Side Ahea had a fight or skirmish with Muley Nacer near Cernou, in which many people on each side were killed, and that Muley Nasser remained in the same Cernou, which is four leagues from Safi. Side Ahea retired near to Safi, where he had his camp in a strong place. And this all took place last Monday, from which one may believe that, if Nuno Fernandes[2] had needed to, he could easily have sent me a message, because there was enough time for this. Furthermore, we frequently saw vessels passing which were coming from Safi and appeared to have brought some help from the Algarve.

I, Sire, have sent a number of Moors by land but until today have not seen anyone, except that yesterday those people from Tit, who came here to trade, said that they had news that Muley Nasser was returning to Marrakesh, and that neither the sherif nor the king of Marrakesh himself would help him nor other people he had been expecting. And although I cannot be more certain of this, from what I have heard and from what to me seems likely, if that were the case, there would be much news about his departure. It also appears to me that, if Nuno Fernandes needed any help, his message could reach me by sea at any time. Among all these uncertainties I am trusting in Our Lord for some good news. And if I delay from today until tomorrow, it will be necessary to send two ships with some more people, because such a delay seems to me to be a sign that there is a siege. And if this harbour were not so difficult to enter and leave, I would already have gone myself to see what is happening, but unless there was a real need, I did not want to spend time away from this place, which only has half its garrison, because the whole number would not be enough to protect it if it were besieged.

[Estevão Rodrigues] Berrio confirms that the weather is very good for sending me a message and that every other day one could be sent if I was needed, and in addition, Our Lord be praised, as well as the people of the place, they have more than 600 men from outside, namely 200 crossbowmen, or rather fewer, from Ilha [Madeira] and 140 crossbowmen from here who went with Nuno Gato and some gentlemen; and from the fifty ships which were in the port and which will remain at anchor, he is able to draw 400 men; and from the caravels which we subsequently saw sail past, we have hopes of there being more people, for they also ought to come to offer help given the time it takes to send to the Algarve to ask for it.

And this, Sire, is what can be written to Your Highness about what is now going on. For the future I do not know what remedy Your Highness can find for this land and this city, because the people who have been here up to now certainly cannot remain any longer. And although the *fidalgos* and men of honour can be valuable for one day, at all other times when they are not fighting or are not in combat, they are wasted because, if two of them lose their sense of honour by being here, all lose it. Moreover, they are [your] vassals and are less accustomed to obedience than other men and neither desire nor are able to put up with hardship. They all now openly say that they do not have to stay here to begin the war all over again and that, even should Muley Nasser attack these lands, they will all have to leave so as not to be besieged, and that Your Highness should send others who can stay here for the same amount of time. Now, Your Highness will recall how many times I have begged and advised you not to engage any more *fidalgos* for the war except those who are content to be posted here. I am not talking about lances, even though they are *fidalgos*, but those who, whenever four get together stir up trouble and cause the others to jump whenever they jump themselves. Therefore, as Your Highness knows, there are not even two men who should remain here.

And if you think there are settlers here, forget it. Of those that are here, the greater part desires to leave because they see that this city is very big and they have done nothing to defend it and fear to remain in it as it is. And in order to have a shelter in the fortress, they have already made some houses and other habitations where the fortification ought to be, and I think they are larger than they should be, though they are in the manner that was ordered by Pedro Correa and Rui Barreto. On top of all this, there came two *regimentos* signed by Your Highness in which it was ordered that they should be given the same pay as is given in other places, which would be less than half what they all receive now.

This appears a very great grievance to them. For these reasons added to all the others, there will be very few who desire to remain here.

For this reason I would disabuse Your Highness of the idea that there is any basis for ordering this place to be defended. I will be able to leave the 300 mounted crossbowmen with Rui Barreto, as Your Highness ordered, and the very few servants of Your Highness who at present do not have any shipping [to leave] and some residents. And I do not believe that Rui Barreto, together with his relatives and men, will be able to hold out many days, for this place, in its present state, needs not less than 2,000 men to guard it from the people of the land, and I do not believe this can be done because nobody wants to live in this place.

Notes

1   Today Tit Mellil.
2   Nuno Fernandes de Ataíde, senhor de Penacova,

---

6   THE PORTUGUESE OF AZAMOUR RAID THE BEDOUINS, 1519

Letter of Dom Álvaro de Noronha to Dom Manuel I, 15 December 1519.

From Pierre de Cenival ed., *Les Sources Inédites de l'Histoire du Maroc: Archives et Bibliothèques de Portugal, Tome 1 (1486–1516)* (Paris, 1934), pp. 260–3.

The original document is in Arquivo Nacional de Torre de Tombo, Cartas dos Governadores de Africa, n ° 74.

Translated by Malyn Newitt.

This letter describes a typical raid mounted by the Portuguese of Azamour on the surrounding populations with the intention of rounding up camels and cattle, and obtaining ransoms for important individuals. This type of warfare had changed little since the days of the Reconquista *and was favoured by the fidalgos on whom the kings of Portugal still relied to make up their armies. These were brutal encounters with the local populations and show how the Portuguese understood the local pattern of crop sowing which made the camel herders and Bedouins vulnerable to raids at certain seasons of the year.*

To the King our Lord,

I hope that before the time for sowing these, Moors of Cherquia[1] will return to their lands to sow [their crops], and this is in accord with some messages they have sent to me about this. And now I see that they have sown in Emxouvia and because, before being there, together with the people of Bolçoba they had robbed the caravans of the Moors of Oley Sobeta, who was here, and had taken prisoner two of his sheikhs and had taken horses from him, it seems right, my Lord, that there should be some punishment. Lest it appear to the Moors that I failed to punish them while they were here but waited instead for them to mend their ways, and because, my Lord, I knew where these Moors of Cherquia were sowing their crops, I set out from this city in search of them on Sunday, 11 December, with 200 or so lances and 40 foot soldiers. And going up the river[2] on the Duquela bank, I crossed it by a ford which was about eight leagues from that city on the Monday about one o'clock in the afternoon. There I rested until night and sent my spies to see if the Cherquia camp was in the place where they had said, and I told them a certain place where they would find me with all the people. And at the ford, my Lord, I left some of the weaker horses and all the foot soldiers.

Three hours after nightfall the spies returned, my Lord, with news of where the camp was, and bearing in mind the place where it was, I took advice and formed the people into a column so that they would not be noticed until we got close. I placed the guides in the front with Lourenço de Freitas and the armed men in the rear with João de Freitas. I ordered twenty-five men to dismount to cover the entrance to the village, while I, with five or six mounted men, went to control the columns and the people to see that they did as I desired.

We found out, my Lord, that this was the village of a very important sheikh of the Oleid Aquo[3] who has done a great deal of disservice to Your Highness in this land. He is called Nasser Benduma and has carried off many Christians and Jewish fishermen from the bar of this city and has raised the Oleid Aquo throughout the land. And it pleased Our Lord that we took him and with him another seventy persons, people of importance, and we killed all the others we found. And we took 300 camels and a lot of cattle, which, as they did not wish to cross the river, we had to kill there. And with all this, my Lord, we returned, God be praised, without anyone opposing us.

And Mafamede ben Mafamede, who was another man I desired to meet, was so fortunate that I passed through his village without meeting him, so I remained behind. Nasser Benduma was ransomed for 100,000 *reis* but, God willing, I hope to get more for Mafamede.

Before this, my Lord, I went to look for Gharbiya in the Serra Verde,[4] where my spies told me he was to be found, but he had already left. However, if he does not come back to Safi to serve Your Highness, I will strive to be as bad a neighbour to him as I can.

In all these past labours, Álvaro Caiado has served Your Highness well, and in everything he is a person who is very well informed and knows how to serve you. And, therefore, my Lord, he is very worthy of the reward which he will be requesting from Your Highness, and if he obtains it, I will kiss Your Highness's hands for it.

Tit has already more than a hundred settlers and seems to me to be well populated. The Bedouins[5] of Oley Sobeta live in the neighbourhood and have already sown their crops there. They give us a lot of wood and meat. Those sheikhs who have their women and children here also live with them.

> May Our Lord enrich the life and state of Your Highness.
> From Azamour the 15th day of December [1519]
> My Lord, I kiss Your Highness's hands
> Dom Álvaro de Noronha

Notes

1 Possibly the modern Chekaoua.
2 The river is the Oum er Rbia, the second largest river in Morocco, which enters the sea near Azamour.
3 Cenival thinks this should be Ouled Ya'koub.
4 According to Cenival this was the Djebel-el-Akhdar (today Jbel Ahmar Lakhdar).
5 The word used is 'Alarves'.

2

THE EARLY VOYAGES TO WEST AFRICA

---

7 PRINCE HENRY 'THE NAVIGATOR' IS REMEMBERED

From Duarte Pacheco Pereira, *Esmeraldo de Situ Orbis*, Damião Peres ed., 3rd edition (Lisbon, 1988), book 1, chapter 33.

Translated by Malyn Newitt.

Duarte Pacheco Pereira probably made several voyages to west Africa before accompanying Afonso de Albuquerque to the East in 1503. There he was involved in the defence of the factory of Cochin and in the first serious fighting between the Portuguese and the Indians of Calicut. He returned to Portugal in 1505 and appears to have busied himself with the manuscript of his book, mysteriously entitled Esmeraldo de Situ Orbis.[1] *This work provides the first comprehensive account of Portuguese explorations and activities in western Africa. It is largely a compendium of geographical information, but the author incorporates much historical detail and gives his reflections on the peoples of the region and their relations with the Portuguese. He abandoned the manuscript unfinished around 1506, although he himself lived until 1533. It was first published in 1892.*

This extract shows how the reputation of Henry 'the Navigator' had developed in the forty years since his death. Duarte Pacheco does not share either the doubts expressed by many modern historians concerning Henry's role in the peopling of the islands and the discovery of the upper Guinea coast or twenty-first century reservations about the slave trade. It was the wealth brought to Portugal by these discoveries, including the trade in 3,500 slaves a year, which for him was the principal reason why Portugal should honour the prince and pray for his soul.

Further, he [the Prince] ordered the peopling of the islands of the Azores. ... All this and many other good things, which I need not relate, were done by this virtuous prince, besides discovering Guinea as far as

Serra Leoa. ... [2] And therefore we must pray to God for his soul; he ended the life in this world on the thirteenth day of the month of November in the year of Our Lord Jesus Christ 1460, and lies buried in the monastery of Santa Maria da Vitória da Batalha, in the chapel of king João his father. The benefits conferred on these kingdoms by the virtuous Prince Henry are such that its kings and people are greatly indebted to him, for in the land which he discovered a great part of the Portuguese people now earn their livelihood and the kings [of Portugal] derive great profit from this commerce; for, from the Rio da Çanagua[3] on the frontier of the kingdom of Jalofo,[4] where the first negroes are ... as far as, and including, Serra Leoa, when the trade of this country was well ordered, it yielded yearly 3,500 slaves and more, and many tusks of elephant ivory, gold, fine cotton cloth and much other merchandise. Therefore, we must pray God for the soul of Prince Henry, for his discovery of this land led to the discovery of the other Guinea beyond the said Serra [Leoa] and to [the discovery of] India, whose commerce brings us an abundance of wealth.

Notes

1   There have been numerous attempts to interpret the title. In the edition published by the Academia Portuguesa de História in 1988, Damião Peres concluded with José Dentinho that the title had to be understood as meaning 'About the green sea of the world'. See Damião Peres ed., *Esmeraldo de situ orbis* (Lisbon, 1988) p. 211. This was dismissed by Joaquim Barradas de Carvalho, who observed that the Indian word for an emerald was *pachec* and Pacheco used the Italian word *smeraldo* as a witty, Italianate translation of his own name. The title would then mean 'Pacheco's De Situ Orbis'. See Joaquim Barradas de Carvalho, *À la Recherche de la Spécificité de la Renaissance Portugaise*, 2 vols. (Paris, 1983) vol. 1, p. 123.
2   It is widely accepted that Sierra Leone was the furthest point on the African coast that had been reached by Portuguese traders at the time of Prince Henry's death in 1460.
3   The Senegal River.
4   For the Wolof kingdoms, see Docs. 10, 18, 20 and 56.

8   SLAVE RAIDING ON THE SAHARA COAST, 1445

From *Crónica de Guiné* by Gomes Eanes de Zurara.

Translation by Malyn Newitt based on C. R. Beazley and Edgar Prestage, *The Chronicle of the Discovery and Conquest of Guinea*, 2 vols., (Hakluyt Society, London, 1896–9), pp. 143–6, and Léon Bourdon trans., *Chronique de Guinée (1453)* (Paris, 1994), pp. 140–3.

Zurara's Crónica de Guiné *was probably begun around 1453 but incorporated material from an earlier chronicle that is now lost. It was commissioned shortly after the death of the former Regent, Dom Pedro, at the battle of Alfarrobeira in 1449 and was designed to enhance the reputation of Prince Henry and to confirm his standing* vis à vis *the new regime, which was dominated by the Duke of Bragança. Zurara was very well-educated in classical literature and took immense trouble to inform himself about the events of his day. He was the author of three other chronicles, all modelled on the chronicles of chivalry made popular by Froissart. All the incidents are described in the light of the ethos of the military class of* fidalgos *and are seen as affairs of honour, even when they are nothing more than slave raids and, as in this case, the Portuguese suffer humiliating defeats.*

In the 1440s the Portuguese were still mounting slave raids along the Sahara coast, though shortly afterwards slave raiding gave way to slave trading, which proved less hazardous and more profitable. Zurara liked to employ classical conceits such as invocations to Fortune, but he also attempted to understand what was happening in the encounters that Portuguese raiders had with non-Christian peoples. His discussion of the rumours of ritual cannibalism show him to be a man who was trying not to be credulous, but who was nevertheless disposed to believe the worst of those who had killed so many Portuguese.

Fortune would contradict its own nature were it always to turn in the same direction. So, in its usual fashion, it would not permit our ships to come back in an altogether happy state with their share of victory. ... Very early the next day, the boats returned to the island, according to the decision that had been taken, but our men did not find there the nets nor the other fishing tackle, but only the turtles, which were tied with ropes. This made them assume that the Moors, although they had removed their fishing tackle, could not be very far away. So, as they looked round them in all directions, they saw another island, from which they were separated by an arm of the sea that ran between the two, namely the one where they were and the other one they could see. However, as they were very keen to confront those Moors and thought that fortune could not be less favourable to them in that encounter than it had been in all the others they had had on that voyage, they decided to go to the said island to see if they could find there what they wanted so much to find.

They did not know the secret design that contrary Fortune had in store for them. So they quickly got into their boats and crossed over to the said island, but as they were men who lacked prudence and were unwilling to reflect on the harm which they might suffer, they began to spread out over the island as boldly as if they were taking a walk safely in their own land. However, as Bernard said in the instructions which he gave to Richard, Lord of Castello Ambrosio, upon the government of his household,[1] he who does not realise that his enemy is able to think of the same things that he can think of exposes himself to danger. So the Moors had the same thought that our men had had and, being more carefully on the watch, had arranged three ambushes as well as they could behind some dunes located there. There they waited until they saw that our men were near. Then the Moors, seeing they were much more numerous than our men, sprung their trap and advanced strongly against them, as men who sought to avenge the capture of their relatives and friends. And although the crowd of these Moors was very great in comparison to the small number of our men, the latter did not retreat, but faced the enemy like men who would not let fear get the better of them. They fought for a long time, during which the Moors suffered great losses for the blows of the Christians were not inflicted in vain. However, at last our men saw the great danger they were in and the need to retire, and began to retreat, not like men taking to flight, but calmly and with all the courage that such a situation required. It is certain that the fight was very violent and worthy of men who fought with good courage. Up to the point when both parties reached the boats most of the casualties were suffered by the Moors, many of whom were killed in the course of this retreat, whereas, although many of the Christians were wounded, not one had yet fallen.

When they reached the boats, because that of Álvaro Gil was the nearest or the easiest to board, most of the Christians climbed aboard that one and also Mafaldo's.[2] The others who were still on the shore wanted to get into the boat belonging to Gonçalo Pacheco's ship, but found themselves in extreme danger because, although it had the lightest load, it was large and could not be launched, remaining stuck on dry land because the tide was in the last quarter of its ebb. So some of the men who knew how to swim, seeing danger so near at hand, threw themselves into the water and saved their lives by swimming. Others, who did not know that art, were forced to prepare themselves to meet their fate, and they met a sad death, albeit not without defending themselves as long as their strength gave them aid. In this way seven of them perished. May God, in His mercy, receive their souls in the habitation of the blessed and, as Holy Scripture says that he who prays for another prays for himself, may it please all you who read this history to address your prayers to God, that by your intercession their souls may receive some increase in glory.

When the men in the other two boats saw their companions die in this way, they regained their caravels and, filled with great sadness, departed to Arguim[3] to take in water, of which they had begun to run short. The Moors took [Gonçalo Pacheco's] boat to the River Tider,[4] where they broke up most of it in order to obtain the planks with the nails, but I do not know to what end because they were quite unable to make any use of them. Afterwards some people said that they had been told by some of the Moors who chanced to fall into our hands that their countrymen ate our fallen men. Although others of our Moor captives denied this, seeking to excuse their countrymen from a matter so monstrous, it is nevertheless certain that their custom is to eat the liver and to drink the blood of dead men, not as a general rule but only, as was said, in the case of those who had killed their fathers, or sons, or brothers, considering this to be a very great revenge. It seems to me that there is no reason to doubt this because it is stated in the book of Marco Polo that such things were customary in many of the nations in the East.[5] Moreover, I see that the idea is still among us today, for we say of one person who hates another that he shows such ill will towards his enemy that, if he could, he would eat his liver and drink his blood.

Notes

1   This is apparently a reference to *Epistola de Cura Rei Familiaris*, a copy of which was in the Portuguese Royal Library.
2   Mafaldo de Setúbal.
3   Arguim was the site of the first permanent Portuguese trading factory on the west African coast south of Morocco. It was probably established after 1443 and was situated on an island off the coast of modern Mauretania.
4   This is situated just south of Arguim.
5   A copy of this work had been brought from Venice by the Infante Dom Pedro and was in the Royal Library.

---

9   THE PORTUGUESE RUN INTO OPPOSITION, 1446

From *Crónica de Guiné* by Gomes Eanes de Zurara.

Translation by Malyn Newitt based on C. R. Beazley and Edgar Prestage, *The Chronicle of the Discovery and Conquest of Guinea*, 2 vols. (London: Hakluyt Society 1896–99), pp. 258–61 and Léon Bourdon trans., *Chronique de Guinée (1453)* (Paris, 1994), pp. 244–7.

This voyage marks a significant change in Portugal's relations with the people of Africa. Up until this time the Portuguese had been raiders, attacking the coastal communities for slaves. On this voyage they met formidable opposition from well-organized African societies. The Portuguese showed little inclination to fight these people, not least, as Zurara says, because of their use of poisoned arrows. From this time onwards slave trading was to replace slave raiding.

There are four particular points of interest in this passage. First, it shows the relationship of slaving to exploration. The caravels would head for a section of the coast which had not been raided before. If the attempt to capture slaves met with resistance, the ships would then sail farther on, in the process exploring new lengths of coastline. Second, it describes a voyage made, not at the direct instigation of Prince Henry or one of the royal princes, but by one of the captains of Madeira. Slave hunting and exploratory voyages were widely supported by the Portuguese nobility. Third, the passage shows that Dom Pedro was apparently as much a sponsor of voyages as Prince Henry himself. There is a possibility that Zurara made use of a chronicle, since lost, that was written about Dom Pedro, and this passage might well have come from such a source. Finally, it is worth noting that Zurara shows himself to be very sensitive to the human issues involved in slaving. Although in the famous account of the landing of slaves at Lagos (Doc. 35) Zurara finds arguments to condone the trade, the account in this passage of the capture of the African woman shows once again his unease with this type of activity.

One of the signs by which a noble heart is recognized is that it is not content with small matters, but always seeks to do better in order to increase its honour and to surpass the deeds of the most noble, both in its own land and abroad. This can justly be said of João Gonçalves,[1] captain of the island [of Madeira], because he was not satisfied with the voyage that his ship had made in the previous year to the land of the blacks. He wanted to send the same Álvaro Fernandes again with his well-armed caravel, and charged him to sail as far and to try to obtain some prize which, by its novelty and importance, might give proof of the great desire he had to serve the lord who had brought him up. Álvaro Fernandes accepted the mission with great good will because he was a man who desired to carry out what he had been charged to do by his uncle.

Once the ship had been provisioned they took the route directly to Cape Verde, where the previous year they had captured the two Guineans of whom we have spoken in another place. Then they continued to the Cape of Masts,[2] where they stayed to put some men on shore. Seven men assembled for the sole purpose of seeing the land and, when these had been landed on the beach, they discovered human footprints, all leading in the same direction. So they followed them, and came to a well where they found goats, which it seemed the Guineans had left there. I think this was because they must have seen that they were being followed. The Christians went as far as this but lacked the courage to push on farther.

They returned to their caravel and continued their voyage. Upon launching their boat, they found elephant droppings which, in the opinion of those who saw them, were equal in size to the height of a man. However, because this did not seem a likely place to take a prize, they returned again to their caravel.

Continuing their journey along the seacoast, after only a few days they went ashore again and came upon a village, the inhabitants of which came out like men determined to defend their homes. Among them was one man armed with a great shield and with a spear in his hand. As soon as he saw him, Álvaro Fernandes, thinking that he was their chief, advanced quickly towards him and gave him such a wound with his lance that he fell dead. He then took his shield and spear, which he brought back for the Infante, together with other things to be described later. When the Guineans saw [the villager] lying dead, they gave up the fight. As for our men, they thought it was neither the time nor the place to allow the Guineans to overcome their fear, so they returned to their ship.

The next day they landed a little further along and saw some Guinean women who seemed to be collecting shellfish on the shore of a little inlet. They seized one of the women who must have been about thirty years old, with her son who was two, and also a young girl of fourteen, who did not lack a certain elegance of form and, for a Guinean, a certain beauty of face. The strength of the woman was astonishing because the three men who seized her had great trouble getting her into the boat. So one of our men, seeing the slow progress they were making, which might allow time for some of the inhabitants of the land to surprise them, had the idea of taking her child and carrying him to the boat, so that her maternal love made her follow him, without her being further forced by the two men who were leading her.

From this place they continued for a certain time until they found a river up which they could venture in their boat. In the houses they found there, they captured a woman and, after they brought her to the caravel, they returned once more to the river, intending to sail farther upstream in order to try and capture a good prize. As they continued in this way, four or five boats of Guineans came at them, with the air of men who were determined to defend their land. The men in the boat were unwilling to fight them because they saw the superiority of their enemies, and especially because they feared the great danger that lay in the poison the [Guineans] used on their missiles. So they began to retreat to their ship as well as they could, but seeing that one of the [Guinean] boats was a long way ahead of the others, they turned round ready to face it. However, it turned aside towards the others. Our men wanted to capture this boat before it could escape, because it seemed to be sufficiently distant from its companions. The boat came so near that one of the Guineans discharged an arrow, which by chance hit Álvaro Fernandes in the leg. However, because he knew well the effect of the poison, he drew out the arrow very quickly and had the wound washed with urine and olive oil, and then anointed it very thoroughly with theriac.[3] And it pleased God that this saved him, although his health was in very great danger, and for some days he was at death's door.

Although the others on the caravel saw their captain thus wounded, they continued to sail along that coast until they reached a narrow strip of sand stretching in front of a great bay. They launched their boat and entered the bay to see what country they would find. When they were in sight of the beach, they saw coming towards them about 120 Guineans, some with shields and spears and others with bows. As soon as they came near the water's edge, the Guineans began to play music and to dance like people who had no cares in the world. However, our men declined the invitation to these festivities and returned to their ship. All this happened about 110 leagues beyond Cape Verde, with the direction of the coast always tending to the south.[4]

This caravel went farther this year than all the others, which was worth 200 dobras[5] by way of reward, that is to say 100 dobras, which the Infante Dom Pedro, who was then Regent, ordered to be given, and another 100, which they received from the Infante Dom Henrique. Had it not been for the illness of Álvaro Fernandes, which tormented him greatly, the caravel would have gone farther still. However, it was obliged to turn back at the last place I mentioned and return straight to the island of Arguim, and from there to the Cape of the Ransom, where they found Ahude Meymam, of whom we have already spoken in this history. They did not carry an interpreter, yet by making signs they obtained a black woman, whom the Moors gave them in exchange for some cloths they had brought with them. Had they not brought so little they could have obtained much more, so great was the desire that the Moors showed [to trade]. From there they came back to the kingdom, where they received the dobras, as I have already said, together with many other rewards from the Infante their lord, who was very pleased at their return because they had pushed on with their voyage so far.

Notes

1   João Gonçalves Zarco, who had been knighted while on the Tangier campaign of 1437, was given the captaincy of Funchal, which covered half the island of Madeira.
2   Today known as Cap Naze on the coast of Senegal.
3   An antidote to poison, especially to snake bite, the use of which dated back to classical antiquity.

4   It is not clear what was the farthest point reached by this caravel. It may have reached
    as far as Sierra Leone, but a place nearer Cacheu is more likely. See the discussion in
    Léon Bourdon trans., *Chronique de Guinée (1453)*, pp. 340–1
5   *Dobra* was the name given to gold coins minted in Morocco and Castile. Monetary
    reform in Portugal led to the minting of *escudos* in 1435–36, which had a parity with
    the *dobra*. In 1457, the Portuguese broke with the *dobra*, and its replacement, the *cru-
    zado*, was linked to the Venetian ducat.

10   DUARTE PACHECO PEREIRA TRIES TO COME TO TERMS WITH 'DIFFERENCE'

Duarte Pacheco Pereira, *Esmeraldo de Situ Orbis*, Damião Peres ed., 3rd edition (Lisbon, 1988), book 2, chapter 11 and book 1, chapter 29.

Translated by Malyn Newitt.

Duarte Pacheco Pereira's account of western Africa is a rich compendium of geographical information, history and anecdote. It represents a comprehensive attempt to gather together all that was known about western Africa and to interpret half a century of contact and experience in the light of the classical texts of Pliny and Pomponius Mela. Duarte Pacheco, like so many educated people of his day, was half scientist and half believer in the myths inherited from classical literature and medieval legend. He was a typical man of the Renaissance, in that he tried to reconcile 'ancient' knowledge with scientific observation and his own experience. In his thoughts on skin colour, he allowed observation to displace ideas that, until that time, were accepted without question. Yet he still relied on stories accepted since the days of ancient Greece for matters that fell outside his direct experience, as can be seen in his account of the 'dogfaces' and the silent trade.

The Mysteries of Skin Colour

This Cabo de Lopo Gonçalves[1] lies just below the Equator, and as many people live there who are negroes as in any other part of the world. And during the many years we have sailed and operated in this part of the Ethiopias of Guinea, experience has taught us how to take the height of the sun and its declination in order to tell the degrees of latitude by which each place is separated from the Equator and one of the poles. And we have found that this promontory lies directly over the Equator, and have discovered that in this place the days and nights throughout the year are equal, and if there is any difference it is so small as to be scarcely noticeable.[2]

Many of the ancients said that if two lands lie to the east and west of one another, both would have the same degree of sun and would be in all things alike. As to their equal share of the sun this is true, but such is the great variety employed by the majesty of nature in her work of creation and procreation that we find, from experience, that the inhabitants of this promontory of Lopo Gonçalves and of the rest of Guinea are very black, whereas the people who live beyond the Ocean Sea[3] to the west (who have an equal amount of sun with the blacks of Guinea) are brown, and some almost white. These are the people who live in the land of Brazil, of whom we made mention in the second chapter of our first book. If any want to claim that these are protected from the heat of the sun because there are many trees in that region which give them shade and for this reason they are almost white, I would say that there are also many trees as great and as thick in this land of Guinea on the eastern side of the ocean. And if any should say that they are black because they go around naked and that the others are white because they go clothed, I would say that both of them give the same privilege to nature because all go around just as they were born. So we can say that the sun does not affect one more than the others. Now it only remains to find out if they are both descended from Adam.

Silent Trade

A great fair is held at Sutuco,[4] to which the Mandingas[5] bring many asses; these same Mandingas, when the country is at peace and there are no wars, come to our ships which, at the command of our prince, visit these parts. The Mandingas trade with the said ships – they trade red, blue and green cloths of small value, and buy scarves and silks of different colours, brass bracelets (*manilhas*), caps, hats, the stones called *alaquequas*[6] and much more merchandise, so that in time of peace, as we have said, five and six thousand dobras of good gold are brought from there to Portugal. Sutuco and the other places nearby belong to the kingdom of Jalofo,[7] but being on the borders of Mandinga they speak the Mandinga language. This Rio de Gambia divides the kingdom of Jalofo from the great kingdom of Mandinga, which in their language is called *Encalhor*,[8] as I have said above; Rio de Gambia[9] itself is called in the Mandinga tongue *Guabu*.[10] When ascending the Guabu the kingdom of Jalofo is to the north and that of Mandinga to the south,[11] extending nearly two hundred leagues in length and eighty in breadth. The king of Mandinga can put into the field twenty thousand horsemen and as many infantry, [for] they take as many wives as they desire, and when their king is very old and cannot govern, or if he has a prolonged illness, they kill him and make one of his sons or near relatives king.[12]

Two hundred leagues from this river of Mandinga is a region where there is much gold, which is called Toom. The inhabitants of this region have the faces and teeth of dogs and tails like dogs.[13] They are black and shun conversation, not liking to see other men. The inhabitants of the places called Betu,[14] Banbarrana[15] and Baha go to this country of Toom to obtain gold in exchange for merchandise and slaves, which they bring there. The way these people trade is as follows: Anyone who wishes to sell a slave or other article goes to a certain place appointed for the purpose, ties the slave to a tree and makes a hole in the ground as large as he thinks fit. Having done this he goes a good way off. Then the dogface comes and, if he is content to fill the said hole with gold, he fills it, and if not, he covers up the hole with earth and makes another smaller one and goes away. When this is done, the seller of the slave returns and examines the hole made by the dogface and, if he is satisfied, he goes away again, and the dogface returns and fills the hole with gold. This is the way they conduct their commerce both in slaves and other merchandise, and I have spoken with men who have seen this. The merchants of Mandinga go to the fairs of Betu and Banbarrana and Baha to obtain gold from these monstrous people.[16]

Notes

1 Cape Lopes is half a degree south of the Equator.
2 By the end of the fifteenth century, navigators were able to calculate latitude with considerable accuracy; the calculation of longitude had to await the invention of the chronometer in the eighteenth century.
3 The Atlantic.
4 Sutuco, also known as Sutukoba, was situated north of the Gambia opposite Cantor.
5 Mande-speaking traders who were Muslims and originated in the Mali empire had been penetrating the forest zones, probably since the twelfth century A.D.
6 Bloodstones.
7 Wolofs. See also Docs. 7, 19 and 55.
8 This presumably refers to Cayor. See Doc. 16.
9 The Gambia River.
10 The name Guabuu, more usually Kaabu, was given to the state established by Mandinka invaders whose ascendancy depended on their cavalry and that grew to include most of the savannah country between the Gambia and Geba Rivers.
11 The original has *'da parte do sul ou meio-dia'*.
12 This is an early reference to the idea of 'divine kingship', which the nineteenth-century anthropologist Sir James Fraser believed to be the archetypal form of human government, traces of which could be detected in cultures throughout the world.
13 The belief in the existence of dog-headed people can be found in Book Four of Herodotus's *Histories* and was widely accepted by educated and uneducated alike in

the Middle Ages. It was referred to by Marco Polo and more recently was revived in the popular but entirely fictitious account of the travels of Sir John Mandeville, which was written in the mid-fourteenth century.

14 According to E. W. Bovill, *The Golden Trade of the Moors* (Oxford, 1968) p. 149, Bitu was another name for Bonduku in northern Ashanti.

15 Possibly Bambara in modern Mali.

16 The 'silent trade' is first described in Book Four of Herodotus's *Histories*. Another detailed discussion of this 'silent trade' is contained in Alvise da Cadamosto's *Voyages*, which were written in the 1460s.

3

THE ATLANTIC ISLANDS

---

11 MADEIRA AND THE CANARY ISLANDS IN THE FIFTEENTH CENTURY

From Rinaldo Caddeo ed., *Le Navigazioni Atlantiche di Alvise da Cá da Mosto* (Milan, 1929) in *Viagens de Luís de Cadamosto e de Pedro de Sintra*, Academia Portuguesa da História (Lisbon, 1948), pp. 9–13.
Translated by Malyn Newitt.

From as early as the sixteenth century the account written by Alvise da Cadamosto of his two voyages to west Africa has been recognized as of great importance. It is the only account of one of the early 'Portuguese' voyages written by an eyewitness and it contains a wealth of observation and information on which any account of western Africa and of the Portuguese slaving and exploratory voyages in the fifteenth century must be based. Cadamosto was from a noble Venetian family and first saw service as a crossbowman in the Venetian galleys. Returning from a voyage to Flanders in 1452, he found his family in difficult financial circumstances and decided to go with his brother to try to redeem the family fortunes. He obtained a licence from Prince Henry to undertake two trading voyages to the upper Guinea region, visiting the Gambia, the Senegal, the Rio Grande and the Cape Verde Islands, which he claimed to have discovered. He returned to Venice around 1463, and his account was completed by 1468.

The two following passages constitute one of the earliest detailed accounts of the Atlantic islands. The legend of the burning of the forests on Madeira may have been an account of an actual event, but to modern readers it seems more like an allegory of the environmental disaster which has so often accompanied European overseas expansion. Cadamosto was impressed by the fertility of Madeira and the prosperity of the settlements there. The sugar plantations and vineyards needed slave labour, and the Madeirans were among those who pioneered slaving voyages to west Africa (Doc. 9). The description of the

Canary Islands is one of the few dating from the years before the Spanish conquest and shows the willingness of Cadamosto to try to gather first-hand evidence of the areas about which he was writing. His emphasis on the various ways in which Canarian society differed from that of Christian Europe must be seen in the context of the debate over whether it was justifiable to enslave such people.[1]

Madeira

Twenty-four years ago the said Lord Infante had this island of Madeira, which had never previously been inhabited, settled by Portuguese. He made two of his knights its governors. One of these, called Tristão [Vaz] Teixeira, had that half of the island around Machico; the other half on the side around Funchal was governed by João Gonçalves [Zarco].[2] This island is called the island of Madeira, which means the island of wood because when it was first discovered by the Infante's men, there was not a palm's breadth of land which was not covered by immense trees, in such a manner that the first people who wanted to settle there were forced to set them on fire. This fire burned throughout the island for such a long time and so fiercely, that in order to escape the inferno and a certain death, the governor, João Gonçalves, his wife and children, and all those who were on the island, had to remain in the sea for two days and nights without anything to eat or drink and with the water up to their necks. In this way a large part of the wood was cleared to make farmland.

Four parts of this island are inhabited: The first is called Machico, the second Santa Cruz, the third Funchal and the fourth and last Câmara de Lobos.[3] Although there are other places that are inhabited, these are the principal ones. There are 800 men, a hundred of whom are mounted. The island is about 140 miles round and, although it does not possess any port, there are very good anchorages. The land is fruitful and abundant and, although it is as mountainous as Sicily, it is always very fertile and produces 30,000 Venetian *stara*[4] of wheat each year, sometimes more and sometimes less. At one time the land yielded sixty or seventy to one, but at present this is reduced to between thirty and forty, because day by day, the land is becoming exhausted. The region is very productive and has abundant water and beautiful springs, and there are six or eight small streams that flow through the island. Along these watercourses are built sawmills where they continually work wood and make planks of various kinds, which are supplied to Portugal and other places. Among the different kinds of wood there are two which I will mention. The first is cedar, which is strongly scented and is like cypress, out of which fine long and wide planks, chests and other objects are made; the second kind is the wood of the yew, which is of a beautiful reddish colour.

As the island is known to be well watered, the said Infante had sugar cane planted, which grows to perfection. Different kinds of sugar, amounting to 400 *cantara*,[5] are produced, which are useful for cooking or blending, and I understand that they will soon produce a good quantity because this crop is suited to the warm and temperate climate where, as in Sicily and Cyprus, it never gets really cold. Sugar also grows well because there is an abundance of water. Many different types of sugar-coated sweetmeat are made to perfection, and wax and honey are also produced though in small quantities. The new settlers have planted vines and their wines are good and fine. They produce enough for their needs and allow a part of it to be exported. Among these vines are malvoisie grapes of Candia,[6] which the Infante had brought directly from the Levant. The soil of this island is so good and fertile that the vines produce almost more grapes than leaves and the bunches are enormous, being two palms and I might almost say four palms, long – it is the most beautiful thing to be seen in the world – and there are also black trellis grapes, which have no pips and grow to perfection.

The most excellent and beautiful bows and crossbow bolts of yew are made in this island, and are exported by ship to the mainland.[7] Wild peacocks are found, some of which are white, but they have neither partridges nor other game except quails and some wild pigs in the mountains. I have heard it said by trustworthy islanders that at first a large number of pigeons were found in this island and the people used to hunt them with a small noose on the end of a pole. This was placed around the neck of the pigeon, which was then pulled down from the trees without their having any fear of men. This happened because they did not know anything about men and were not accustomed to being hunted. This can be believed because I have heard the same thing said of another recently discovered island. The island of Madeira abounds in all kinds of meat. Many of the inhabitants are rich, like the country itself, since the island resembles a garden and everything that grows there is like gold. There are monasteries of friars of the Observant Franciscan Order who live a holy life.[8] There are many trustworthy people who, because of the perfection of the country for agriculture, have reported seeing ripe grapes in holy week, which is a thing more amazing than anything I have seen.

Canary Islands

... There are ten Canary Islands, seven inhabited and three uninhabited. ... Of these seven islands, four are inhabited by Christians, that is Lanzarote, Fuerteventura, Gomera and Ferro. The other three [Gran Canaria, Teneriffe and Palma] are inhabited by idolators. ... [9] The inhabitants of the four Christian islands are also Canarians,[10] but they speak languages so different that they have difficulty understanding each other. There are no walled places in these islands except a few villages, but they have strongholds in the mountains, which are very big and high and access to them is so difficult that no one in the world could capture them except by starvation.

That applies to the four islands inhabited by Christians, all of which are large since the smallest is at least ninety miles round. The other three islands inhabited by idolators are larger and very populous, especially two of them, namely Gran Canaria, which has more than seven or eight thousand souls, and Teneriffe, the largest of the three, which is said to have fourteen to fifteen thousand people. Palma is not so populous but is a very beautiful island to look upon. It should be noted that because these three islands are so populous and have many people to defend them, and because the islands are very high and their settlements difficult and dangerous to attack, the Christians have never been able to subdue them. Teneriffe, which is the most populous, deserves a particular mention as it is one of the highest islands in the world, so that in clear weather it can be seen from a great distance at sea. Trustworthy sailors have assured me that they have seen it at a distance of between sixty and seventy Spanish leagues, which are about 250 Italian miles, because in the middle of the island arises a peak, like a diamond, which shines continuously.[11] This is also confirmed by Christians who have been made prisoner in this island and who maintain that this mountain measures from the base to the summit fifteen Portuguese leagues or sixty of our Italian miles.

In this island there are nine lords, which they call dukes. These are not lords by natural right, where the son succeeds the father, but whoever is the strongest becomes the lord. These lords are frequently at war and kill each other like beasts, having no other weapons than stones and sticks from which they fashion a kind of javelin. And some of them fix a pointed horn in place of an iron tip. Others which do not have a horn are burnt at the point, which makes the tip as hard as iron. It is with these weapons that they fight having no iron or other weapons. They go around quite naked except that some wear the skins of goats, one before and one behind. They cover their bodies with the fat of goats, which they mix with the juice of certain herbs to toughen the skin. This protects them from the cold although, because these regions are situated towards the south, it is never very cold.

They do not have houses either of stone or of straw but live in caverns and caves in the mountains. They eat barley and the meat and milk of goats, which they have in abundance, and especially figs. Because this is a hot country, they harvest their crops in March or April. They do not have any religion and do not recognize God. However, some of them worship the sun, others the moon and still others the planets, and they have peculiar pagan practices. They do not have wives in common but each one is able to have as many as he wishes. However, no one ever takes a virgin until she has first slept one night with the lord, and this they consider to be a great honour. If you should ask how I learned these things, I would reply that the inhabitants of the four Christian islands are accustomed to come secretly by night in their boats to these islands to attack the idolatrous Canarians and to capture men and women who they send to be sold as slaves in Spain. It sometimes happens that some of the men from these vessels are taken prisoner. These are not killed by the Canarians but are given the job of killing and skinning the goats and preparing the meat, because they consider the profession of butcher to be most vile and to humiliate [their captives] they are made to do this until in some manner they gain their liberty. ... [12]

Notes

1 For the most recent discussion of all the early sources for the Canary islands, see David Abulafia, *The Discovery of Mankind* (New Haven and London, 2008).

2 In the Italian they are called Tristan Tesera and Zuan Conzales. For Zarco, see also Doc. 9.

3 In the Italian these are rendered Monzicho, Sancta Croxe, Fonzial and Camera de Loui.

4 The *stara* or *setier* as a measure of wheat was the equivalent of 152 litres.

5 The *cantara* was the same as the *alqueire* or 13.8 litres.

6 Candia was the capital of Crete.

7 The Italian has "in ponent".

8 The Observant Franciscans, known as *zelanti*, were those who followed the strict rules of poverty laid down by St. Francis in his Testament.

9 In Italian the names are Lanzaroto, Forteventura, Gran Canaria, Teneriffe, Gomera, Palma, Farro.

10 Usually called Guanches.

11 This is the Pico del Teide, which is 3718 metres high.

12 Cadamosto's account of the customs of the Canary islanders is similar to the information given by Zurara, which may suggest that both writers may have relied on the same source. See the discussion in David Abulafia, *The Discovery of Mankind* (New Haven and London, 2008) pp. 63–4.

12 HOW TO SURVIVE TROPICAL HEAT AND DISEASE

From Anon, *Viagens de um pilôto português do século XVI à costa de África e a São Tomé*, Arlindo Manuel Caldeira ed. (Lisbon, 2000), pp. 117–8. Translated by Malyn Newitt.

This anonymous text was first published in Italian in 1550 by Giovanni Battista Ramusio in his collection of voyages entitled Navigationi e Viaggi.[1] *The Portuguese original is no longer extant. The author is described as being a 'pilot' and evidence in the text suggests that he came from Vila do Conde, a prosperous sea port just north of Porto which had extensive commercial ties with São Tomé. The text describes São Tomé and Príncipe, two of the four islands in the Gulf of Guinea that the Portuguese had settled at the end of the fifteenth century, which were in their heyday as producers of sugar. The Portuguese 'pilot' knew the islands well and gives a vivid description of a slave-owning society trying to come to terms with a hostile environment and seeking solutions to problems of climate and disease. The passage shows how the Portuguese treated the malarial fevers that were endemic in the islands and the extent to which they relied on the medical knowledge of their African slaves.*

In the town[2] there is a very common custom that when the atmosphere is cloudy and without wind, which lasts for a few days (during which they experience an extraordinary heat and such humidity that it appears that a cauldron of water is boiling), four or five neighbouring families come together to eat in some large ground-floor rooms with their wives and children, and to these houses each one brings whatever he has prepared in his own house. Everything is laid out on a wide table, and each one serves himself freely from the dainty dishes of his neighbour rather than from those prepared in his own house, so weak and dispirited do they feel. They pass these suffocating[3] days in conversation, without being able to do any business outside their houses. And so great is the heat that the earth gives off, that they wear leather shoes with double soles and also large clogs with cork inside them.

Throughout the year the white inhabitants of the town usually suffer a sort of intermittent fever every eight or ten days as follows: First comes cold and then heat, and it all passes off in two hours according to each person's constitution. This complaint happens to those who live permanently there, and they are accustomed to bleed themselves three or four times a year. However, for foreigners who come there on board the ships, the first fever which attacks them usually lasts twenty days and is often fatal. They are bled without any reckoning being taken of the quantity, drawing almost a tankard-full[4] of blood from a vein in the arm, and after they have been bled, they make for them a soup of bread cooked in water with a little salt and olive oil. If they survive the seventh day, then they can expect to last till the fourteenth, and after that they can consider themselves saved unless they suffer a relapse. And in proportion as the fever declines the quantity of food is increased, first with chicken and at the end of the fever with some pig meat.

The French disease[5] and scabies are also common in this island, diseases which the blacks take little notice of, and some black women make a sort of plaster with alum and mercury and use it together with an infusion from certain roots, which they drink.

Notes

1   In the original Italian the title was *Navigazione Da Lisbona All'Isola Di san Thomé posta sotto la linea scritta per un pilotto Portoghese, & mandata al Magnifico Conte Rimondo della torre, gentiluomo veronese, & tradotta di lingua Portoghese in Italiana.* A popular Portuguese edition was published with the title *Viagem de Lisboa a Ilha de S.Tomé* Portugália (Lisbon, 1960) by Augusto Reis Machado who updated an earlier eighteenth century translation by Sebastião Francisco de Mendo Trigoso.

2   The author refers to it as the *Povoação*. The main town of São Tomé is situated on the north of the island in the bay of Ana de Chaves.

3   Augusto Reis Machado rendered this *tormentosos* meaning 'stormy', which would be a strange way to describe days 'without wind'.

4   The Portuguese term is *pichel*.

5   Syphillis.

---

13   SUGAR AND SLAVES

From Anon, *Viagens de um pilôto português do século XVI à costa de África e a São Tomé*, Arlindo Manuel Caldeira ed. (Lisbon, 2000), pp. 105–6.

Translated by Malyn Newitt.

São Tomé and its sister island of Príncipe in the Gulf of Guinea were the first of the European colonies given over wholly to sugar production. Here the plantation system, dependent on slave labour, was developed and a monoculture established, which made it necessary for the settlers to import everything they needed, including food. São Tomé took on all the characteristics later assumed by the islands of the lesser Antilles; it was a Caribbean island on the wrong side of the Atlantic. This account, first published in Italian in 1550,[1] describes São Tomé's sugar industry at its height in the middle of the sixteenth century, for by the end of the century most of the sugar production had moved to Brazil, where plentiful land enabled a rapid growth of the industry. The Portuguese planters preferred to buy both male and female slaves in order to establish slave households, which is in marked contrast to the preference of the English and Dutch for male slaves only.

São Tomé was not just a sugar plantation island but played a major role in Portuguese relations with mainland Africa. Traders from São Tomé were active in all the African coastal ports of the Gulf of Guinea and as far as south Luanda, where they founded a settlement and developed the trade in currency shells. São Tomé islanders were also accused of undermining the trade monopolies which the Portuguese Crown tried to develop at Elmina and in the kingdom of Kongo, and even of providing military backing to rebels against the Kongo king.

The principal occupation of the inhabitants [of this island] is to manufacture sugar and sell it to the ships, which come in search of it every year. These ships bring kegs of flour, Spanish wines, olive oil, cheese, leather for shoes, swords, glasses, beads and a kind of small white shell which the Italians call *porcellete* and we call *búzio* and which in Ethiopia are used as money.[2] If the ships that bring these goods did not come, the white merchants would die because they are not accustomed to the food of the blacks.

Each inhabitant buys black slaves with their women from Guinea, Benin and Manikongo, and they employ these couples to cultivate the land and to plant and extract the sugar. And there are some rich men who possess a hundred and fifty, two hundred and even three hundred black men and women who are obliged to work the whole week for their master, except on Saturdays when they work for their own maintenance. On these days they sow sorghum,[3] of which we have already spoken above, yams and many green vegetables such as lettuces, kale, turnips, beetroot and celery, which, once they have been sown, grow in a few days and are of very good quality. However, the seed that they produce is not suitable for sowing.

The earth is a red-yellow colour, rich with thick clay and, because of the heavy dew that falls continually every night, it never becomes powdery but remains with the texture of soft wax and for this reason anything that is planted in it grows very well. A good idea of the fertility of the land is seen in the fact that if the blacks cease cultivating some of the lowland areas for a time, immediately trees grow up there and in a few days they grow as large as would take many months with us, so that it is necessary to cut them down and then reduce them to ashes. In the place where they cut and burn the trees it is good to plant sugar cane, which in this way matures in the space of five months. The canes that are planted in the month of January are cut at the beginning of June, while those planted in February reach maturity by the beginning of July, and in the same way they plant and cut cane every month. Nor does the sun do any harm when it is directly overhead in March and September, because at these times the weather is misty, with heavy cloud and continuous rains, which is very good for the sugar cane.

This island yields a hundred and fifty thousand or more arrobas[4] of sugar ... and from this amount is deducted the tenth that is paid to the king, which ordinarily amounts to between twelve and fourteen thousand arrobas, although there are many who do not pay in full. There are around sixty sugar mills powered by water where they mill and crush the cane. They pour the juice into very large cauldrons and, after boiling it, pour it into moulds from which they make loaves of fifteen to twenty pounds. They purify the sugar with ashes in the same way that we use sieved chalk. In many parts of the island, where there is no water, this work has to be done by manpower of the blacks and even by the horses. After being crushed, the cane is left for the pigs of which there are a great number. As they do not eat anything other than the said cane, they grow extraordinarily fat and their flesh is so delicate and healthy that it is easier to digest than chicken and for this reason is usually given to the sick.[5]

Notes

1   See Doc. 12.
2   *Búzios* were a kind of cowry found on the coast of western Africa, especially on the coast near the future city of Luanda. They were also known as *nzimbu*. See Docs 26, 32 and 55.
3   The Italian miglio zaburo may also indicate one of the many varieties of pennisetum.
4   The author adds 'each *arroba* corresponding to 31 of our *libras'*. An *arroba* was equivalent to 15 kgs (or 33 lbs).
5   See Doc. 12.

14   HUNTING ESCAPED SLAVES IN SÃO TOMÉ

A Letter from the Justices of São Tomé to the Royal Officials, 6 September 1535
António Brásio, *Monumenta Missionaria Africana* (Lisbon, 1952), 2, pp. 46–7.
Translated by Malyn Newitt.

In the early sixteenth century São Tomé developed as a plantation society dependent on a large slave population. The island was mountainous and covered with tropical rainforest and, in spite of its small size, much of the interior was inaccessible. Slaves who escaped into the mountains were difficult to find and recapture. The planters lived in continual fear of slave revolts, of raids by bands of fugitives and of attacks by pirates. A major slave revolt in 1595, led by the legendary Amador, proved to be a major factor in convincing the planters that it was time to move their operations to Brazil. It is now thought that it was a group of escaped slaves that formed the nucleus of the modern population of Angolares with their distinctive dialect.[1]

At the time this letter was written, São Tomé was largely self-governing. The captaincy had been abolished in 1522, and the island was supposed to be ruled by a governor sent from Lisbon. However, because of the prevalence of disease, many governors never took up their offices, and the islanders effectively governed themselves through their Senado da Câmara, which was granted its charter in 1524. The Crown was only represented on the spot by the royal trading factor, who levied duties on slaves that were exported. The church was also largely self-governing. São Tomé had become a bishopric in 1534, but few bishops went to the islands, and the church was run by the canons of the cathedral, most of whom were drawn from the local free black families.

To the *Senhor* Factor and the Officials of our Lord the King

Gonçalo Álvares and Rodrigo Ayres, common justices and justices for orphans in this island of São Tomé[2] and so forth, make known to Your Excellencies[3] how it is true and well known that a *mocambo*[4] with a large population exists in the forest, and they do what damage they can, killing and robbing men and destroying plantations, all of which brings loss and damage to the people of this island and its settlers,[5] and a disservice to the king our lord and much loss to his treasury and the revenues which he has in this island. In order to restore everything to law and order henceforth, Your Excellencies should give money for the war in the bush, part to be provided by the said lord and the other part by the people, as has been done up to now both in the time of *senhor* Henrique Pereira[6] and after his death. And now, *senhores*, we have armed men ready to go against the said escaped blacks and the fortified *mocambo*, but we do not have any money to give them and every day the forest is filling up with escaped blacks, and we are all terrified, waiting for the day when the said *mocambo* and its people will do some evil which is contrary to the will of God.

We request Your Excellencies, on behalf of the king our lord and on our own behalf, to order us as a favour to be given forty thousand *reis* so that we can send armed men against the said *mocambo*.

And if Your Excellencies will do this, they will perform what needs to be done and will fulfil their duty to the king our lord and to the people and the land. If Your Excellencies are not willing to do this, we protest that you will be liable for all that happens to us and for the loss that will occur and which the blacks will cause us. And the said lord will be surprised, and it will be much to his disservice that all the people of this island cry out every day for people to go into the bush. For this reason we order this letter to be passed to Your Excellencies,

Signed by us Gonçalo Álvares and Rodrigo Ayres

Notes

1   For the slave revolts in São Tomé and the identification of the Angolares as descendants of maroons see Gerhard Seibert, 'Castaways, Autochthons, or Maroons? The debate on the Angolares of São Tomé Island', in Philip J.Havik and Malyn Newitt eds., *Creole Societies in the Portuguese Colonial Empire*, (Bristol, 2007), pp.103–26
2   Written 'Samtomé'.
3   *Vossas merçês*.
4   Known in Brazil as *quilombos*, these were settlements of escaped slaves.
5   *Moradores*.
6   He had been nominated *corregedor* of São Tomé in 1531.

---

15   NEW CHRISTIANS HAVE POISONED THE BISHOP OF SÃO TOMÉ

From Lorenzo Tramalho to Cardinal Francesco Barberini, Lisbon, 14 February 1632.

J. Cuvelier and L. Jadin eds., *L'Ancien Congo d'aprés les archives romaines*, Mémoire de l'Académie des Sciences Coloniales (Brussels, 1954), p. 498.

Translated by Malyn Newitt.

After the expulsion of Jews from Portugal in 1495 and the continued persecution of New Christians, which culminated in the Lisbon massacres of 1506, many Jews and New Christians left for Morocco and also for west Africa (see Docs. 4 and 56). In the west African trading stations Jewish rites could be practised with little disturbance from the ecclesiastical authorities. By the early seventeenth century New Christian influence in western Africa was widespread and flourished alongside other kinds of religious heterodoxy. The São Tomé islanders acquired early on the reputation of being strongly influenced by Jewish practices.

This may have had its origin in the story that large numbers of Jewish children, who had been taken away from their parents, were among the settlers who were sent to São Tomé in the late fifteenth century,[1] but it was certainly encouraged by the heavy mortality among priests and governors sent from Portugal, who, it was only too easy to believe, had been poisoned. In 1621, one bishop even fled the island claiming that Judaism was so rampant that he had seen a secret night-time procession carrying a 'golden calf'. At a deeper level, these accusations of Judaizing probably reflect the metropolitan frustration at the long-established opposition of the islanders to any form of control from Lisbon.

This week a canon and two secular priests from São Tomé have arrived from Holland, having been taken by the Dutch after the capture of their ship. The bishop [of São Tomé], a Dominican, died two years ago.[2] He was poisoned by some New Christians, among them ecclesiastics as well as laymen, against whom he had held an inquest and had produced the deposition of witnesses. The canon says that the island is so infested with New Christians that Jewish practices are carried on almost openly. They have poisoned the bishops and governors who try to punish them. It is requested that New Christians should no longer receive benefices and canonries and that the capitular vicar, who they say is of that race and one of those principally guilty of the poisoning, should be removed from his office. This should be done if he is found guilty.

Notes

1 This story appears in fol 197r of the manuscript assembled by Valentim Fernandes, who gives the number of children as 2,000. See Th. Monod, A. Teixeira da Mota and R. Mauny, eds. and trans., *Description de la Côte Occidentale d'Afrique (Sénégal au Cap de Monte, Archipels)* (Bissau: Centro de Estudos da Guiné Portuguesa, 1951), p. 119. See Doc. 18.
2 Fr. Domingos da Assunção was enthroned as bishop in 1627.

4

THE UPPER GUINEA COAST AND SIERRA LEONE

16 CADAMOSTO MEETS BUDOMEL

From Rinaldo Caddeo ed., *Le Navigazioni Atlantiche di Alvise da Cá da Mosto* (Milan, 1929), in *Viagens de Luís de Cadamosto e de Pedro de Sintra*, Academia Portuguesa da História (Lisbon, 1948), pp. 33–8.
Translated by Malyn Newitt.

Cadamosto's[1] trading voyage to Budomel's country, fifty miles beyond the Senegal river, took place in 1455. Budomel has been identified as the ruler or Damel of Cayor. The account that the author gives of his visit is one of the most remarkable early accounts of the meeting of Europeans and black Africans. In this encounter there was a high level of trust arising from the mutual advantage of the exchange of horses for slaves. Cadamosto, it appears, handed over his valuable trade goods ahead of any payment by the ruler. It is clear that European traders were already being treated as honoured strangers by the African rulers, who stood to gain so much from the trade. Cadamosto has an extraordinary curiosity about African society and how it functioned, and his account shows little if any trace of the medieval legends that had previously coloured the way Europeans viewed the equatorial regions. Particularly noteworthy is his understanding of the function of polygyny, the ruler moving round the villages of his wives who were able to support him and his entourage.

I passed the aforementioned river Senegal with my caravel and, sailing on, reached the land of Budomel, which place is about eighty miles from this river along the coast. This coast from the said river to the land of Budomel is all low lying and without mountains. The name Budomel is the title of this lord and not his personal name: The land is called the land of Budomel as one would say the land of such a lord or count. I stayed there with my caravel in order to speak with this lord, because I had heard from other Portuguese who had traded with him that he was a good person and a lord who could be trusted, and that he paid handsomely for what was brought to him. And because I had brought with me some Spanish horses,[2] and other things which were in much demand in the land of the blacks (among the many other things I had with me were woollen cloths, Moorish silks and other merchandise), I made up my mind to try my luck with this lord. So I decided to anchor at a place on the coast of his country, which is called the Palm of Budomel and which is an anchorage rather than a port.

I announced my arrival to Budomel through my black interpreter and told him I had come with horses and other merchandise to be of service to him if he should need it. As soon as the said lord received this information, he mounted his horse and came down to the beach with 15 mounted men and 150 men on foot. And he sent [a messenger] to tell me that I should disembark and go to see him, and that he would treat me with honour and profit. And so, knowing of his good reputation, I did this and he gave me a warm welcome. After exchanging many words I gave him my horses and everything that he wanted, so great was my trust in him. He asked me if I would be willing to go inland with him to his residence, which was about twenty-five miles distant from the coast. There he would give me what he owed me, which would take some days for he had promised me a hundred slaves in exchange for the horses and other merchandise. So I gave him the horses I had with me with their accoutrements and other things which did not cost me less than 300 ducats and determined to go with him. Before I left, however, he gave me a very pretty black girl of twelve or thirteen years and he told me he was giving her to me for service in my chamber.[3] I accepted her and sent her to my ship. And certainly my journey inland was more to see and learn about new things than to receive my payment.

So then I left to travel inland to Budomel. He gave me horses and everything I needed, and when we were about four miles from his residence, he entrusted me to his nephew, who was called Bisboror and who was the lord of a small town which we had reached. This Bisboror took me to his house and treated me honourably and hospitably. I was there about twenty-eight days (this was the month of November) and during these twenty-eight days I went many times to meet Budomel, and his nephew was always with me. During this time I saw something of the customs of the country, which I make mention of below. However, the more I saw the more necessary it became for me to go back to the river Senegal because, if bad weather should occur on that coast and I wished to embark, it would be necessary to send the boat to that river and for me to go there by land.

Among other things that I saw in that place, I will describe this incident. Desiring to send a letter to those in my ship to let them know that they should come to that river, to which I would have to go by land,

I asked the blacks if there was anyone who knew how to swim well and who had sufficient courage to take my letter to the ship, which was about three miles away. At once many of them said yes, but because the sea was high and there was a lot of wind, I said that I did not think such a thing was possible for a man to do. The principal reason was that about a bow-shot off shore, there was a reef and bank of sand and other banks two bowshots farther still, and between these banks such a current ran now one way and now another, that it was a very difficult thing for any man swimming to withstand it and not to be carried away. So great a sea broke over these banks that it appeared impossible to pass them. In spite of this, two blacks offered to go and when I asked what I should give them, they said that they should be given two manilhas[4] of tin each, which is some-thing they greatly value. So for sixteen marchetti each, they took on them-selves to bring the letter to the caravels and went into the sea. I cannot describe the difficulty they had in passing those sand banks in such a sea. Sometimes they remained for so long without being seen that I thought they had drowned. Finally one of them could no longer withstand the force of the sea which broke over him and turned back. The other strug-gled on bravely across the bank for the space of an hour. Finally he passed it and took the letter to the ship and returned with a reply, which seemed to me to be a remarkable thing. From this I conclude that the blacks of that coast are the greatest swimmers which there are in the world.

What I was able to observe of this lord, of his customs and his resi-dence, are as follows. First I must tell you that, although these men are called lords, it should not be thought that they have castles or cities, as has been noted earlier. The king of this kingdom[5] only reigns over vil-lages made of straw houses and Budomel was lord of only a small part of this kingdom. In truth, those like him are not lords because they are rich in treasure or in money, because they do not strike any coinage nor do they have any. However, in terms of ceremony and in the number of people in their retinue, they are indeed as much lords as any other, for they go about always accompanied by many people and are much more reverenced and feared by their subjects than are ours by their subjects.

So that you can understand the nature of this lord's residence, it is not a palace or a building with walls. This is the manner in which the king lives. There are some villages in the country which are reserved for the habitation of the lord, his wives and all his family because they are never fixed in one place. In whatever village he resides, which is called his resi-dence, there may be forty-five or fifty straw huts grouped to form a circle and surrounded by a fence of stakes made from large trees, leaving one or two openings through which one can enter. Each one of these houses is surrounded by a courtyard which is also fenced, and one goes from courtyard to courtyard and house to house. In this place Budomel has nine wives and he has many other wives who are distributed, as I have said, in various places. Each wife has five or six black girls who wait on them and it is permitted for the lord to sleep with his wife's servants as well as with the wives themselves. And his wives do not feel injured by this because it is the custom. In this way Budomel has a different dinner each night.[6] These black men and women are very lustful, and one of the first things that Budomel asked me on being informed that we Christians knew how to do many things, was that, if by chance I could teach him how to increase his desire so that he could please many women, he would pay me richly. From this you can judge how greatly he tries to indulge himself, which results in these lords being very jealous of their wives. For this reason they allow no one except themselves to enter the houses where the women are, and they do not even trust their own sons.

This Budomel has at least 200 blacks in his retinue who continually go with him and follow him around. In fact, some come and others go and he never lacks number of people since they come to wait on him from different places. On entering the residence of Budomel, before one comes to the place where he sleeps, there are seven large enclosed courtyards, which lead one into the next. In the centre of each one of the courtyards is a large tree so that those who are waiting in the courtyards can stay in the shade. These enclosures correspond to the standing and condition of different persons. In the first enclosure are the servants and the people of lower rank; beyond that are others of higher category and further in, in the third enclosure, still others; and thus by degrees up to Budomel's doorway according to who they are. Very few men dare approach his door, except the Christians who are allowed to go about freely whenever they are met with and the Azenegi who are those who teach the law of Mahomet.[7] These are given more freedom than his own native blacks, or anyone else.

This Budomel shows his rank in this way. He only allows himself to appear for one hour in the morning and for a short time in the afternoon. During this time he remains in the first of his enclosures at the door of his house where, as I have said, only men of importance are allowed to enter and especially foreigners. When these great lords give an audience to anyone, great ceremonial is employed. When anyone comes before Budomel to speak with him, no matter what his rank or his relationship with the great man, he has to throw himself onto his knees at the entrance of the enclosure and place his head on the ground and with both hands throw sand onto his back and onto his head, being entirely naked. In this manner he greets his lord since no one dares to come before him to speak with him unless he is completely naked except for some pieces of leather which they wear to cover their shame. They remain in this posture for some time, throwing sand over their backs.

Then they approach him, not getting to their feet but crawling along the ground on their knees. When they are two paces away from the lord, they start speaking and explaining their case to him, still throwing sand over their backs and with their heads lowered as a sign of great humility, as I have described. The lord scarcely appears to notice them and continues to speak to one person or another. Then, when the vassal has spoken a lot, with an arrogant gesture he gives him a reply in two words. In this way he shows such dignity and reserve that if God himself came to earth I do not believe that greater honour or reverence would be shown to him than these blacks show to their lords. And all this stems from the great fear and terror which they have of him because, at the smallest fault which they are guilty of, the lord orders their wives and children to be seized and all of them to be sold as slaves. It is in these two ways that he shows he is lord and demonstrates his state – that is, in seldom allowing himself to be seen and in being reverenced by his subjects.

Notes

1 For more detail on Cadamosto, see Doc. 11.
2 For the importance of horses in the trade of this region, see Docs. 17 and 18.
3 The Italian has 'per servisio dela mia chamara'. Cadamosto's exact meaning is open to interpretation.
4 Copper or brass rings used as trade currency in western Africa. Although Cadamosto uses the word 'stagno' meaning 'tin', these were probably brass.
5 At this time Cayor was part of the larger Wolof empire. It did not become a fully independent kingdom until a hundred years after Cadamosto's visit.
6 The Italian reads 'budumel muda ogni noto pasta'. Again Cadamosto's intention in using this phrase is open to interpretation.
7 These were Sanhaja who lived in the western region of the Sahara. Sanhaja migrants who entered the upper Guinea region were Muslims and combined trade with the practice of religion and medicine.

---

17   MARKETS AND DANCES: AFRICA RESPONDS TO EUROPE

From Rinaldo Caddeo ed., *Le Navigazioni Atlantiche di Alvise da Cá da Mosto* (Milan, 1929), in *Viagens de Luís de Cadamosto e de Pedro de Sintra*, Academia Portuguesa da História (Lisbon, 1948), pp. 46–9.
Translated by Malyn Newitt.

Cadamosto's[1] open and inquisitive mind is shown to best advantage when he tries to describe African society and its reaction to the European traders. As usual his eye is most immediately attracted to matters of trade, and the cost of slaves measured against the value of a horse indicate to him one of the most profound differences between the two societies.

Because I happened to be in this land for many days, I determined to go to see one of their markets or fairs, which were held every Monday and Friday on an open plain not far from where I was lodged, and which I visited two or three times. To this market men and women came from four or five miles around. Those from farther away went to other markets which they were accustomed to hold in other parts. In these markets it became quite clear to me, from the goods that they brought to the market to sell, that these people are very poor. First, there were small quantities of cotton (but not spun thread), a few woven cotton cloths and vegetables, millet, oil, wooden mortars, palm mats and all the other things that serve them in their everyday life. These things are brought as often by men as by women. The men also sell weapons and some bring a little gold for sale but very little. Nothing is sold for money because they do not have any coins but exchange one thing for another, or two things for one thing, so that the whole market is conducted through exchange.

The blacks, both men and women, came to look at me as a marvel and it seemed to them to be a strange thing to see a Christian in that place, something they had never seen before. They were astonished at the whiteness of my skin and at my clothes, which were in the Spanish[2] style with damask surcoat[3] and a grey cloak. They particularly noticed and marvelled at the woollen cloth because they do not have any wool and at the surcoat. Some touched my hands and arms and rubbed them with spit to see whether my whiteness was paint or flesh, and finding that the flesh was white they remained astonished.

I went to these markets to see new things but also to see if there was anyone with quantities of gold to sell but I only found a little, as I have already said.

Horses are much prized in this country because they only obtain them with great difficulty, since they are brought by land from Barbary[4] by Arabs or Azenegi;[5] and also because they cannot live for long due to the great heat, as I have said above. They also become very fat so that most of them die from a disease which prevents them from urinating so that they burst. The food which they give to the horses in these parts consists of the leaves of the beans which remain in the fields after the beans have been harvested. They cut them in small pieces and when they are dry, they give this to the horses to eat instead of hay. And in place of oats they give them millet, which makes them grow very fat. A harnessed horse with its accoutrements fetches between nine and fourteen slaves according to its quality and appearance. When a lord buys a horse, he sends for his horse doctors[6] who make a large fire with branches and herbs in their manner. This makes a lot of smoke and they lead the horse by its bridle through this smoke and utter some words. Afterwards they smear the whole horse with a fine ointment and keep it for fifteen or twenty days since they do not wish anyone to see it, and they hang round its neck some Moorish amulets which appear to be prayers, folded and folded again into quarters and covered with red leather. They believe that by carrying this amulet around the neck, these horses go more safely into battle.

The women of this country are very happy and good humoured and always want to sing and dance, especially the young ones. However, they do not dance except at night by the light of the moon, and their dances are very different from ours.

These blacks marvel at many things of ours, among others the ingenuity of our crossbows and even more of our bombards, for some of the blacks came to our ship and I made them see a bombard fired, at the noise of which they were terrified. I told them that a bombard could kill more than one hundred men at one blow, and they were astonished and said that this must be an object of the devil. They also admired one of our bagpipes on which I got one of my sailors to play, since they have no knowledge of such an instrument; and seeing it covered with multicoloured cloth and with some pieces of cloth at the top, they persuaded themselves that it was some living animal which could sing in different voices. With this they were at the same time both pleased and astonished. However, seeing the mistake they had made, I told them that this was a [musical] instrument, and I placed it in their hands deflated. And seeing that this was an instrument made by hand, they said that this was a heavenly thing, and that God had made it with his own hands since it spoke so sweetly with different voices. They said they had never seen such a beautiful thing.

They were also astonished at the ingenuity of our ship with its equipment, its masts, sails and anchors.[7] They also thought that the eyes that were painted on the prow of the ship were real eyes and that in this way the ship could see where it was going at sea. Afterwards they said that we must be great magicians, almost comparable to the Devil, saying that men who travelled by land had difficulty going from one place to another but that we travelled across the sea and they had heard that it was a very difficult thing to travel many days without seeing land. They knew that we did this, which was something impossible except by the power of the Devil. And it appeared like this to them because they had no knowledge of how to navigate with the help of compass and map.

They also greatly wondered at seeing a candle burning at night in a candlestick, and this because in their land they have no way of producing light other than by a fire. And seeing a candle, which they had never seen before, it appeared to them an astonishing and excellent thing. Although honey and wax are found in their country, they suck up the honey and throw the wax away. Seeing this, I bought a piece of honeycomb from them and showed them how to extract the honey from the wax. Afterwards I asked them if they knew what was the substance left over from the honey. They replied that it was nothing of any use. So in their presence I made some candles from the substance which they thought was valueless, which was wax, and lit it. Seeing this they were very astonished saying that we knew how to do everything.

Notes

1   For more detail on Cadamosto, see Doc. 11.
2   The adjective Spanish at this time would have referred to the whole Iberian peninsula.
3   The word in Italian is 'zupon'.
4   In Italian the phrase is 'barbarie nostre' by which Cadamosto wants to emphasize that it is the same Barbary, or North Africa, known the Venetians.
5   Sanhaja.
6   In Italian 'incantadori da cavalli'.
7   This interest in the details of the Portuguese ships brings to mind the carved ivory salt cellar from Benin in the British Museum that features a European ship complete with masts, rigging, anchors and crow's nest.

---

18   THE WOLOF KINGDOM AT THE END OF THE FIFTEENTH CENTURY

From *O Manuscrito de Valentim Fernandes*.
Original in Bayersiches Staatsbibliothek, Munich. Codex Hispanus No 27.
Th. Monod, A. Teixeira da Mota and R. Mauny, eds. and trans., *Description de la Côte Occidentale d'Afrique (Sénégal au Cap de Monte, Archipels)*, Centro de Estudos da Guiné Portuguesa (Bissau, 1951).
Translated by Malyn Newitt.

Valentim Fernandes was a German who originally came from Moravia and who settled in Lisbon some time around 1495 and remained there until his death, probably in 1518. By profession he was a printer and combined this with active

*work as a translator and as the official representative of the German community
in Lisbon. He had good connections at court through his friendship with Queen
Leonor de Lencastre, wife of Dom João II, and this, added to the information he
obtained from his compatriots, enabled him to have access to the latest information about Portuguese voyages. The information, often in the form of letters,
which he sent to correspondents in Germany, was collected together by Conrad
Peutinger in Augsburg. Although this material was seen by humanists and
scholars like Damião de Goes who appreciated its importance, the collection was
never published and was lost sight of in the Staatsbibliothek in Munich until
rediscovered in 1847.*

*Fernandes never travelled to west Africa but he obtained a great deal
of information from ships' captains. By the end of the fifteenth century the
Portuguese had fifty years' experience of trading in upper Guinea, and many
had settled along the tidal reaches of the rivers. Fernandes's account reflects the
detailed knowledge the Portuguese had acquired of the Wolof kingdom south of
the Senegal river, which was one of the principal trading areas. In this extract
Fernandes's informant tried to understand the role of the professional bards
or praise singers. These formed a distinct caste in Wolof society similar to
smiths and leather workers. Bards had influence and prestige but, although the
Portuguese understood the separateness of this group, they believed they were
despised by the ordinary people. This apparently led the Portuguese to compare
them, and possibly to confuse them, with Jews with whom they were familiar
in Portugal.*

*The importance of the horse trade is also clear from this passage. Although
horses were used in warfare and were the basis for political power through much
of the Sahel and forest regions, Fernandes also emphasizes that the ownership of
horses was so much a matter of status that they were even valued if they were
dead, for their tails could be displayed as objects of prestige.*

*Fernandes also describes the important role played by itinerant Muslim
preachers or holymen who spread Islam not least through the provision of amulets which were worn as a means of protection by horses as well as people.*

The river Çanaga[1] separates the Azenegue Moors[2] from the province
of Geloffa,[3] which begins on the opposite bank. ... This first river of the
blacks separates the Azenegues with their desert and their land, which
is dry, sterile and arid, from the fertile land which belongs to the blacks.
It is a miraculous thing that on one side of the river are men who are
tanned and verging on the white, and are small and lean, and on the
other side they are completely black and of tall stature while the land is
green and full of trees.

This river Canaga is large and is half a league or more wide. Almost
a hundred leagues upstream is a mountain or very high cliff over which

the river cascades. Beyond this mountain the river comes from such a distance that the blacks know nothing about it. Some say that it extends to Tambucutu[4] and beyond, and for this reason it is assumed that this river is a branch of the Nile.[5] Along this river a little gold and a lot of black slaves are traded.

The kingdom of Gyloffa extends from this river to the river Gambia, which is also called Cantor[6] although there are other people there such as Barbacijs and Tucurooes[7] and so forth. ... However, they are all Gyloffos. This land has luxuriant trees and vegetation. At the mouth of this river lives the king who is called the king of Gyloffa and who is the lord of 8,000 horsemen. Very few horses are bred in this province, the others are brought by the Christians and by the Moors from the interior. They have men of rank like dukes and counts and they have many people who are subject to them.

The king and his people have many canoes, boats made from a single tree trunk. The king is as powerful as the king of Marmelle.[8]

They are such good swimmers that they can swim across the river and they do not have, nor have they ever had, boats other than these canoes which are long and hollowed out from a tree.

The king and all the nobles and lords of the province of Gyloffa are Muslims and have white bischerijs who are priests and who preach [the doctrines of] Mohammed and know how to read and write. These bischerijs[9] come from a long way in the interior, for example, from the kingdoms of Fez and Morocco, and they come to convert the blacks to their faith by their preaching. These bischerijs make amulets[10] written in Arabic and the blacks hang them around their necks and also those of their horses.

When the Christians bring the horses which a great lord has bought or which he intends to buy, he brings one of the bischerijs with him who, before the horse is handed over, writes his blessings on a tablet of wood. He then takes a wooden basin full of water and washes the letters off the tablet and then gives the water to the horse to drink. After this the lord leads him away.

One part of the ordinary people believes in Mahomet but the majority are idolaters, although all the men in that province are circumcized like the Moors. The idolaters of the Gyloffa country take an old clay pot and throw into it some blood of a chicken, feathers and dirty water, and cover the pot and place it at the entrance in a little hut, which is covered and made of straw, and around it place a lot of rice flour and other things. It is there that they make their prayers and ceremonies each morning.

In this country and in Mandinga there are Jews who are called Gaul[11] and they are black like the people of the country. However, they do not have synagogues and do not practice the ceremonies of other Jews. They do not live with the other blacks but separate from them in their own villages.

These Gaul are usually jesters and singers and play on viols and cavacos.[12] And because they do not dare to enter the villages, they take up a position behind the houses of the lords of the village, and at daybreak they sing his praises until he orders them to be given a ration of millet, and then they go away.

And when the lord leaves his house, these Jews go in front of him singing and calling out their jests. If the Jews did not know these jests and if they did not greet the lord in this way, they would not be tolerated by the blacks. For so great is the ill will felt towards them, that they are barred by the blacks and do not dare enter one of their houses except that of the lord. And if they are found in the village, they are beaten with sticks.

No Gaul, whether a Jew or a Jewess, may take water from a spring until everyone else has finished drawing water. And then the last person will give them water. Or if they live in a country where there is a lot of water, they have some spring of their own set apart.

The lords of Gyloffa have as many women as they can support in this manner, for there are some who have four, five or even more villages.[13] For the lord is always attending court and in each one of his villages he has a wife, her children and the slaves who serve them. And in this way such a lord is going to live with one of his wives one month and with another the next month, and then they return to the court.

The slaves in this country work and produce for their lords during six days and on the seventh they produce for themselves what they need to maintain themselves on the other six.[14]

And when one of these lords has to go to war, he has some cows killed, three or four or more according to his rank, and these cows are cut into pieces and the pieces are thrown into the road which the lord has to take to go to the war. And the said lord and his people have to walk over these pieces of meat, which no one can eat and which are left for the birds and the beasts.

And when they go to war each one takes ten, fifteen or twenty assegais in his hands because they are small and slender and the iron tips are small.

. . .

The Portuguese merchants purchase a great many hides of cows and other animals and a lot of slaves but little gold. And they bring there *alquices*[15] and *bedees*,[16] red and blue cloth, and horses.

When the caravels of the Christians arrive and a lord wants to buy some horses, he immediately descends on the first village he finds, whether it belongs to a friend or an enemy, and rounds up as many men and women as he needs for this occasion and with whom he can get away.

He then buys the horses less for war than for prestige. Even if the horse is ill and he knows that it will die the next day, he buys it all the same because everyone keeps the tails and these are hung up in their houses. And when they go to a festival, the women carry the tails in their hands to let it be known that their husband has possessed so many horses.

Notes

1 The River Senegal.
2 Sanhaja.
3 Wolofs.
4 Timbuktu.
5 The limits of Portuguese geographical knowledge did not allow them to distinguish between the Senegal, the Niger and the Nile, which were all thought of as being part of the same river system.
6 Cantor is the name of the region south of the Gambia rather than of the river itself.
7 According to Monod, these are the Serur (sometimes called Barbacins by early writers) and the Takrur who had been incorporated in the Mali empire but later came to dominate the state of Futa Toro on the middle regions of the Senegal.
8 Probably a reference to the empire of Mali.
9 Also *bixerim* and *bicherin* from Arabic el-Mubecherin who were itinerant preachers, called by Monod 'marabouts'.
10 For a discussion of amulets and their role in the hybrid religious practice of west Africa, see Roger Sansi-Roca, 'The Fetish in the Lusophone Atlantic', in Nancy Naro, Roger Sansi-Roca and David Treece, eds., *Cultures of the Lusophone Black Atlantic* (Basingstoke, 2007) pp. 19–39.
11 This is a rendering either of *geuwel* (Wolof) or *gaulo* (Fulfulde). They have no connection with Jews and the reason Fernandes calls them 'Jews' seems to be that they are a group in society who are widely despised and who keep themselves separate from the rest.
12 The *cavaco* (more commonly *cavaquinho*) is a small, stringed instrument with four strings.
13 The Portuguese word used is *quinta*, which describes a country farm or estate.
14 This organization of slave labour was adopted by the Portuguese of São Tomé. See Doc. 13.
15 Cloaks.
16 Short tunics.

19 RELATIONS BETWEEN THE COASTAL PEOPLES OF UPPER GUINEA AND THE CAPE VERDE ISLANDS

From André Donelha, *Descrição da Serra Leoa e dos Rios de Guiné do Cabo Verde*, A. Teixeira da Mota and P. E. H. Hair, eds., Junta de Investigações Científicas do Ultramar (Lisbon, 1977), pp. 108–14.

The original of this account is in Biblioteca da Ajuda 51-IX-25.
Translated by Malyn Newitt.

André Donelha was probably born in the Cape Verde Islands sometime between 1550 and 1560 and went to school in Santiago. His father traded in slaves and he himself made at least three voyages to Guinea in the 1570s and 1580s.

The Portuguese had traded in the Sierra Leone region ever since the 1440s and had acquired a detailed knowledge of the local peoples and states. In this extract, Donelha is describing the impact of the Manes on the area. The Manes were invaders of Mandinka origin who devastated the coastal regions in the sixteenth century and brought about far-reaching changes to the political configuration of Guinea, as well as feeding the slave trade.[1] Donelha shows how the Mane wars increased the dependence of the coastal people on the Portuguese, so that many Sapes became, in effect, clients of the Portuguese and adopted Christianity. Portuguese residents on the mainland, who were known as tangomaos,[2] had their own towns on the rivers of upper Guinea, where rulers ousted by the Manes were able to take refuge. Members of ruling families had also settled in the Cape Verde Islands, where some had been educated and had become Christians although, when famine struck in the islands, they returned temporarily to Guinea. Donelha describes the process by which the Afro-Portuguese ethnic groups established their separate identities. He emphasizes the privileged position of strangers in west African society, which provided the foundation for the trading success of the Portuguese tangomaos. The tangomaos and the Africans who adopted Christianity merged to create the Afro-Portuguese community, which played such an important part in the commerce of western Africa until the nineteenth century.

Donelha intersperses his account of the history of the region with information on every aspect of African culture, taking a particular interest in religious matters and medicine. This extract gives an early description of Africans maltreating their fetishes if they have not brought good luck, and he reflects on the effects that arrow poison has on the human body, causing lockjaw, which, he thinks, accounts for the custom of removing front teeth – an early example of a functionalist interpretation of ethnic custom. His reference to cannibalism among the Manes may refer to war rituals which involved eating human flesh but may merely reflect the fear which the Manes inspired in the Afro-Portuguese community.

After this lady[3] died, her principal captains continued their march and invaded the lands of Sierra Leone in the year 1545. They had many conflicts, wars, sieges, skirmishes and battles with the native Sapes,[4] in which many people were killed. The Manes[5] behaved very cruelly towards these people, and they established their dominance over the Bolons[6] who live on the right bank of the Tagarim River.[7] The Bolons immediately adopted the voracious practices of the Sumbas by eating human flesh and, as they were familiar with the country, they joined with the Manes and became excellent soldiers.

Together they conquered and made themselves lords over the above-mentioned nations and many others. They treated the kings and great lords with such cruelty that two of the kings, with their wives and children and some vassals, and with some gold and ivory, escaped on board some Portuguese ships which had come from this island to trade there. They came to the São Domingos River,[8] where they were well received by the king of that land, and they built separate villages near the town of the tangomaos, and lived there. The Portuguese who run off to [live in] Guinea are called tangomaos.

I knew one of these kings at São Domingos who was called king Beca Caia. In the ancient language of the Sapes 'Beca' means 'king', just as 'bera' means 'queen'. Today there is a daughter of this king on this island. She became a Christian and came to this island of Santiago. During the great famine which occurred in the year 1583, she went to Guinea and stayed in the town of her father who was then still alive. Then, when the famine was over, she returned to this island. Her name is Brizida [Brigida?] Beca Caia.

The other king, who was called Beca Bore, who was a great lord in his country and a cousin of king Beca Caia, sent one of his sons to this island. He became a Christian and at school was my fellow scholar in learning to read and write. When he left he could write very well, because the Sapes have great talent and skill at everything they learn. He also went to Guinea during the famine of 1583 and, on the death of his uncle king Beca Caia, who had succeeded his father king Beca Bore, he inherited his uncle's estate. However, his subjects in that town rose up against him because he wanted them to become Christians. With the help of his cousin, who was also a Christian and had lived in this island, the king was driven out of the town, without the tangomaos offering him any help, though if they had supported him they might have restored him to power.

He lived among the whites as a poor man, but God, who does not forsake His people, came to his aid through the death of a king in another part of Sierra Leone, who was a relative of his and subject to the Manes. As he had no nearer heir, the king declared that the kingdom belonged to him, with the result that he was summoned there and made the king. He wrote to me about all about this, as a friend and schoolfellow, and asked me to get a ship and to join him (which I had no licence to do). He was very eager to convert his people to the faith of Our Lord Jesus Christ, or else to leave Guinea and come to live in this island, if he could earn a livelihood here.

Sierra Leone should be settled if God is willing, so that with our help he can make his people Christian. He is known as Ventura de Sequeira, because his father entrusted him to one Jorge de Sequeira, who was captain of the *estância* [watering place?] and the bastion above the port of this city, and who was his godfather and brought him to this island.

. . . .

The Manes have no faith nor belong to any religious sect. They worship pots into which they put feathers which they then sprinkle with the blood of hens which they kill so that the feathers stick to the blood, and the pot is covered with feathers outside and in.[9] They also fashion many idols of wood, in the form of men or monkeys or other animals. These they call *corfis*,[10] and they are placed on the roads, some near to the villages and some far away. They say that they are protectors of the settlements of that district. They make idols for war, for rain, for sunshine, for famine or for whatever else they wish to undertake; and if things do not turn out as successfully as they hope, they throw the idols down and beat them and make new ones, or else they take up the original ones and implore them, caressing them and placing roasted and boiled meat, rice, wine and fruit before them in order to make them happy, and they beg them to help them in whatever they undertake.

They are simple people and if there were a settlement of Christians in the Sierra, they would very soon all be Christians. They have many wives and are not jealous for when guests come to their houses, they entertain them with much festivity, and to demonstrate greater friendship they allow their guests to choose the most beautiful from among their women, whom they may then use as long as they stay. They do the same thing for whites who want to sleep and lodge ashore. These women are called *cabondos*. They show great respect to their guests, and even risk their lives for them.[11]

If it is desired to settle Sierra Leone, it will have to be done in friendship and peace through the giving of presents, because this behaviour would greatly please the people and would be of great assistance in all the work that would have to be done, and it would [ensure] the ready supply of provisions. Going about it any other way or engaging in warlike action would cost much blood, because they have the advantage in war over any other nation in our commercial sphere. People who have engaged in war with the Manes say that, though the Wolofs are very brave and skilful horsemen, they are not their equals.

The Manes do not make use of horses because there are none in their country. Their arrows are poisoned and anyone injured by them soon dies. However, they employ many medicines against the poison, which they take if they are hit; and they carry the tails of unicorns, which they soak in water and lash their wounds with, and in this way many escape. Because the [arrow] poison makes the wounded man clench his teeth, they all have their front teeth removed so that the medicine can be poured into their mouths.

Notes

1 For the origin of the Manes, see Andreas Massing, 'The Mane, the decline of Mali and Mandinka Expansion towards the South Windward Coast', *Cahiers d'Etudes Africaines*, 25 (1985), pp. 21–55 and for their links with the Poro initiation society George F. Brooks, *Eurafricans in Western Africa*, James Currey (Oxford, 2003), pp. 63–7.

2 The origin and exact meaning of the term *tangomao* is uncertain. In Valenim Fernandes's manuscript, there is a tantalizing reference to an African lineage with the name *tangomas* that provided the priests (*clerigos*) who supervised an important shrine (*ydolo universal de todas estas terras*). Monod, Teixeira da Mota and Mauny *Description de la Côte Occidentale d'Afrique (Sénégal au Cap de Monte, Archipels)*, pp. 100–3. It has been argued that this may refer to an Afro-Portuguese family that had become so Africanized that it had acquired a prestigious role in an important religious cult. See José Lingna Nafafé, *Colonial Encounters: Issues of Culture, Hybridity and Creolisation* (Frankfurt am Main, 2007), pp. 169–72.

3 This is a reference to Macarico, a Mandinga noble woman who left Mali with her followers sometime early in the sixteenth century.

4 A general term used by the Portuguese for the coastal peoples of Sierra Leone 'in the same way that in Spain several nations are called "Spaniards"'. Quoted in Rodney, *A History of the Upper Guinea Coast*.

5 The Mane and Sumba are the same warrior group, though the Sumba appear to have been made up of men from conquered groups co-opted into the Mane army. Their invasion of the coastal area after 1545 was described by the Portuguese who bought slaves from them.

6 The Bullom-speaking ethnic group lived along the Sherbro River.

7 The Tagarim River is the Rokell, one of the rivers that feed into the Sierra Leone River.

8 Today known as the Cacheu River.

9 Compare this with the description of Wolof religious custom given by Valentim Fernandes (Doc. 18).

10 From the Temne *korfi* meaning spirit or spiritual power.

11 This custom is recorded by Valentim Fernandes early in the sixteenth century and is mentioned in many other contemporary accounts of upper Guinea, including Manuel Álvares who uses the same term.

---

20 TRADE AND PIRACY ON THE SENEGAL COAST

From Manuel Alvares SJ, *Etiópia Menor e Descripção Géografica da Província da Serra Leoa*, chapter 8.

A. Teixeira da Mota and Luís de Matos, eds. (unpublished).

The manuscript is located in the Biblioteca da Sociedade de Geografia de Lisboa.[1]

Translation by P. E. H. Hair; revised by Malyn Newitt.

Manuel Álvares SJ was born in 1573 and joined the Jesuit mission in upper Guinea in 1607. He travelled to a number of the trading ports and worked there until his death in 1616 or 1617. This extract from his account of upper Guinea, probably written before 1615, describes the increasing activity of French and Dutch interlopers, who were directly challenging the commercial monopoly which Portugal had enjoyed for over one hundred years. The activities of these 'pirates' were undermining the relations Portugal had established with the peoples of the coast. Álvares's account is also of interest, as it shows the diversity of the trade carried on with the peoples of upper Guinea. He does not mention slaves at all, but refers to other exports including a considerable quantity of hides and even cloth, which was woven in west Africa and fetched a high price in Europe.

Although the coastal Jalofo[2] whom we are now discussing have only limited social and political organization, nevertheless they have enough rascality and sharp dealing in their trade with foreigners. Many of them, speaking French as if it were their native language, have developed such ways through their regular trade with the pirates. Cape Verde is a true training ground for these pirates. They regularly live there while they careen their ships, and build launches and sloops that enable them to rob the entire coast of these provinces, from which they carry off in an average year 200,000 cruzados worth of goods. Their seizures have left the coast as poor in wealth as it is rich in misery and destitution for the Portuguese, who suffer great losses on the coast because of their enemies. This could be remedied by means of two or three warships, which would patrol the coast, go to the Cape and rout the pirates, in this way greatly benefiting not only our sea routes within Ethiopia, but also those to the Malagueta Coast,[3] to Mina[4] and to Brazil. Of no less value would be the prizes, which by this strategy would be taken from among the ships which anchor in Biziguiche Bay, in its renowned port of Arrecife, nine leagues from Porto de Ale.[5]

Three or four ships anchor here every year; and the French and some Flemings, who also anchor a mile away from Porto de Ale because of the bad bottom and poor anchorage, annually export 50,000 hides and 200 quintals of ivory, together with the ambergris and gold which come to this place and to the renowned port of Joala from the entire coast of Ethiopia.[6] What was stated above about the royal officers who live in the seaports and receive presents [for the king] is the general practice. These officers are admirably punctilious in what they do, in order to cultivate the goodwill of the lords and keep them friendly.

To conclude this chapter, let us speak of the occupations of the heathen. The men work in the fields and they fish and weave, making their very well-known cotton cloths by sowing from six to twelve strips together. Some of these cloths are so valuable that those that are taken from these parts to Spain are worth 6,000 reis. The looms are different from ours.

All of them are traders. The Jalofo people in the kingdom of Lambaia[7] are so enthusiastic that they give pledges to the Portuguese and go up-country to trade in the three fairs, which are normally held every week. The main fair is called Ricai Fair, and 2,000 people go to it. The products of the country are sold; that is, cow-hides, cotton cloths, goats and hens – the last in great quantities and so cheap that one can be bought for four strings of pocate beads worth at most 60 reis. The currency in use here is what the ships bring from all kinds of traders, [such as] coral, and so forth. The main occupations of the women are sewing, cooking and grinding milho in wooden mortars which resemble our grinding bowls, these being an ell in height. They do this last task from midnight onwards, in order not to be seen at work, and during the day they take it easy and treat it as time off. I have spoken about idolatry. For the heathen who live near the sea, the burial rites of the Jalofo are in every respect the same as those of other idolaters, and they have celebratory feasts in which food abounds, and so forth.

Now I come back to Joala. Having given due praise and shown a grateful heart for the love with which they receive us and the welcome they give our boats, we ought to be no less generous in giving our love to the heathen there, because they are exceptionally friendly to the Portuguese nation and have no connection with the pirates. These connections are multiplying among the coastal peoples of the two [kingdoms or ports] of Cape Verde, as we have sufficiently illustrated above, and this is the main reason for the hatred of us which this Jalofo scum has developed.

Notes

1   P. E. H. Hair's translation of the Álvares's manuscript was never published because of the death of his collaborator Teixeira da Mota. Hair wrote a detailed account of all the circumstances surrounding his unfinished translation as well as a critique of the manuscript itself, which can be found at http://digicoll.library.wisc.edu/cgi-bin/AfricaFocus

2   Wolof. See also Doc. 18.

3   The Malaguetta Coast stretched from Sierra Leone to Cape Palmas.

4   Mina is the Gold Coast, modern Ghana. The name refers to the Portuguese fort and trading station of São Jorge da Mina (Elmina).

5   Arrecife is Rufisque (from the Portuguese Rio Fresco). These places all lie just to the south of the Cape Verde peninsula and the Île de Gorée in modern Senegal.

6   The modern Joal-Fadiouh just to the north of the Saloum River, which was the main
    port for the Serer states.
7   Lambaia or Lambaay was the capital of the state of Baol and approximately 100
    kilometres inland from Rufisque.

21 THE SLAVE TRADE AND ROYAL LUXURY IN THE LAND OF THE BUSSIS

From Manuel Álvares SJ *Etiópia Menor e Descripção Géografica da Província da Serra Leoa*, chapter 8.

A. Teixeira da Mota and Luís de Matos, eds. (unpublished).

The manuscript is located in the Biblioteca da Sociedade de Geografia de Lisboa.[1]

Translation by P. E. H. Hair; revised by Malyn Newitt.

In this extract Álvares vividly describes the impact of Portuguese trade on one of the Papel states. The 'kingdom of Bussis' consisted of an island at the mouth of the Mansoa river, near the modern Bissau. Portuguese traders seeking slaves lavished luxury European goods on the king and were in turn granted the position of privileged strangers in his kingdom. Álvares shows how the slave trade was exploited by the king to increase his power, as it gave him access to prestigious imports and enabled him to sell into slavery those who in any way went against his wishes. As a missionary, Álvares was outraged by much of what he saw and this clearly clouded his judgment, but his account provides a wealth of detail about conditions on the upper Guinea coast and about what incorporation into the economy of the Atlantic world meant to the peoples of the region. On the other hand, he also tried to locate and define the moral basis for action in defining certain types of trade as 'illicit'. His comments on the relationship of witchcraft accusations to the slave trade show that African responses to the slave trade, and the wealth to be derived from it, involved adjustments to traditional communal values and concepts of morality as marked as those by which the Portuguese justified to themselves the enslavement of human beings.

The king of Bussis[2] is unique in that there is so much to be told about his household and royal state, as well as his person and all his possessions, for the whites have turned him into a lascarin.[3] He is well acquainted with what comes from Spain, indeed he benefits more from these things here than many do there. Heathen as he is, those who know his lifestyle cannot but speak well of him. They say: 'A good disciple of a good master'. So let us proceed to make a careful examination of this savage. His person is so dainty and sleek as a result of the variety of his delicacies and luxuries that he may readily be envied by those of this district most dedicated to epicureanism. As regards his manner of life, in order to dress well he cuts up silks and other expensive cloths, and does so more lavishly than do those Spaniards who make most use of these. As proof, it is enough to refer to the quantity of silks and other textiles sent to him by his admirers in this Guinea. He has many of such people because he behaves with royal magnificence towards those who gracefully fall down before him. In 1612, one of them sent him a quantity of merchandise of this kind to the value of forty black slaves. His bed is a paradise. No one in Guinea except this tyrant possesses a bed of this style; and he can change it as he wishes with such a variety of bedspreads and canopies that there would be no end to describing them. He is the richest king in all this [part of] Ethiopia. His jurisdiction is the most unrestricted and absolute. Although the country is small, being only about six leagues long and four across, it is so important because of its king that it extends as far as the savage cares to spread its fame.

The result of this independence is that there is no law other than the king's appetites. If he wished to be worshipped, and Divine Omnipotence did not intervene, he could completely achieve his wish. At the human level, he is treated with great respect by his people, wholly because he is powerful and to be feared. Therefore no vassal of his would dare to sell a slave, even if the slave belonged to that vassal's domain, without seeking permission from him; nor may he sell a bullock or castrated goat without first informing the king. If he goes fishing and catches a large fish, he must bring it for the king to see, so that he can take any part he fancies. Anyone who fails to do this could lose his head, unless, to save it, he presents a slave and so is freed from the penalty. No one may give his daughter to a man without first bringing her to the [royal] household, and if she pleases him, the king may take her for himself. Anyone who arranges a marriage and disregards this law may lose his house and family, since nothing of import is allowed to happen in the land without the king being first informed. In this respect, they are all obedient and very punctilious in keeping the law, and are greatly encouraged to be so by the apparatus of spies and informers reporting on breaches of the law which is maintained by the king.

At any time he wishes, he can put in the field nearly 2,000 men armed with shields, spears, swords and knives. He is therefore feared by the neighbouring kings. He can also defend himself successfully against the inhabitants of the Bijagos Islands,[4] three or four leagues out to sea to the southwest, who live by mounting assaults either at sea, attacking Portuguese vessels in their canoes, or on the mainland, where they burn houses, villages and churches. This last they did in 1603 at Biguba, and in 1609 at Guinala, where they fired the House of Our Lady.[5] But they cannot invade this renowned island, the king having ordered such vigilance to be kept all around it that a bird cannot appear out at sea or cross the land without it being generally known, by means of the bambalous.[6] The men who keep watch from the tops of trees are in charge of these bambalous, so that if there is cause, they sound them in order to give the whole land warning of what is happening.

. . . .

As well as the large number of houses [for wives] which the king maintains in this place, he has his own house, which is barred with iron all around. Within this house he keeps many trunks and boxes full of different articles of clothing, such as very elaborate smocks, doublets and breeches, (also) sheets, coverlets and canopies made of different pieces of silk, and items in gold and silver. These goods, apart from the ones left him by his uncle and predecessor, he has bought and continues to buy from the Portuguese who come there with their ships to obtain slaves, a commodity the tyrant's chains never fail to have available. For he has such cruel laws that only the person who is truly a slave [at heart] and does not know the value of life would be willing to live under this king's rule. The Portuguese come ashore in full security and they are received with all the signs of friendship, since this king is fond of saying that, without his permission, only the snakes in the forest can do anyone ill in his land. And this is the experience of the Portuguese even today, for if they cut down a hand of bananas, his vassals will not accept money for it, on account of the respect for the whites which they know their king has, albeit only out of self-interest. On this point, the heathen deserves praise.

His bearing is solemn. More often than not he is seated on a chair lined with velvet, for he has several of these and makes most use of them when delivering judgments. The captains convey goods to him on his verbal request, and he pays them well, although what he buys is usually related to how much an individual pleases him. He shows great respect to captains of vessels, but they are expected to give him handsome presents; and he consents to eat with them, though he never eats with anyone else, a restriction arising from his sense of hauteur. He is in the habit of giving away some of his castrated animals as presents and then adding a slave. Yet all the heathen [give presents merely to obtain] a compensating advantage in return, a characteristic of the people of this Ethiopia, who whether they give little or much never do so except in the hope of getting more back. They have a proverb 'Give a hen, hope for a goat: give a goat, hope for a cow!'

Because these savages have no horses, they use oxen instead, after castrating them to make them fatter. The oxen become so tame and tractable that they insert a rope through their nostrils to act as reins so that they can ride them, and they can travel on these oxen for a fair number of leagues. However, the oxen tire easily because of their great size. To make them go more quickly they beat them with sticks shaped to the thickness of a palm, and give them such thwacks on the belly that they can be heard a good distance away. These oxen provide the mounts for the Papels and for the other heathen inhabiting these lands.

Now let us be more specific. In material power this savage is far above all the other kings and lords of Ethiopia. As everyone concedes, he alone is king, and he behaves accordingly, requiring obedience appropriate to the royal dignity. He maintains an elevated royal state befitting his royal person; and this is more extreme than if his state were one due to grace. But he has such false instructors in the faith that, instead of providing him with a good reputation deriving from the fundamental virtue of the House of the Lord, they disparage this with their hellish works. For these people sell their own Christian slave-women to serve the appetite of this savage, as Jorge Fernandes Granjo and other captains have done, while another of those lançados, about whom I have spoken, fortified the king's port with two cannons, a scheme in which Captain S[ebastião]. B. Fernandes has been very active. I am sure that their lordships, the ecclesiastical visitors of Cacheu, must know about these acts which are so contrary to the Christian faith and religion. Equally contentious are other acts practised on the Windward Coast by the sale to the people there of many kinds of prohibited goods. Prohibited goods are those which do not meet the test of being morally indifferent and applied to various uses. For only goods meeting this test are licit and the others are illicit, which have a single use and that a diabolical one, in idolatry for instance. Hence the sale of paper[7] is not licit, nor is the sale of animal horns or heads, since these are ingredients for their magic medicines. And it should not be said: 'So what! Someone else will sell these goods and they will continue to practice idolatry!' Those who obtain these goods for the heathen are accessories to their actions. I say the same thing when slaves procured unjustly are offered for sale. 'But if I don't buy them, their own people will kill them, because they are witches!' That is a poor argument, for as long as witches are sold they will be uncovered daily.

Notes

1 P. E. H. Hair's translation of the Álvares's manuscript was never published. See note 1 in Doc. 19.
2 The island is called Pecixe.
3 Lascar. Persian: *lashkar*. Indian sailor.
4 The twenty inhabited Bissagos Islands (Arquipélago de Bijagós) lie thirty miles off Bissau.
5 Biguba (more usually Buguba) was the land that lay upstream on the right bank of the Rio Grande. Guinala was the country lying between the Rio Grande and the Geba River.
6 A *bambalou* was a kind of drum.
7 Paper was used in the manufacture of amulets that contained verses of the Koran.

5

ELMINA AND BENIN

---

22 THE FOUNDATION OF THE CASTLE AND CITY OF SÃO JORGE DA MINA, 1482

From Rui de Pina, *Crónica de El-Rey D.João II*, edited by Alberto Martins de Carvalho, Atlântida (Coimbra, 1950), pp. 7–13.
Translated by Malyn Newitt.

In the sixty years following the capture of Ceuta in 1415, the Portuguese established three more fortresses in Morocco and a fortified factory at Arguim on the coast of modern Mauretania. The fortified towns in Morocco were originally intended to be bases from which to undertake the conquest of Morocco. However, as a result of the war with Castile (1474–79), these plans were largely abandoned and the coastal forts became centres of commerce and cultural interaction with the local populations (see Doc. 3). The decision taken in 1481 to build a fortified trading factory at Elmina on the coast of modern Ghana was not, therefore, a radically new idea. It was the king's intention to make the gold trade an exclusive royal monopoly, which would be administered thousands of miles from Lisbon, that made this a major new departure in Portuguese policy and anticipated developments in the Indian Ocean in the sixteenth century.

Rui de Pina was appointed the official royal chronicler in 1490. His reputation has never stood high in comparison with his predecessors Fernão Lopes and Gomes Eanes de Zurara or with João de Barros, but he was as assiduous a recorder of Portuguese enterprise in Africa as Zurara had been. Like his predecessors, he wanted his narrative to bestow legitimacy on the actions of the king, and the narrative of the building of Elmina is a good example of his style. Dom João's decision to overrule the doubts of his Council and to select Diogo de Azambuja to carry out his plans is seen as a demonstration of the soundness of his judgment. The chronicler also wants to show the benevolent and peaceful intentions of the Portuguese, and the story of the unintentional

*destruction of the sacred rock, and the skilful diplomacy by which the problem
was smoothed over, is made to carry deep symbolic meaning. Although Pina's
account is clearly a propaganda exercise, the contrast between the actions of the
Portuguese in establishing peaceful trade with the local population is nevertheless in marked contrast to the behaviour of the Castilians when they discovered
the existence gold in the New World.*[1]

At this time the city of São Jorge was built on the Mina coast. It
should be known that the king,[2] when he was still prince, had received
the government of all the places in Africa as a royal gift from the king
his father[3] together with the revenues and commerce of Mina and of all
Guinea, which at that time had been leased for a small sum to Fernão
Gomes da Mina, a citizen of Lisbon.[4] As the king was a prudent man, he
considered what great profit and what benefit his subjects would receive,
both in body and soul, and how his trade, his honour and his service
would be secured if in those parts of Mina he should have a fortress.
Desiring to know if he should do this, and whether it was possible, he
sought advice and heard many contradictory voices and opinions. Some
thought it would be an easy and profitable thing to accomplish, while
others thought it would be difficult, dangerous and perhaps impossible.
They said that it would be very hard to maintain both because of the great
distance of the land and because there was much illness there. Moreover,
even if the blacks allowed it to be built, they were not to be believed or
trusted. These problems were so great that [the enterprise] should not
be undertaken. However, setting all this aside, the king decided that he
would go ahead with it.

To this end he ordered that all the timber and the stone for the door-
ways, windows and corners of the walls and towers and for other things
that were necessary should at once be cut and prepared so that they
could be put in place without any delay to the work. So, a great quantity
of lime was prepared and sufficient quantities of tiles, bricks, nails, tools,
provisions and all the things pertaining to the project were collected
together. Six hundred men were assembled and got ready, a hundred
to act as master masons and carpenters and five hundred to serve the
fortress and defend it. It was ordered that all this should be carried (as it
was) in urcas[5] and great ships, which were not intended to return or sail
again. Apart from these there were other ships and caravels which were
well and strongly built and which carried provisions, medical supplies
and rich merchandise with honourable men and servants of the king
appointed to command them.

Some men to whom the king wanted to entrust this work had
already excused themselves because they feared the difficulties and

dangers, when Fernão Lourenço who was secretary of the treasury and afterwards was appointed to take charge of the money and the trading factory, became the first man to accept [the command] and to be willing to undertake it. However, although the king gave him great praise and thanks, which his goodwill deserved, he excused him because of the responsibilities he already held. Then, being informed of the goodness, loyalty and great ability of Diogo de Azambuja,[6] a knight of his household who was already experienced in matters of great importance and danger, he entrusted the command to him, expressing the singular confidence he had in him and his hope that he would prove deserving of the rewards and advancement which he promised him. He, together with others whose loyalty and obedience were worthy of praise, accepted this appointment with an open countenance and steady heart. To carry out the [mission], he went at once to Lisbon to get ready and sailed on Santa Lucia's eve[7] in December 1481, having already dispatched the urcas to wait for him at Cape Verde.

He carried with him a regimento to the effect that the fortress should be built in the land of Mina in the place which seemed most suitable between Cabo das Tres Pontas and Cabo das Redes, which are forty leagues apart. So, when they arrived he went ahead of the rest of the fleet and, taking great care and many precautions, he examined all the places in that land to see which was most suitable. In some of them, although the land seemed good, the sea was bad having poor anchorages; in others where the sea was good, the land was either too low or was rocky or lacked water and was rejected. Finally, guided by the Holy Spirit to whom he had commended himself, he anchored before the village, which is known as Of Two Parts, where he went ashore on Wednesday the 19 January 1482. He carefully noted the rise in the land for defensive purposes and for the health of the people, and sounding the anchorages at sea for the ships with care, he realised that he could not find nor imagine a better place, especially as there was a lot of stone and a large population which gave promise of a good water supply and plenty of provisions for the people over a long period of time.

So, on the advice of João Bernaldes whom he found trading there, the next day, which was the feast of Saint Sebastian,[8] he went ashore dressed in brocade and silk and with his people in good order. At the foot of a tree in the shade he ordered a Mass to be said, which he heard and which was the first to be said there. He then called that valley after Saint Sebastian, a name it will always bear. After eating he ordered a splendid platform to be erected on which he sat surrounded by many men of rank and with his trumpets, tambourines and drums, and as an act of peace prepared to receive and to speak with the ruler of the place, who was called Caramansa whom the blacks called their king. The king arrived there accompanied by a great noise of bells, horns and shells, which are their instruments, and a huge crowd of blacks, some with bows and arrows, others with spears and shields. The chief men among them were followed by naked pages with wooden stools like chairs for them to sit on. The king was naked except for chains and ornaments of gold fashioned in many different ways which covered his arms and legs and with bells and long beads of gold which hung from the hairs of his beard and his head. The captain came to receive him in front of the platform with a great fanfare of his instruments, and the king gave the captain the customary sign of peace, which was to place his fingers together pressing one against the other and saying in their language 'Bere Bere', which in our language means 'Peace Peace', and the captain did the same. Then the principal men who came with him did the same, first moistening their fingers in their mouths and wiping them on their chests before touching those of the captain, which among them is an act of courtesy and respect reserved for kings and persons of high rank.

When everyone had sat down, the captain made a signal for silence and began to speak, with a black who acted as interpreter[9] and who immediately translated for him. And this is what he said: that because the king his lord had received favourable information of them and that those of his vassals who came to trade there had met better treatment than among the other people of the land, His Highness had sent him there to treat with them and to secure peace and friendship for ever; that he wanted to make a permanent factory for rich merchandise in that place rather than in any other of that region, so that through good trade they and their descendants should become rich and ennobled. Although various other kings and lords of that land had already sent him gifts in order to seek to have such a factory, the king his lord had made it clear that he desired only to do business with them because of the great belief and trust he had in them. In order to ensure that the merchandise which they had brought, and which they would bring in future, should always remain continually secure and in good condition, a warehouse would be necessary and he requested that [the king] would give him permission as well as a place and help to build it near the mouth of the river so that the warehouse and the Christians which were there would always bring him protection, profit and favour.

The king, together with his principal men, at once replied to him, saying that the Christians who up to that time had come there were few, dishonest and vile, but that those who now came were quite different,

especially the person [of the captain] who from his clothes and appearance must be the son or brother of the king of Portugal. Before they
could proceed further with their speech, the captain replied to them
that he was neither the son nor the brother of the king his lord, but one
of the least of his vassals because the king was so powerful and such a
great lord that in his kingdoms he could command the obedience of two
hundred thousand men who were greater, better and richer than he.
As a sign of their amazement at such a remarkable thing, they clapped
loudly as was their custom. Then, proceeding with his reply, he said
that because of his presence and the assurances he had given in the
name of the king, he could not, in making his requests, be hiding the
truth nor intending treachery or malice.

Meanwhile they gave him a place to build the warehouse because,
when it was built, if the [king] kept his promises, it was certain that
the king of Portugal his lord would be well served, and the Christians
his subjects would be better treated. If the contrary happened, they
would leave the land and the warehouse and take their leave, because
in another land there would be no shortage of wood and thatch to make
another one. And he gave them a sign that they could be sure and certain of all he said to them, for Christians were not accustomed to lie but
rather to carry out what they had promised better than they had said,
and they believed that the king his lord and his descendants would
make this place the most respected, richest and most populous of all
others among them. Then, being very satisfied by all this, they offered
him thanks and with a cheerful clamour rose to their feet and offered
him their help.

Before he withdrew, the captain went with the craftsmen he had
brought to lay the foundation of the fortress [with stone] which they took
from the top of some high rocks which were sacred to the blacks and
adored by them. The captain divided the work into watches between
the different captaincies so that they could begin the next day, which
was the 21 January, which they did. He sent the king and his people
a good present of brass basins and manilhas, shawls and other cloths,
which were to be given to them to obtain their goodwill. He gave this
mission to João Bernaldes who did not start on it until the workmen and
quarrymen had already begun their work. For at the beginning of the
day it was intended to dig the foundations for the tower and to cut stone
to lay for them. When the blacks saw so much damage being done to
their sacred rocks, and their hopes of salvation destroyed, they reacted
very strongly and, burning with fury, took up their arms and treated
the workmen so harshly that they could not resist and fled back to their
boats. Seeing this, Diogo de Azambuja at once sent help and realised

that the cause of the commotion was that his present had not yet been delivered because of the negligence of the messenger. He ordered that the present, to which he added other things, should be delivered without delay, so that the hostility of the blacks might be turned into goodwill and their strenuous defence into a double compliance. So, until the tower had been built as far as the first storey, he did not plan or lay the foundations for any other building, but when it had reached that level he at once began to build the castle walls. For this it was necessary to demolish some houses belonging to the blacks but they and their wives happily and without hesitation agreed to this because of the gifts they were given in compensation.

They now began to have great need for water because the local supply that was nearby was closely guarded and protected by the blacks so that they could not profit by it and, to avoid any commotion, they did not want to take it by force. After looking for many remedies for this situation, they were able, almost miraculously, to find provision elsewhere. They then hurried on with their work so fast that, although many men fell ill and some died, the walls of the fortress were raised in twenty days and the tower and many of the houses inside were finished. And they gave it the name of Castello de São Jorge[10] in honour of the patron [saint] and protector of Portugal and later, when the king was in Santarém, on the 15 March 1486, he bestowed on it a Letter Patent which gave it the privileges and honours of a city.

As there was gold in abundance, the people exchanged all their merchandise to their satisfaction and arranged all the dues. Diogo de Azambuja detailed sixty men and three women to remain with him and the rest he sent away and they returned to Portugal to give a full account to the king of everything that had happened and had been done.

Notes

1 For a discussion of the sources for building of the castle see P. E. H. Hair, *The Founding of the Castello de São Jorge da Mina: and Analysis of the Sources*, University of Wisconsin (Madison, 1994).
2 Dom João II (1481–95).
3 Dom Afonso V (1438–81).
4 Fernão Gomes had been awarded the monopoly of the Guinea trade in 1469. He held this until 1475 with the condition that he should explore 100 leagues of African coastline each year and pay an annual rent to the Crown.
5 Cargo ships.
6 See Doc. 4.
7 The feast of Santa Lucia is on 13 December.
8 20 January.

9 The word used is *lingua*. The Portuguese pursued a policy of taking Africans from the coasts where they traded to Lisbon to learn Portuguese and to act as interpreters for future expeditions. See also Doc. 16.
10 The name of the castle and town was officially São Jorge da Mina but was always known as Elmina by the Dutch and English.

23 THE IMPORTANCE OF REACHING AN ACCOMMODATION WITH THE PRIVATE TRADERS

Letter of Dom João III to Afonso de Albuquerque, governor of São Jorge da Mina, Tomar, 13 October 1523.

António Brásio., ed., *Monumenta Missionaria Africana*, vol. 1 1471–1531 Agência Geral do Ultramar (Lisbon, 1952), pp. 451–2.

Translated by Malyn Newitt.

This letter lays bare the tensions that had grown up between those administering the royal monopoly of the gold trade at Elmina and the private traders who were operating along the coast. The conciliatory attitude adopted by the king acknowledges the vital role that the private traders played in supplying the fortress, obtaining slaves and taking spoiled trade goods off the factor's hands. It is in marked contrast to the hostile attitude of the Crown towards the tangomaos *who operated in the rivers of upper Guinea. These private traders, operating independently of royal control, were to become one of the main ways by which Portuguese influence spread along the west African coast. They were an instance of the informal empire that grew up alongside the formal empire both in the Atlantic and the East.*

Dom Afonso, we the King send you greetings. We are informed that you have behaved harshly towards the *cavaleiros*[1] of this our town[2] of Mina, so that it is becoming depopulated and they are departing from there to other places. For the reasons which they have given, and which have been indicated to us and others, we consider it very prejudicial to our service and to the welfare of this town and its trade. First, because they are Christian and have received the water of baptism, they should be protected, instructed and supported and not driven into exile. Moreover they are our vassals and obedient to us and to you and to our captains in this city. In our name they serve us in everything required of them, and with their canoes and their servants they bring wood to the captains of our ships. Many of them make large purchases from our factory and most of them are accustomed to buy the old cloth which they sell from their canoes.

Among them are said to be many rich men who have slaves, all of whom are, or could be, at our service. If they were supported and were only punished in moderation and were instructed as they should be, they would be of service to us and would secure their own interests. For all these services, these men tells us, they do not expect any reward from us except that we should protect them and behave justly towards them. For this reason, it appears to us that you should not consider it to be your duty to throw them out. And if it is intended to punish them, this appears to be harsh because by expelling them they run two risks, of being robbed or being killed. And it should be sufficient, if they deserve it, that they should pay a penalty to the Church or something similar, like any other person. We therefore recommend and order that you behave better towards them and do not banish them as far as you are able, rather that you should direct them to follow a path which is more in our service and to strive to prevent them from straying from it because this is in the interest of the factory. And [for their part] they should not go around saying things that they ought not to say about you or [the factory]. Otherwise, when they are no longer in the land, as well as losing the service which we receive from these men, merchants will not come with their goods as they used to come.

Notes

1 This word normally means 'knights' but here must refer to freemen.
2 Mina is referred to as *'nossa alldea'*, which would normally be translated as 'our village'. However, by this time, Mina had acquired the size, importance and status of a town.

---

24 CHRISTIANITY AND THE OBAS OF BENIN

Letter of Duarte Pires to Dom Manuel I, Benin, 20 October 1516
António Brásio, ed., *Monumenta Missionaria Africana*, vol. 1, Agência Geral do Ultramar (Lisbon, 1952), pp. 1471–531.
Translated by Malyn Newitt.

The writer of this letter, Duarte Pires, and his companion João Sobrinho, were Portuguese from Príncipe who had opened up trading relations with Benin, which may have included military assistance for the Oba of Benin in his wars. The king of Portugal was hoping to benefit by their presence to bring about the conversion of the Oba and the establishment of a close alliance of the kind that was proving so profitable for the Portuguese Crown in the Kongo Kingdom. It is clear that the Oba gave encouragement to the Portuguese in order to obtain help from them, although no mass conversion ever took place. The Obas remained attached to their traditional religious practices and, to compound this stubbornness (in the eyes of the Portuguese), were ready to trade with French interlopers. They also forbade the export of male slaves, thereby lessening Portugal's interest in the region. The commerce of Benin never became a Portuguese royal monopoly and was largely carried on by traders from São Tomé and Príncipe, whose interests frequently clashed with those of the Crown in west Africa.

The presence of Portuguese in Benin is vividly portrayed by the Benin bronze casters who used the distinctive features, dress and arms of the Portuguese as a favourite motif in their work. However, the contrast between the experience of the Portuguese in Benin and their experience in Kongo is especially noteworthy, and shows how important the adoption of the Christian cult in the Kongo was to the growth of a creole culture and integration of the Kongolese into the burgeoning Atlantic economy.

Sire, you should know that Pero Baroso gave me a letter from Your Highness and I rejoice that Your Highness should remember such a poor man as I. Now I will give Your Highness an account of the matter contained in the letter you sent me. Sire, what you say about my being in great favour with the King of Benin is certainly true, because the King of Benin favours anyone who speaks well of Your Highness and very much desires to be your friend. He never speaks of anything else but matters which concern you and Our Lord. And in this, he and all his nobles and people take the greatest pleasure, and you will soon know of this and the good that the King of Benin does to us for love of Your Highness. As a result, he treats us very honourably and places us to eat at table together with his son. Nothing in his palace is hidden from us but all the doors are open.

Sire, when the priests arrived at Benin, the pleasure of the King of Benin and his people was such that I cannot describe to you. At once he sent for them and they were with him during the war for a whole year. We and the fathers both reminded him of Your Highness' embassy, and he replied that he was very happy with it but because of the war, he could do nothing until he returned to Benin because he had to have time to consider such a great mystery as this. As soon as he was once again in Benin, he would carry out what he had promised Your Highness and he would do what would give great pleasure to you and all your kingdom.

So at the end of a year, in the month of August, the King allowed his son and some of the greatest nobles in his kingdom to become Christians. He ordered a church to be built in Benin and they were immediately baptized. They are being taught to read, and Your Highness's will know that they are learning very well. And, Sire, the King of Benin expects to end the war this summer when we will go to Benin, and I will give an account to Your Highness of everything that occurs.

Sire, I Duarte Pires and João Sobrinho, an inhabitant of the island of Príncipe, and Gregório Lourenço, a black man who was the servant of Francisco Lourenço, are all three at Your Highness' service and we have conveyed Your Highness' thoughts to the King of Benin and have told him what a great lord Your Highness is and what a great lord you can make him.

Written during the war, 10 October 1516.

6

DISCOVERY OF THE KINGDOM OF KONGO

25 THE MANISONYO EMBRACES CHRISTIANITY, 1491

From Rui de Pina, *Crónica de D. João II.*
António Brásio, *Monumenta Missionaria Africana* (Lisbon, 1952), 1, pp. 61, 65–6.
Translated by Malyn Newitt.

The Portuguese explorer Diogo Cão had reached the Zaire River in 1483. He met some Kongo notables and took two of them back to Portugal, returning again on his second voyage in 1485, when he visited the capital of the Kongo kingdom. As a result of these early contacts Dom João II decided to send a full-scale embassy, which was dispatched in 1491 under Dom João da Silva, who died of plague during the voyage. The reception of this embassy is described by Rui de Pina in great detail and shows how the Kongo elites sought to incorporate these new experiences into their view of the spirit world. This account of the reception of the embassy by the ruler of the province of Sonyo[1] shows how important the new religion appeared to the ruling elite of Kongo. The ruler of the province was determined that he would be the first person initiated into the new cult, which he had every intention of controlling. Rui de Pina incorporates much detail about the religious ceremonies of the Kongo, as well as other important information such as the fact that the Kongo kingdom maintained a fleet.

The lord of the land, whose port we entered on 29 March 1491, is a great lord, the uncle of the king and his subject, called Manisonyo,[2] a man of fifty years of age, good natured and wise. He was two leagues distant from the port when he was notified of the arrival of the fleet and was requested to send word of the arrival to the king. The Manisonyo gave signs and demonstrations of great joy at having to attend to the affairs of the king of Portugal, and as a token of respect placed both hands on the ground and then placed them on his face, which is the greatest sign of veneration that they make to their kings. And after he heard of the death of Dom João da Silva, how and in what place it occurred, and how he had died a Christian, he said that whether death came here or there did not signify, for he was fortunate to have made so good an end, as it was in the service of God and of two such kings. And to serve as a memorial on behalf of a king who was so virtuous and so powerful and one who was such a true friend, he desired to hold celebrations and to demonstrate in his own person and that of his subjects what he would have shown to the king himself had he been present.

To this end, there at once assembled a crowd of people with bows and arrows, drums, trumpets of ivory and violas, all according to their custom and apparently well coordinated. All came naked above the waist with their bodies painted in white and other colours as a sign of great pleasure and happiness. From the waist down they were clothed in rich palm cloths and wore headdresses made from the feathers of parrots and other birds, which the noblewomen had made and had given to them for the occasion. The lord wore on his head a cap decorated with a serpent beautifully worked in needlework and very lifelike. The wives of the nobles were present and celebrated with loud voices to please their husbands, each one saying that their man gave better service to the king of Portugal, whom they called Zambemapongo,[3] which means lord of the world.

....

The lord, when asked what name he would have, said Dom Manuel,[4] because they had told him that this was the name of the brother of the queen of Portugal, who was a duke, and he also was a duke and was brother of the queen. His son would be called Dom António. The captain and other principal men of the fleet acted as godfathers, and when the ceremony, which was very long and to which Dom Manuel was very attentive, was finished, they immediately placed the holy oil on his head. It was clearly explained to him through interpreters what each thing signified, which pleased him and at each step made him more content. The nobles of his household did not enter the church, however important they were, but walked round fearful of what was happening to their lord. Eventually he came out of the church, safe and with a very happy face, and said to them:

'Friends, you all know with how much pleasure and good fortune I have conducted such and such of our annual festivals and won such and such victories over my enemies. It now gives me pleasure above everything else to affirm to you that I have never felt so joyful nor so youthful in my happiness as I do at this hour. And the true God be praised, to whom today I give myself, since the desire to be His has been so strong, although according to His law it is impossible to serve him except with the will.'

Then, as his people were looking at the altars and ornaments of the church, he said to them: 'You who are not yet Christian must remain here, as you do not deserve to see such holy things.' And with one voice they all said, 'Lord remember us. And since, as you say, what you receive is such that brings pleasure to young men, give us part of it.' To whom he answered, 'I have already replied to you that I cannot do this now as it is not the right time'.

After all this was finished, the said friars returned in procession with Dom Manuel to his house, all singing *Benedictus Dominus Deus Israel,* and so forth. And as the cross was taken back to the church, both father and son sank to the ground on their knees, and with their hands joined and raised to heaven and their heads uncovered, they bowed to it with much reverence until it had gone by and was out of sight.

When these things had taken place and he was now a Christian, Dom Manuel at once notified the king his lord, who was some fifty leagues away. The king sent a reply at once through a great lord who was cousin of the prince's brother, congratulating him on the honour the Christians of the king of Portugal his brother and friend had bestowed on him, and that he was delighted and rejoiced greatly that he was a Christian as he himself hoped to be, and that for having done this, which he considered to be a great and signal service, he would make him a grant of thirty leagues of land along the seacoast and ten leagues inland, with all its inhabitants and revenues. And the fleet and its crews were entrusted to him since he was their lord and would supply and provide for them as though they were his children. And Dom Manuel who had previously been a good ruler, now ruled even better.

The same Easter day that he became a Christian, great festivities were held after their fashion, and in the evening Dom Manuel took the friars aside and requested that they instruct him in what he needed to know and what he needed to observe if he was to secure his salvation.

Notes

1 This region is now called Soyo.
2 'Mani', or 'Mweni', was the title of a ruler in the Kongo kingdom. So Manisonyo means the 'ruler of Sonyo'.
3 Anne Hilton renders this *nzambi mpungo,* 'the highest other worldly authority of the *mbumba* dimension'. *Mbumba* was the spiritual manifestation of the natural world and *mbumba* spirits 'appear to have been the water and earth spirits' and might be invoked whenever there were issues surrounding fertility (Hilton, pp. 13–7, 31).
4 Dom Manuel succeeded his cousin Dom João II as king of Portugal in 1495.

26 THE ARRIVAL OF THE PORTUGUESE EMBASSY AT THE KONGO COURT, 1491

From Rui de Pina, *Crónica de D. João II.*
António Brásio, *Monumenta Missionaria Africana* (Lisbon, 1952), 1,
pp. 112–6.
Translated by Malyn Newitt.

The Portuguese embassy sent to the Kongo kingdom in 1491 was warmly welcomed. To the royal chronicler this was flattering evidence of the might and benevolence of the king of Portugal. However, the details of the traditional ceremonies, in particular the gathering of dust and the smearing of it on the captain's body, make it clear that the Kongolese saw the Portuguese principally as representatives of the spirit world whose goodwill was essential to ensure the continued fertility of the kingdom. Christianity was thus incorporated as a new and powerful spirit cult in the Kongo cosmology.

After these things had been done and completed, much to the service of God and to the honour and praise of the king of Portugal, the said Dom Manuel[1] ordered that the captain, the friars and the other persons should go with the embassy to see to the affairs of the king his lord. These things were at once quickly prepared and got ready, and after the captain had sent the good news to the ships, he departed by land with two hundred blacks to carry the goods, which included a lot of provisions, and with many other people in addition to protect them. While he was on the road, a fidalgo of the king came to him with a message, rejoicing in his arrival and with a general order that, under pain of death, all the Christians in his kingdom should be given freely whatever they wished. This was fully carried out, because in those lands he is the king and is the person who is most feared and also most loved and obeyed. Having been granted this licence, the blacks in our company did a lot of harm to those through whose land they passed, taking a great many things from them, but in spite of this no one complained or showed any sign of discontent.

Being already near the court of the king, another lord, his principal secretary,[2] came to them with many thousands of nzimbus,[3] which are their coins and which are the small white shells of shellfish that they find in the sea and that are shaped like sea-snails,[4] and that they and all those in the land value as though they were gold or silver coins, which are neither known nor used in that land. And he also brought them many sheep and goats, millet flour, chickens, honey, palm wine, fruit and other things for their maintenance. It was a journey of fifty leagues, so they said, from the port to the king's court and took twenty-three days.

The day that the Christians reached the court, they were received with great noise by countless people, and they were housed in some huts that were new and very suitable [for their rank] and they were provided with everything they required. The mode of receiving them was that the king sent to the captain and friars many courtiers who danced in a demented manner, and after them an infinite number of archers and lance bearers and others with warlike arms, and also countless women all arranged in companies and with ivory trumpets and drums and other instruments, all singing the praises of the king of Portugal and, with great joy, extolling his greatness.

In this manner they arrived before the king who was in a square in front of his palace accompanied by people without number.[5] He was positioned on a rich platform after this fashion, naked from the waist up, with a very tall cap of palm cloth placed on his head, and on his shoulders a horse's tail decorated in silver. From his waist down he was covered with a damask cloth, which the king [of Portugal] had sent him, and on his left arm was a bracelet of ivory. When the Portuguese captain arrived, he kissed his hand and performed other Spanish ceremonies and gave him greetings from the king and said other things to him on his own behalf, which the Manikongo showed that he received with great pleasure. And as a sign of his satisfaction, he took earth in his hand and ran it down the captain's breast and his own, which is the greatest sign of respect that the king could give, taking account of his rank and custom.

At this, all the people of his court turned and ceremoniously raised their hands towards the sea as though indicating Portugal, and crying out, 'Long live the king and Lord of the World,[6] and God grant him favour since he is so good and such a friend of the king our benefactor and our lord.'

After these festivities were over, the king dismissed the captain with great honour, saying that this visit was enough for now, and that later he would listen to him at greater length and in private. As the captain and the Christians were tired from their journey, by the king's pleasure they took their things and placed everything neatly and in good order in one of the huts of the great palace, which was beautiful and covered in carvings and woven strips of multicoloured palm cloth tied with complicated knots. To this the king immediately came accompanied by a few of his trusted nobles and great lords and men, each one of whom could, as the king asserted, serve him with a hundred thousand men.

He was straight away shown the ornaments and things connected with the church, and at each one he wanted to show such happiness and pleasure that many times he jumped up from the path and, embracing the captain, lifted him in his arms, showing that he desired to adopt him in the name of the king, and saying such things that clearly indicated that he thought himself the most fortunate king in the world. Although he had kingdoms and lordships greater than any he had yet spoken about, they seemed to him too small to reward and serve the king of Portugal, who deserved so much and from whom he had received such honour. After he had been shown the religious items, the said captain offered him all the other things, which the king had sent at his request, namely the masons and carpenters and Christian women and artisans with all their tools and apparatus, and afterwards a horse with its saddle and harness. He was also immediately offered and given those presents which the king had sent to him for his person, namely a rich piece of rough and smooth brocade, and many cloths of silk and velvet and others of many colours, and satins and damasks and scarlet and pieces of Holland, and horses' tails decorated with silver, which he valued above all, especially some which were light brown, and large bells and many other things of this kind.[7] And the captain said to him: 'My Lord these things are sent to you by the king my lord, who is your lord and your friend, and there are many like these in his kingdoms and he intends that they should give you pleasure'. In addition he gave him garments richly embroidered, saying to him: 'He also sends you these garments, which are those in which he himself is dressed, so that you may wear them out of love for him, even though these are things you had not requested.'

The king was astonished at the richness and novelty of these things and replied: 'I cannot receive anything from such a king that does not deserve to be constantly before my eyes and in my heart or on my body, which until now I always thought was so dull'. And in addition, the said captain offered to him the whole royal fleet and all its people. He was to make use of these in any way that did him honour and service, until such a time as they should die, because he had been so commanded.[8]

At each thing that the said captain offered to him in the name of the king [of Portugal], the said king bowed with happiness and pleasure, touching the ground with hands and placing them on his breast. And having received them all, he said to his nobles: 'Certainly a king in whom there is so much nobility, so much goodness and so much truth, he alone is the Lord of the World and deserves to be so. And in these things you begin to see it. For I am king of such large lands, but he does not want for anything, and since on one occasion he became my friend (which I do not deserve and can never deserve) and helped me and sent me everything that I asked of him, all as completely as you can see, what will he do to others who can and will serve him still better?'

Notes

1 This was the baptismal name taken by the Manisonyo in 1491 (Doc. 25). He also adopted the lineage name of Silva, presumably after the dead ambassador.
2 *Privado.*
3 Currency shells; a kind of cowrie. See Docs. 13, 32 and 55.
4 *Caramujos.*
5 The Manikongo at the time was Nzinga a Nkuwu. He was later baptized João I and died in 1506.
6 This is the name *nzambi mpungu*, which the king of Portugal had been called from the time of the first contacts. See Doc. 24.
7 Compare this with the value attached to horses' tails by the Wolof. See Doc. 18.
8 See Doc. 36.

---

27 THE KING OF KONGO IS BAPTIZED AND GOES TO WAR, 1491

From João de Barros *Da Ásia*, Década 1, book 3, ch. 9.

António Brásio, *Monumenta Missionaria Africana* (Lisbon, 1952), 1, pp. 84–5.

Translated by Malyn Newitt.

João de Barros is widely recognized as the most important Portuguese historian of the early days of overseas expansion. In 1525 he was appointed treasurer of the Casa da Índia, which appointment he held until 1568 and which gave him access to wide-ranging sources of information. The first volume of his great history, the Décadas da Ásia, *appeared in 1552. The king of Kongo had intended that his baptism and the building of the church would give him exclusive access to the power of what he believed to be a new spirit cult. However, he was forced to allow some leading nobles (Mwissikongo) and the queen to receive baptism, thus widening the circle of those involved in the cult.*

Just as our people arrived, news reached the king that the Mundequete people, who inhabited certain islands in the lake from which issues the River Zaire, which flows through this kingdom of Kongo, were in rebellion and were causing much destruction in neighbouring lands. The king went in person to bring help, and for this reason the baptism of the king was not carried out with all the ceremony that he had planned when the building of the church should be finished. So he received this sacrament, so necessary for his salvation, the very same day that the first stone was laid. And as King Dom João [of Portugal] was the author of this work, he desired that he should be called João after him.[1] Six nobles[2] from among those who accompanied him to the war were baptized with him, and a 100,000 people assembled because of it and also because of the arrival of our people. He took with him to this war a banner emblazoned with a Cross, which Rui de Sousa[3] delivered to him, by virtue of which sign he was promised that he would triumph over his enemies. This banner, which was given to him by the king, belonged to the Holy Crusade and had been given to him by Pope Innocent VIII[4] for use in war against the Infidels.

When the queen saw that the king was leaving and that Frei João, the leader of the clerics, was dead and that the others fell ill as soon as they set foot on the land, she began to complain to the king, demanding of him that it would be a good idea if she were baptized before his departure. She asked why she should wait until the prince, who was at the front with the enemy, arrived, as he had ordered, saying that by that time the church would already be finished, the wait would be very long and she feared that the ministers of the sacrament would die as had already begun to happen. Seeing how just was her request, the king thought that it was a good idea that she should be baptized and gave her the name of Leonor, after the queen of Portugal, the wife of King Dom João, so that both husband and wife, being now Christians, had the same names as those two most Christian princes, the authors of this conversion, who were joined through matrimony and also through blood, both being grandchildren of Dom Duarte.[5]

The king departed for that war, which was now pressing, and according to our people who were there, there were more than 80,000 people with him. And, because of the faith and the symbol that he carried with him, he won a victory more swiftly than [would have happened] as a result of any preparations [made before] his departure. Returning to the city, Rui de Sousa was sent back to Portugal, leaving behind for the conversion of the people Frei António, who was the second person after Frei João, four other friars and also some laymen to keep them company. Others were also detailed to travel into the interior of the land with some of the natives as the king, Dom João, had commanded, so that they could discover the interior of that great kingdom and pass beyond the great lake, which we have mentioned.[6]

Notes

1 Dom João II of Portugal (1481–95).
2 *Principaes fidalgos.* From other sources it is clear that these took the names of senior Portuguese noblemen.

3   He had taken over as head of the mission when his father, Gonçalo de Sousa, the commander of the fleet, and João da Silva, the ambassador, died of the plague during the voyage to Kongo.
4   Innocent VIII was pope from 1484 to 1492.
5   Queen Leonor was Dom João's first cousin, the daughter of Dom Afonso V's younger brother.
6   The outcome of this exploratory journey into the interior is not known. This refers to the current belief that the major rivers of Africa all flowed from a great central lake.

28   THE PROVINCE OF MBATA AND ITS RELATIONS WITH THE PORTUGUESE AND THE KONGO KING

From Filippo Pigafetta, *Relatione del Reame di Congo et delli circonvicine contrade tratta dalli scritti & ragionamenti di Odoardo Lopez Portoghese*, Grassi (Rome, 1591).

Translation by Malyn Newitt, based on M. Hutchinson, trans. and ed., *A Report of the Kingdom of Congo and of the Surrounding Countries* (London, 1881), pp.60–2; Filippo Pigafetta e Duarte Lopes, *Relação do Reino do Congo e das Terras Circunvizinhas*, António Luís Alves Ferronha, ed. (Lisbon, 1989), pp. 54–6.

In the dedication of this work to Antonio Migliore, bishop of San Marco and head of the hospital of Espirito Santo in Rome, dated 7 August 1591, Pigafetta says he was asked to record the life story of a Portuguese 'pilgrim', Duarte Lopes. Although the story was told to him in Portuguese, Pigafetta translated it into Italian and, as he confesses, used his own words to render what he was told. Lopes left for Africa in 1578 on board a trading ship owned by his uncle, and spent twelve years in the Kongo. When Pigafetta knew him, he was acting as ambassador of the king of Kongo in Rome. The Pigafetta/Lopes text is the earliest authoritative European account of the Kongo kingdom, and gives important information about its origin and structure.

Mbata was a frontier province situated in the east of the kingdom and, according to Lopes, had been voluntarily incorporated into the Kongo kingdom. It was ruled by the Nsaku Lau kanda (a matrilineal descent group), which traditionally provided the chief wife of the Manikongo. However, children of this wife were debarred from the succession, a system that the Europeans found hard to understand and that Lopes struggled to interpret. Nevertheless, the accession of Afonso as Manikongo in 1506 brought to power a prince of the Nsaku Lau, and from this time the rulers of Mbata became, in effect, members of a royal dynasty (see Doc. 54).

This passage introduces the Jaga, who were to play such an important part in Kongo history, first as invaders in the 1560s, and then as mercenaries providing soldiers for the Portuguese. Lopes claims that the Manikongo restricted access to firearms, preferring to depend upon Portuguese musketeers to defend him rather than allow these arms to fall into the hands of rival lineages. To this, however, the rulers of Mbata were exceptions. Not only did they need firearms to defend their frontiers, but they were more to be trusted than other lineages, and the kings came to depend on their loyalty to maintain their authority.

Of the Fifth Province which Is Called Mbata

This province is bounded on the north by the land of Mpangu[1]; on the east it crosses the River Barbela and extends to the Mountains of the Sun[2] and to the foot of the Salnitro range; and south of the said mountains it passes the junction of the Barbela and Cacinga rivers to the Burnt Mountains.[3]

Within these limits lies Mbata and its principal city, the residence of the prince, who is also called Mbata. Formerly it was known as Aghirimba, but afterwards the name was corrupted and now it is called Mbata. The kingdom was formerly great and powerful, and voluntarily became united with the kingdom of Kongo without any war, doubtless to avoid dissensions among its great men. In consequence, it is more favoured and enjoys greater privileges and freedoms than any other province in the Kongo kingdom. The government of Mbata is always given to one of the blood royal of this country, according to the king's pleasure, without having regard to one person more than to another, beyond keeping to the royal race and lineage. Neither the eldest nor the second son inherits this post, but the king of Kongo gives it, as we have said, according to his pleasure, to avoid either usurpation or rebellion. He considers himself closer to the king than any other governor or lord in the kingdom of Kongo, being the second person in the kingdom, nor can anyone alter his decrees as they can those of others; and on the failure of the royal line, the succession devolves upon him. He is styled Dom Pedro Manimbata.

Sometimes he eats at the king's table, but at a lower place, which is a privilege not granted to any other noble in Kongo, not even to the sons of the king himself. His court and attendants are scarcely inferior to those of the king of Kongo, with trumpets, drums and other instruments going before him as befits a king. He is commonly called prince of Mbata[4] by the Portuguese because, as has been said, if the kings of Kongo lack heirs, the kingdom would pass to one of his blood.

He is always waging war against the heathens who live near him, and he can bring into the field seventy or eighty thousand men. As he is continually at war with the neighbouring peoples, he is allowed to maintain arquebusiers among his native vassals, the king permitting no governor of other provinces, not even his sons, to employ native arquebusiers, but only Portuguese.

Duarte Lopes having once asked the king why he did not permit other governors to keep musketeers, he replied that, if there happened to be a rebellion against him [by a governor who had] one or two thousand arquebusiers, there would be no possibility of resisting them. And, as we have already mentioned, the king only permits the use of native arquebusiers to the prince of Mbata, but it is right to add that he does this for a necessary reason, because to the east of Mbata, beyond the Mountains of the Sun and Salnitro, on the western and eastern banks of the Nile,[5] and on the borders of the kingdom of Moene Muge,[6] live a people called Jagas by the people of Kongo but known in their own country by the name of Agag.[7] They are a very savage and warlike people, much given to fighting and robbery, who make constant raids into the neighbouring countries and from time to time into Mbata. So there is a need for the people of the latter country to be constantly under arms and on their guard, and to maintain arquebusiers to defend themselves.

The prince of Mbata has many lords under him, and the native peoples are called Mozombos,[8] their language being understood in Kongo. The people are much less civilized than the Mwissikongo,[9] and slaves coming from there prove extremely obstinate. The trade is the same as amongst the other people of whom we have just spoken, but the revenues and profits which the king draws from Mbata amounts to more than double that of the provinces mentioned above.

Notes

1   Mpangu was another of the traditional provinces of the kingdom.
2   Monti del Sole in the Italian.
3   Monte Bruciato in the Italian.
4   From their first contacts the Portuguese had employed titles used by the European nobility to describe the different ranks within the Kongo kingdom. The Kongolese themselves adopted these titles.
5   Pigafetta published a famous map to accompany his account of the Kongo. In this he tried to relate the geography of western Africa to what was known of the Nile and eastern Africa. In so doing, he had, of course, grossly underestimated the width of Africa.
6   The kingdom of Moene Muge appears on Pigafetta's map and is located in east Africa. From there it was copied by many subsequent cartographers, and in the nineteenth

century appears as the kingdom of Moenemoezi, which was thought to lie north of the Makua territory and east of the great lakes.

7 The Jaga first enter the known history of the region in the pages of Pigafetta's narrative and he is the only source for the invasion of 1568, which almost destroyed the Kongo kingdom. See Doc. 39.

8 Monsobos in the text.

9 Mociconghi in the text. The Mwissikongo were members of the ruling lineages from which the Manikongos were chosen.

---

29 THE ACCESSION OF DOM AFONSO I OF KONGO

From João de Barros *Da Ásia*, Década 1, book 3, ch. X.

António Brásio, *Monumenta Missionaria Africana* (Lisbon, 1952), 1, pp. 141–7.

Translated by Malyn Newitt.

Barros's account of the events in the Kongo kingdom that preceded the accession of Afonso I in 1506 is a miraculous religious narrative, but barely concealed within it are the realities of Kongo power politics. Barros makes it clear that the insistence of the Portuguese priests that the king keep only one wife meant that all the other wives lost status. As it was from their children, and not the children of the principal wife, that the next Manikongo would traditionally have been chosen, this stricture threatened the whole stability of the kingdom. This account also reveals that the majority of the ruling elite of Kongo supported Mpanzu and considered Christianity to be a form of witchcraft, the nature of which was graphically illustrated in Barros's narrative. Afonso's victory over his brother was attributed by the Portuguese and by the king himself to the intervention of Saint James, and the king incorporated a reference to this in the coat of arms he adopted. Afonso's accession as Manikongo broke with Kongo tradition but conformed to Portuguese ideas of primogeniture and confirmed the power of the ruling lineage of Mbata (see Doc. 28). The royal authority was now to be inextricably tied to the Christian cult, and the spread of Christianity in its turn rested on the authority that the king and the ruling lineage of Mbata could exercise from the centre.

When Rui de Sousa had left for this kingdom, the prince, the son of Dom João, the king of Kongo, came from the hostile frontier districts where he was and, as the church was already completed, he was baptized with many fidalgos, both those who came with him and those who arrived for the occasion. And out of love for Dom Afonso,[1] son of Dom João II, the king of Portugal, he took the same name.[2] However, because the devil lost so much of his jurisdiction through the baptism of so many people every day, he worked to keep some members of the royal family loyal to himself, through whom he might be able to make good the loss. A son of the king, called Panso Aquitimo,[3] who was unwilling to receive the water of baptism, removed himself from the influence of his father and gathered around him some of those who agreed with his intentions.

To the hard-heartedness of his son, the devil added a new temptation for the king when the priests tried to make him separate himself from the many women he had and remain with only one, as prescribed by the Church. Through the precept of these priests, these [women] lost their status as royal wives and had the support of other women who were wives of the king's councillors who, because this was a matter which also affected them, worked on their husbands to advise the king not to consent to it. Because the king was old, he heeded the advice of his councillors and, as he was inclined to the old ways, the early fervour which he had shown [for Christianity] began to cool, and he turned again to his former rites and customs.

The prince, Dom Afonso, was firmer in matters of the faith and, as he was not happy with this change, he defended what he believed with all his might. Those he denounced began to turn the king against him until they expelled him from the [king's] favour and replaced him with the pagan son, Panso Aquitemo, with the objective that, if he should become king, they could continue to live according to the customs of the past. And as all the people of this part of Ethiopia are much given to witchcraft,[4] in which they put all their faith and belief, these servants of the devil who plotted these things told the king that it was certain that Dom Afonso, his son, by means of the magic which the Christians had taught him, came flying every night from the Cabo do Reino where he was some eighty leagues distant, and went in to those women, who had been removed from him [the king], and had intercourse with them and returned immediately the same night. And apart from this injury which he did him, he knew how to dry up rivers and spoil the crops, all so that he could prevent him having so much income from the kingdom as he had had previously, and would therefore not have enough to give to those who served him faithfully, with the result that the kingdom would rise against him.

These and other fables aroused the indignation of the king against his son, so that he stopped the income that was given to him to maintain himself. Some fidalgos who were friends of the prince protested against this, saying that these things were lies, since his son had been seen both by day and by night in the place where he was residing. So, in order to make himself more certain of the truth concerning his son, the king ordered a charm[5] which is in use among them. Hiding this charm in a cloth, he sent it by one of his servants to one of his women, called Cufua Cuanfulo, whom he suspected, saying, on behalf of the prince Dom Afonso, that he sent her that charm to deliver her from the death sentence that the king had ordered for her and also for all the other women. However, because she was innocent of any crime and because it was to her that the present was sent, she told the servant to place the cloth on the ground and went to the king telling him of the present sent by his son, and other words, which revealed to the king that she was innocent so that he agreed that what had been said to him about his son was malicious. And a few days later, without telling anyone about the matter, he ordered the prince to come and restored his revenues to him, with a further increase in his lands. He made a public announcement about this when those who had aroused these suspicions were present, and to make their confusion even greater he ordered them to be killed.

It was not long before the devil found a new route to follow. When the prince returned to his land, as one who had received the light of God and the favour of his father, he made a public proclamation that, if anyone was discovered with an idol in his house, he would be killed. This action was immediately reported to the king by the prince's enemies, who made the situation worse by making him believe that the people were so agitated that, if he did not intervene, they would rebel against his royal person.

The prince was summoned to Court and agreed that, rather than forfeit his life, in this matter he would obey his father and would not allow this work, which was to the glory of God, to continue. And because in his company there was Dom Gonçalo, one of those who had been baptized with him, a prudent man and by faith a Christian and zealous to honour God, the king tried to have him near him. However, through his own prudence, through the words of the prince and through the aid of God who ruled them, they ordered and delayed his departure. And feigning now one thing and now another, all to do with the service of the king, the government of the land and the collection of the revenues which they owed him, God willed it that this persecution of the prince should cease by bringing such an illness on his father that he died.

This death also brought relief to our people,[6] many of whom remained in exile with the prince, because of the life that the king lived and the small progress they had made with him. By means of the priests, the prince had been converted and the people of a very great part of his domain,[7] which they call Nsundi,[8] had been baptized, which was a cause of great indignation to the king and to those who had returned to their old ways. The prince knew about this indignation, and for this reason, while his father was ill, he did not trust these messages, although he was summoned by some fidalgos who told him that [the king] was at the point of death and that his brother, Panso, was about to arrive in the city with a view to taking possession of it with the people he brought with him. It appeared to [Afonso] that this illness was feigned in order to bring him there. However, when the death of the king was confirmed, he reached the city in three days because, after he had begun to hear news of his illness, he had already started his journey there. Before he entered the city he was warned by the queen, his mother, that he should enter by night secretly and without a crowd of people, and that those who came in his company should come a few at a time with baskets on their heads in which they carried their arms, saying that this was food which was being brought for her.

Having made his entry in this manner, the next day the prince went out to the great square, where he summoned the chief men of the land who were in the city and made a speech to them. At the end of this, according to their custom and before they could change their minds, they declared him to be king, with a great fanfare of music and shouts in such a way that the noise was heard in the houses outside the city, where his brother was waiting for more men to make himself king by force of arms.

When the reason for this din was discovered, in spite of the small number of men his brother had with him, he began to enter the city without waiting for the people he expected. At this time, king Dom Afonso had with him only thirty-seven Christians and, as he was a man skilled in the arts of war and was obedient to God, he ordered his men not to molest his brother but to wait for his entry into that great enclosure, because he trusted in God's mercy, in which he believed, to give him victory over his enemies. He was not deceived in this expectation because, when he began to fight with his brother, who was the first to enter the square, arrows began to rain down, which was a truly miraculous thing since so few men accompanied the king. And all called on the apostle Saint James,[9] while he called on the name of Jesus for help, never ceasing to invoke both of them until in the battle his brother had turned his back on him, and the one had routed the other.

So God gave complete victory to this Catholic king, and in his flight the brother went through the bush and fell into a trap which had been prepared for some wild animal, where he was taken by those who were pursuing him and with him his principal captain. This captain feared for his life and, before reaching the king, he sent to ask him to agree, by the God in which he believed, to his being baptized before his death, because he did not want to lose his soul since he had already lost his body, and because he believed he [Jesus Christ] was the true God whom men should worship. And during the time of the battle, he had seen many armed men on horseback, who followed a sign such as the Christians worship and which was the cause of his destruction, for these were the people who had fought. When the king knew of his penitence and of his request for baptism, he not only ordered it to be given to him but he also pardoned him. And to commemorate this act, he and all his lineage would be obliged to sweep and clean the church and bring water to baptize all the heathen. This penitent was delivered to that honourable and Catholic baron, Dom Gonçalo, who had greatly assisted the king in matters of the faith, and because this captain at the time of his baptism took the name Dom Gonçalo, he made him captain of a part of his lands to collect his revenues.

Panso Aquitemo, the brother of the king, died from the injuries received in the trap into which he had fallen, from anger and from disgust at his situation.

Having settled his affairs, the king remained at peace in his kingdom, although he had much trouble with some of his chiefs who in many areas rebelled against him because of their idolatry. However, God always gave him victory over them and Our Lord granted him such a life in that royal estate that he reigned for fifty-odd years and died aged eighty-five.[10] And in all this time, after he received the faith until the last day of his life, he showed not only the virtues of a most Christian prince, but he also fulfilled the role of an apostle, himself preaching and converting a great many of his people, and showing such zeal for the honour of God that he employed most of his life in doing this. And in order better to carry out his role as preacher, he learned to read our language and studied the lives of Christ and the evangelists, the lives of the saints and other Catholic doctrines, which he was able to learn with the instruction of our priests, and he expounded it all to his barbarous people. He also sent his sons, grandsons, nephews and some noble youths to our kingdom of Portugal to learn their letters, not only ours but also Latin and sacred [texts], to such good effect that there are now two members of his family who are bishops in his kingdom and who, by exercising their office, serve God and please the kings of this kingdom of Portugal, at whose expense all these things were done.[11]

Notes

1   The Infante Afonso was killed in 1491 in a fall from a horse.
2   His African name was Mbemba Nzinga (or Mvemba a Nzinga).
3   Mpanzu a Kitima.
4   The word used here is *feitiço*, which the Portuguese used to described many different African religious practices and beliefs. In the Kongo, belief in *nkisi* was strong. These were images or objects which were endowed with supernatural power.
5   *Feitiço.*

6 The Portuguese.
7 *Senhorio.*
8 Isundi in the text. This was the northeastern province of Nsundi.
9 'Santiago' was the traditional war cry of Portuguese knights in battle.
10 Dom Afonso I reigned 1506–43.
11 See Doc. 42.

30 RELATIONS BETWEEN KONGO AND THE PORTUGUESE OF SÃO TOMÉ

Letter of King Dom Afonso I, the king of Kongo, to Dom Manuel I, 5 October 1514

António Brásio, *Monumenta Missionaria Africana* (Lisbon, 1952), 1, pp. 294–9.

Translated by Malyn Newitt.

This is an extract from a very long letter, which sets out the problems that Dom Afonso was now having with the Portuguese. In his attempt to establish Christianity in his kingdom, the king was continuing to meet a lot of opposition. His main support was coming from his own close relatives of the Nsaka Lau, the ruling elite of Mbata, and from the few Portuguese in the kingdom. He records here the difficulties he was encountering sending letters to Portugal and the devious tactics of the captain of São Tomé, Fernão de Melo. The island of São Tomé was the nearest Portuguese settlement to the Kongo kingdom, and Afonso was hoping to establish close relations with its captain. What he required were priests to maintain the new royal cult of Christianity and firearms. Fernão de Melo, for his part, wanted to monopolise as much of the trade with the kingdom as possible, and had no interest in the wider objectives of the king of Kongo or the king of Portugal. Indeed his behaviour undermined the Crown's objectives in establishing Christianity as the basis for an alliance with Kongo.

The extract also refers to Dom Afonso's destruction of the 'great house of idols' (translated by Anne Hilton as 'the house of the Nkisi-fetishes'[1]). It is not clear exactly what this was, but it refers to the territorial deities which were revered by the Kongolese and which Afonso wished to replace with a royal (Christian) cult, which would be under the king's control.

To the most high and powerful prince, king and lord

We, Dom Afonso, by the grace of God, king of Kongo and lord of Ambundos,[2] and so forth, greet Your Highness as a king and lord whom we greatly love. And we inform him how, in the lifetime of our father, I and my cousin Dom Pedro, a fidalgo from our land, being Christians and believing firmly in the faith of our Lord Jesus Christ, told the king our lord that I and Dom Pedro[3] were Christians and that we believed in God and not in his idols.[4] At this, the king our father said that he desired that the said Dom Pedro should be brought to his Court so that he could order him to be killed to see if God would deliver him. He would also take away our revenues and leave us to go about as vagabonds[5] until we died or he ordered us to be killed. In all this, he wished to see if Our Lord God would give us other people [to support us], since we believed in him so much. And when the message reached us that our father wanted to order me and my cousin to be killed, we gave thanks to God for, however much pain and torment our bodies would receive, great would be the pleasure that our souls would receive if we died for the love of Our Lord and not because of any evil we had done to our father. This was the state of affairs when our father died and we, with the aid of Our Lord and of the glorious Virgin his mother, came to this city to take control of the kingdom. All the people, including my relatives and brothers, were against us, and we had no other aid than that of Our Lord and of Fathers Rodrigo Eanes and António Fernandes, who gave us a great deal of support.

They prayed to Our Lord that he would give us victory against our enemies, and it seemed good to Him in his mercy that He should give us such a victory, and we defeated them. A ship belonging to Gonçalo Roiz then reached our kingdom from Mina,[6] and these Fathers, who had been here a long time, departed in it. We then sent and gave to them and to Gonçalo Roiz one thousand five hundred manilhas[7] and one hundred and fifty slaves. And we wrote a letter to Your Highness, which was written by Francisco Fernandes, in which we gave him an account of the great victory and triumph which Our Lord had given us and of how our kingdom was now a land of Christians, and therefore Your Highness should send us some priests and friars to teach us and help us to spread the faith. And we sent our son, Dom Henrique,[8] and Rodrigo de Santa Maria, our nephew, so that Your Highness could order them to be educated.

By the same ship we wrote a letter to Fernão de Melo[9] in which we asked him to send some priests to visit us and to teach us the things of God. When the priests and Gonçalo Roiz arrived at the island [of São Tomé], Fernão de Melo saw him bring so many trade goods that he became jealous and sent a ship here with nothing on board except a bed cover, a carpet,[10] a bed canopy and a glass bottle. And in the said boat he sent us a priest, and Gonçalo Pires came as captain and pilot, and

João Godinho as secretary. We received this ship with a great deal of pleasure because we supposed that he came in the service of God, but in fact he came because of his great greed. We then asked Gonçalo Pires if Fernão de Melo had some ships in which he could send us guns and muskets to help us when we burned the great house of idols, because if we burned it without having any help from Christians, they [the people] would immediately start a war to kill us. And he told us no, but that if we sent him some trade goods, he would buy them for us and would send us all the help that we needed.

Then, my lord, we desired to send [to Fernão de Melo] everything we had in the kingdom, because we would rather that everything should be spent than that we should lose the faith of Our Lord. This was because we considered that as we, who were heathen and had so little, were prepared to suffer that we might be taught the things of God, how much more would Fernão de Melo, who was a Christian and the son of a Christian. And for this reason it seemed to us that he would suffer [make sacrifices] for the faith of Our Lord and that with the trade goods that we had sent him he would buy some ships, which he would send to us as quickly as possible to help us to spread the faith of Our Lord Jesus Christ and destroy the worship of the devil, and to enable us to burn as many idols as were there. So we asked the said Gonçalo Pires whether Father Rodrigo Eanes and Father António Fernandes were in Portugal and whether they had delivered our letter to Your Highness. He told us that one had died at sea and the other in the Cape Verde Islands, at which we suffered extreme distress both because of their deaths and because Your Highness would not see our letter nor have anyone to give news of the great victory we had won.

Then, my lord, we decided to write another letter to Your Highness, and we sent with it our nephew, who is called Dom Gonçalo, and a servant of ours called Manuel, and we sent them in the said ship of Fernão de Melo. And so that the said Fernão de Melo could buy us the help of which we had need, we sent eight hundred manilhas and fifty slaves for himself and for his wife, and five hundred manilhas for his son and thirty for the captain and for the secretary twenty. And we shed many tears, beseeching Fernão de Melo, for the love of Our Lord, to send aid to us, so that the faith of Our Lord should triumph because the only Christians here are myself and Dom Pedro our cousin and our servants, and all the rest of the people are opposed to us and inclined towards the worship of idols. Then the ship departed for Portugal, and we remained, waiting for a message from Fernão de Melo, with Dom Pedro our cousin and Francisco Fernandes with the Christians from Nsundi[11] who helped us to win the battle. And we waited a whole year without receiving any message.

Then, my lord, we determined to burn all those idols as secretly as we could, and we did not care to wait any longer for help from Fernão de Melo, because the help from heaven is greater than that from earth and [we knew] Our Lord would help us. Moreover, should the people of our kingdom rise against us and kill us we would receive death with resignation for the salvation of our souls.

So we began to burn all the idols, and when the people saw this, they all began to say that I was a very bad man and carried tales about us to Jorge Moxuebata, who was the head[12] of our kingdom, that he should burn and destroy us. However, Our Lord inspired him in such a manner that he desired to become a Christian and replied to those who spoke ill of us to him that he desired to know the faith of our Lord Jesus Christ and that if he, who was our uncle, destroyed us, who else could become king who was a closer relative than he. And in this manner, my brother, we preserved our kingdom and Christianity.

Shortly after this, the fathers from Santo Elói,[13] whom Your Highness sent us, arrived and as soon as we knew that they had reached our kingdom, we ordered all our fidalgos to receive them on the road, and so that they could arrive at the city in good time we went out into the square and preached a sermon to all our people ....

Notes

1 Hilton, *Kingdom of Kongo*, p. 62.
2 The king of Kongo appears to have added this title after his raid on the Mbundu for slaves in 1512. At the beginning of the sixteenth century, most of the Mbundu polities recognized the overlordship of Kongo. The Mbundu states were located south of the Dande River and west of the Kwango.
3 Dom Pedro was also from the Nsaku Lau lineage and was made governor of the central province of Nsundi after Afonso's accession. He became one of Afonso's principal supporters in maintaining the trade in copper and slaves with the interior states.
4 See Doc. 28.
5 *Homem de vento.*
6 The royal fortress of Elmina on the coast of modern Ghana.
7 Brass or copper rings or anklets, which were a form of trade currency in western Africa and were one of the major exports of the Kongo kingdom.
8 Dom Henrique later took holy orders, went to Rome and was made a bishop by the Pope.
9 The captain of São Tomé.
10 *Alcatyfa.*

11 The province of Nsundi of which Afonso had been governor before his accession.
12 The word used is *cabeça*, which is probably to be understood as chief minister. He was also from the Nsaku Lau lineage and was head of the ruling house of Mbata (Manimbata). It is clear that his support was vital in strengthening Dom Afonso's position as king.
13 This was a college of secular canons in Lisbon.

7

ANGOLA, PAULO DIAS AND THE FOUNDING
OF LUANDA

31 EARLY RELATIONS WITH ANGOLA

Extracts from a letter from Francisco de Gouveia SJ to his Superior, 1563.
António Brásio, *Monumenta Missionaria Africana* (Lisbon, 1952), 2, pp. 518–20.
The letter is to be found in Biblioteca Nacional de Lisboa, MS 8123.
Translated by Malyn Newitt.

The Mbundu kingdoms to the south of the Kongo state were nominally subject to the king of Kongo, but had taken the opportunity of the presence of traders from São Tomé to assert their independence. Fear of the Kongo attacks, however, prompted the ruler of Ndongo (called the Ngola) to seek official Portuguese aid by offering to be baptized. A mission was sent in 1520, which included a Kongolese priest, and which remained in the country until 1526. Eventually, in 1560, a Portuguese embassy consisting of two Jesuit priests, two lay brothers and an ambassador, Paulo Dias de Novais, was sent. After making their way to Ndongo, Paulo Dias and the Jesuits were detained as hostages. It became clear that the intention of the Ngola was to use the hostages to obtain as much in the way of presents and trade goods as possible. Paulo Dias was eventually sent back to Portugal in 1565, but Father Gouveia, on whose letters these extracts are based, died a captive in Ndongo in 1575.

The Jesuits were anxious to obtain their own mission field in Africa, and 1560 was the year in which they sent Gonçalo da Silveira to start a mission on the coast of eastern Africa. The experience of Father Gouveia, who was being held hostage, and Silveira, who was murdered in 1561, convinced the Jesuits that conversion could not be achieved without conquest. In his letters, Gouveia mentions the possibility of opening a route across Africa (the elusive policy of contra costa), and eventually in 1608, a Portuguese, Baltasar de Aragão, made the first attempt to cross the continent.

Firstly he says that, however disappointed they were at the beginning of their journey to stay in that profitless country, it now seemed to them that these were signs from God of His help and salvation of that province. It now transpired that, although these people are docile, it is necessary to subdue them in order to convert them properly, for without being subjected, neither this nor any other barbarian people, however well inclined they may be, can be kept in the faith. This can clearly be seen in the Kongo since Christianity has been so badly maintained there. So he says that such a long stay was permitted by God so that they could learn all about the country and, if it turns out that this information becomes the means by which it comes to be subdued, all the annoyances and labours that have been suffered will have been worthwhile. For the subjection of this country will be its remedy and salvation.

As he was kept, or rather imprisoned, there for three years, he and the ambassador[1] were continually observing and noting things about the country, and during this time they came to know everything very well. He said that, in his experience, this is a temperate country in respect of the productivity and fertility of the land and the mines that are contained in it. These are matters so important that in a very short time they could repay all expenses and beyond this show great profit. And it seemed to them that Your Highness[2] should not hesitate to conquer this land, provided there is someone who can give reliable information about the profit to be derived from it and about the truth of this, and above all about the great service that this would be to God.

So, as it seemed to him that this was for the service of God and that, for his part, Our Lord must desire this to be carried out, he determined to write about the temporal profits to be found in the land, and also of the justice of the intention which Your Highness has in conquering it. He wrote everything and sent it to his superior so that, if it appears to be something that should be done, he [the king] may do with it what seems to him to be in the service of God, and if not, to leave it wholly aside.

It would be important to describe how rich and strong the people of the country are, how hard they work and how long they live. The previous king is said to have lived for two hundred years, and the present one is said to be eighty and is held to be still a youth. They eat little and sustain themselves more by drinking palm wine than by eating. And for this reason there are many old people in that land.

In the method of building their towns and cities, and in the construction of their houses, the people are much like those of Guinea. And he says that the principal city is like Évora or a little smaller. And there are others quite large, all surrounded after their fashion with palm groves and woods. And the [roofs] are made of straw woven into cords, and their houses are plastered and lined with good clean mats. It does not appear that in all Guinea there are any people who would be more disposed to civilization if they were made subject to a Christian prince, for their vassals are extremely obedient to their lords and the lords to their king. They serve them less as vassals than as slaves, and in this they are very happy.

The Father also says that it is well known that one can easily go from there to the other sea in the east, which is that of Sofala, Kilwa, Mombasa and Mozambique, as it is not thought to be far. Speaking of people from Dambia Songe,[3] a large kingdom to the east of Angola, and of a celebrated fair which is held there from which people come to the fairs of Angola in search of salt and copper, he says these words: These people of Dambia Songe give us news of the sea on the other coast, and they speak of it so freely and with such certain signs that we consider it proved that they speak the truth. And we met some people who had seen it. And the great journey which they make from this Cabeça[4] lasts seventeen days. Others do it in twelve without loads, from which it appears that it is not far from here to the other sea. These people seem to be more simple and less devious than those of Angola, and in our opinion are more content. From all this, it can be concluded that the passage from here to Mozambique would be very easy.

Notes

1 Paulo Dias de Novais (see Doc. 32).
2 The king of Portugal, who was still a minor at the time this was written, was Dom Sebastião (1557–78).
3 This is the African kingdom of Songo, whose people were related to the Lunda.
4 A marginal note reads 'this is the village of the king where he resides'. The capital of the Ngola was called Kabasa. See Doc. 33.

---

32 DONATION CHARTER TO PAULO DIAS DE NOVAIS, 1571

António Brásio, *Monumenta Missionaria Africana* (Lisbon, 1952), 3, pp. 36–51.

The original document is in Arquivo Nacional de Torre de Tombo, Chancelaria de D. Sebastião (Doações), livro 26, fls 295–9.

Translated by Malyn Newitt.

When Paulo Dias was released from captivity in Ndongo (see Doc. 31) he returned to Portugal with a proposal for the creation of a captaincy in the region. Hereditary captaincies had been used as a device to promote the settlement of the Atlantic islands and Brazil, and the acceptance of this proposal was an indication that the Crown was prepared to implement a radical change of policy in Africa. The idea of establishing Portuguese influence by means of alliances with Christian kings had involved Portugal in expensive wars on behalf of its protégés. A Portuguese army had had to be sent to rescue the Ethiopian king in 1541 and another to protect the Kongo against the invading Jaga (see Doc. 40). In eastern Africa it had led in 1561 to the murder of the Jesuit Gonçalo da Silveira as he tried to secure the conversion of the Monomotapa. Now the Crown was determined to undertake the permanent occupation of the areas of Africa where it believed there were mines of gold and silver, and to achieve this, the country would need to be systematically conquered and settled. In 1569, an army was sent to eastern Africa to conquer the 'mines' of Monomotapa, and in 1571, the Crown agreed to establish a captaincy, on the Brazilian model, in order to secure the conquest of Angola as well.

This lengthy document has been included because it illustrates the official mind of Portugal and the way it viewed its imperial mission in the sixteenth century. The proposed colonization of Angola was couched in the legal terminology that applied to land grants and other forms of donation made by the Crown to its vassals in Portugal and the Atlantic islands. Unlike Kongo and the settlements in upper Guinea, Angola was going to be part of the sovereign territory of Portugal. It would become the 'kingdom' of Angola to sit alongside the other kingdoms of Portugal – the Algarve and the Estado da Índia. The legal jargon of the donation, however, presents some problems of translation, as there is often no English equivalent for what is being declared.

The opening makes clear the basis on which grants were made by the Portuguese Crown. While the past services of the grantee and his family are a major consideration, equally important is the anticipation of further service in the future, as well as the expenses that will be or have been incurred in royal service. The charter confirms Paulo Dias's right to nominate judicial and other officials and the alcaides-mores (governors of towns or fortresses). This was a right that the Crown had progressively clawed back from the nobility in metropolitan Portugal. The charter also tries to prevent the captain from acquiring too much land himself. His land holdings are to be divided into four parts, and there are restrictions on him and members of his family leasing additional land or acquiring it in any other way.

The charter bears all the signs of tough bargaining between the Crown's lawyers and those representing Paulo Dias. The captain was determined to try to protect his captaincy from royal interference, so he tried to get the exclusion of royal corregedores written into the charter, as well as his own right to appoint judges. He also tried to ensure that all holders of the captaincy would

*bear his family name. The Crown, for its part, reserved to itself the right to try
the captains for any crime they might commit and to appoint special tribunals if
this seemed to be in the Crown's interest.*

Dom Sebastião[1] – to those to whom my Charter will come, know
that I have seen and considered how much it is to the service of Our
Lord, and also to my service, to order the conquest and subjection of the
kingdom of Angola, both so that divine worship and the offices of religion shall be celebrated there, and for the increase of our Holy Catholic
Faith and for the promulgation of the Holy Gospel, as well as for the
great profit that will result for my kingdoms and lordships, and also
for the natives of the country when the said kingdom of Angola is subdued and conquered. Hear then that by the opinion and advice of my
Council, and of the deputies of the Mesa da Consciência[2] and of two
learned theologians and canon lawyers, whose opinion has been sought
on the conquest of the said kingdom, it is agreed that for the reasons
given above, which are in conformity with the apostolic Bulls granted
to the kings of this kingdom, my predecessors, I have the obligation to
undertake it.

So I entrust this [conquest] to Paulo Dias de Novais[3] because of the
great confidence that I have in him, and because of the knowledge and
experience he has of the affairs of that kingdom from the time he was my
ambassador there. For this reason, I have regard to the services which
the said Paulo Dias has rendered me both in the said kingdom of Angola
and in other parts where he has served me, in which he has always given
a good account of himself, and to those services which I hope he will
do me in the conquest of this kingdom, and to the great expense which
has to be met without my treasury giving any aid in money or anything
else. I also have regard to the services rendered to the Crown of these
kingdoms by Bartolomeu Dias de Novais,[4] his grandfather, in discovering the Cape of Good Hope. For all these reasons and for others equally
just, which move me to do this of my own will, certain knowledge and
royal and absolute power, I hold it good and it pleases me to make, as
by this Charter I do so make, a grant and irrevocable donation valid
among those who are living, from this day and forever, by right and
heredity, to him and all his children, grandchildren, heirs and successors who will come after him, both descendants, transversals and collat-
erals, according to what will be declared hereafter, of thirty-five leagues
of land on the coast of the said kingdom of Angola which will start at the
River Cuanza and the waters flowing from it towards the south, and will
extend inland as far as he can penetrate and go into my conquista. This
land, according to this demarcation, I grant and donate to him forever

by right and heredity as has been said. I also desire and it is my pleasure that the said Paulo Dias, and all his heirs and successors who will inherit and succeed to the said land, may call themselves and be called captains and governors of it.

In addition, I grant and make donation, by right and heredity for-ever, to him and all his descendants and successors in the above-men-tioned manner of the civil and criminal jurisdiction in the said land, which the said Paulo Dias and his heirs and successors will exercise in the following form and manner, namely: He will be able by him-self or through his *ouvidor* to choose the justices and other officials of the towns and settlements which will be established in the said land, approve and amend rules, and issue letters of confirmation for the said justices and officials who shall be nominated by the said captain and governor; he will appoint an *ouvidor*, who will be able to hear new cases up to ten leagues distant, and appeals and complaints; he will take cog-nizance throughout the captaincy and governorship, and the said jus-tices will send appeals to the said *ouvidor* in the judicial areas where my ordinances are promulgated and where the said *ouvidor* acts as judge, either concerning new cases or those on appeal or complaint; and in civil cases up to one hundred thousand reis, there will be no appeals or complaints, and above this sum he will hear appeals for those who desire to appeal.

In criminal cases, I think it well that the said captain and governor and his *ouvidor* shall have jurisdiction, including the right to inflict the death penalty, over slaves and heathen and also over Christian prison-ers who are freemen, in all cases both to acquit and to condemn without appeal or complaint. However, in the four following matters, namely heresy, when the accusation is made by an ecclesiastic, treason, sodomy and coining false money, they will have jurisdiction over everyone, of whatever rank, to condemn the guilty to death and to carry out their sentences without appeal or complaint. In the said four cases, in order to remit the death penalty, if they wish to give another penalty less than death, they may hear appeals and complaints, and appeals will be made on the grounds of justice; and in the case of persons of higher rank, they will be able to sentence up to ten years as a convict and fine up to a hun-dred cruzados without appeal or complaint.

It also pleases me that the said *ouvidor* take cognizance of appeals and complaints which he will hear in any town or place in the said cap-taincy in which he is, even though it is far removed from where he is living, so long as it is in his own captaincy. And the said captain and governor can appoint a bailiff[5] for the said *ouvidor*, and secretaries and other officials who are necessary and are customary in these kingdoms, both in the jurisdiction of the judge as in all the towns and places of the said captaincy and governorship. And the said captain and governor and his successors will be obliged, when the said land is populated and has grown to such an extent that it is necessary, to appoint another *ouvidor* to a place on which I or my successors shall decide.

It also pleases me to allow the said captain and governor and all his successors of their own accord to create whatever towns and settlements appear to them ought to be made, and these will be designated towns and will have the boundaries, jurisdiction, liberties and insignia of towns according to the rights and customs of my kingdoms. By this it is understood that they will be able to create all the towns they desire from the settlements that exist along the coast of the said land and on the rivers which they navigate, because on the mainland in the interior,[6] they cannot be established less than six leagues from each other, so that each town will have boundaries that will include at least three leagues of territory.[7] At the time that these towns are made, each one will be assigned its own limits and boundaries, and thereafter it will not be permitted without my licence to establish any other within the lands which they have been given as boundaries.

It also pleases me to allow the captain and governor and all his successors to whom this captaincy will come, to create, appoint and provide by their letters patent, both now and in the future, as many public and judicial notaries in the towns and settlements of the said land as seem to them to be necessary. And they will give them their letters of appointment, signed and sealed by them with their seal, and they will administer the oath to them that they fulfil their offices well and truly; and the said notaries shall serve with the authority of these letters without obtaining others from my Chancellery, and whenever these positions become vacant through death or resignation or through mistakes that occur, they will be able to give the same and draw up their *regimentos*[8] by which they are to serve to conform with those of my Chancellery. And it is right that the said captain and governor should be able to appoint the said notaries and they shall pay him the fees as laid down in the *foral*,[9] which I now order to be made for the said land, and I now make donation of these fees by law and heredity in perpetuity.

I also grant and make donation to him by right and heredity in perpetuity of the positions of *alcaide-mor* of all the said towns and settlements of the said land, with all the revenues, rents, rights and tributes which belong to them, as is declared in the *foral* which the said captain and governor and his successors will have and receive for themselves, in the mode and manner which is contained in the said *foral* and according to their form; and the people to whom these offices of *alcaide-mor* are given by the hand of the said captain and governor will carry out their duties according to my ordinances.

It also pleases me to grant to the said Paulo Dias and all his successors to whom this captaincy and governorship will come, that they have and hold by right and heredity in perpetuity, all the water mills, land and sea salt-pans and any other mills of whatever kind they may be, which can be made in the said captaincy and governorship. And it is well that no one shall be able to construct the said water mills, salt-pans or mills except the said captain and governor or those to whom he shall give permission for this purpose, for which they will pay him whatever rent or tribute is reasonable and is agreed between them. I also grant and make donation to him by right and heredity in perpetuity of twenty leagues of land along the coast of the said captaincy and governorship, I permit him to enter inland as far as he is able, and it will be my conquista. And this land shall be his, free and exempt, without his having to pay any rent or due or tribute of any kind for it, but only the tithe to the Order of Christ[10]; and within twenty years of the date on which the said captain enters the kingdom of Angola, he may choose and take the said twenty leagues of land in whatever part he most desires, but they may not be adjoining and must be divided into four or five parts, each one being not less than two leagues from the next. These lands the said captain and governor and his successors can rent out or lease 'em fatiota'[11] or 'em pensões' or as they desire and seems good to them, for whatever rent or payment they shall agree and shall be just; and the said lands, if they are not rented, or the rents of them if they are, shall always accrue to whoever succeeds to the said captaincy or government in the manner set out in this donation. As for the harvests which God bestows on the said lands, neither the captain and governor nor those persons who have them and bring them in with their own hands shall be obliged to pay to me any rent or due for them, but only God's tithe due to the Order of Christ, which generally will have to be paid in all the other lands of the said captaincy, as will be declared below. And he will be obliged to cultivate and develop the said lands for fifteen years from the day that he takes them; and if he does not do so, the lands will revert freely to me to do with them what best suits my service.

Neither the said captain and governor, nor anyone who comes after him, may take any land in the said captaincy in sesmaria,[12] either for himself or for his wife or for the son who is the heir, but rather all the said lands can and should be given in sesmaria to persons, of whatever quality or condition they may be, who seem good to him, freely and without any rent or dues except only God's tithe, which they will be obliged to pay to the said Order on all that they have in the said lands, as is declared in the *foral*. In the same manner, they will be able to give and apportion them to their children and to their relatives outside of a *morgado*.[13] However, their sons and relatives will not be able to give any land, of that which they are given or will have been given, to any other extraneous person. All the said lands which in this way are given in *sesmaria* to one person or another will be given in conformity with the law of *sesmarias*[14] and with the obligations that go with it, which lands neither the said captain and governor nor his successors can at any time take for themselves nor for their wives nor heirs, as has been said, nor can they be given to another person so that they may acquire them later in any way whatsoever, except that they will be able to obtain them through genuine purchase from those persons who desire to sell them after eight years have passed, during which the said lands have been put into cultivation. Otherwise, not.

I also grant and make donation to him by right and heredity in perpetuity of half the tithe on the fisheries of the said captaincy, which will be one fish in every twenty, that I have ordered to be paid, apart from the full tithe which belongs to the Order [of Christ], as is declared in the *foral*, and this half tithe is to be taken to extend to all the fish which are taken in the whole of this captaincy outside the twenty leagues of land belonging to the said captain and governor, since these twenty leagues shall be his land free and unencumbered, as has been declared above.

It also seems good and pleases me to make a grant and donation to the said Paulo Dias during his life of the third part of all the rents and dues which in any way belong to me and to the Order of Christ in the said captaincy and governorship and to the kings my successors, both by the foral that is to be made for them, or in any other mode or manner whatsoever, but his heirs and successors, who inherit and succeed to the said lands after his death, will have by right and heredity in perpetuity only the fourth part of the said rents and dues. And if it happens that in that land they open up some exchange and commerce of the kind that I desire to be traded and transacted only by myself or my officials,[15] in this case I will order the said Paulo Dias during his life to be paid and given, as is said, a third part of all that is gained through this trade or exchange, having first deducted all the capital and costs which this trade incurs, and to his successors I will give a fourth part of the said profits in the manner described above. And it will be understood that this shall be done even when it happens that the said trade and exchange is rented out or is carried on or transacted by any persons to whom I give licence and permission. And if it should happen that the said trade and exchange is of such a kind that anyone, whether from this captaincy and governorship and from these kingdoms or from any other of my sovereign territories, can take part in it in addition to my officials, in that case I will not remain obliged to pay the said captain or his successors the said third or fourth part, and will only give him the same rights as other persons have to give and pay and which have been ordered and put in place for the said trades and exchanges.

I also grant and make donation to the said captain and governor and to his heirs and successors to whom the said captaincy and governorship shall come, that from the River Dande[16] southwards no person may take *búzios*[17] from the sea except those to whom he shall give licence for this.

It also pleases me to grant to the said captain and governor and his successors by right and heredity in perpetuity, to send forty-eight 'pieces'[18] of the slaves that they trade or hold in the said land, to this kingdom each year, to do with them what they want. These slaves will come to the port of the city of Lisbon, and not to any other port, and with them will be sent certification from the officials in the said land that they are theirs, by which certification these slaves will be dispatched freely without paying any dues nor the five percent. And apart from these forty-eight 'pieces' which they can send freely each year, I am pleased to grant them the right to bring as many slaves as they wish or are necessary as sailors and grumetes[19] in their ships, and all the additional slaves who are brought will pay 1,600 reis in dues for each 'piece'.

It also pleases me to grant to the said captain and governor and to his successors and also to the citizens and settlers in the said captaincy, exemption in perpetuity from sisas,[20] impositions, soap and salt taxes and any other dues or tributes of whatever sort they may be, except those that have been ordered for the benefit of this donation and its charter.

It is my pleasure that the succession to this captaincy and governorship and its revenues and goods be inherited and succeeded, by right and heredity in perpetuity, by the said captain and governor and his descendants, their legitimate sons and daughters, with this proviso that a daughter may not succeed while there is a male heir of the same degree, even if she is older than the son. If there is no male heir, or if there is one but not as closely related to the last possessor as the female, the female will then succeed. While there are legitimate male or female heirs, no bastard may succeed to the captaincy, but if there are no legitimate male or female heirs, then male or female bastards may succeed provided they are not from *danado coito*,[21] and may do so in the same order as the legitimate heirs, first the males and then the females of the same degree, with the condition that, if the owner of the said captaincy desires, when he has no legitimate heirs, to leave it to a transversal relative rather than to a bastard, he may do so; and if he has neither legitimate male nor female heirs nor bastards in the manner that has been outlined, in that case the male and female descendants will succeed, first the male and in default of them the female; and if neither descendants nor ascendants exist, the transversals[22] may succeed in the above-mentioned fashion, always first the males who are of equal degree and then the females; and in the case of bastards, the possessor may, if he desires, leave the said captaincy to a legitimate transversal and refuse it to the bastards even though they are descendants in a much closer degree; and this will hold good notwithstanding the *lei mental*,[23] which says that neither bastards, nor transversals nor ascendants shall succeed, for notwithstanding all this, it pleases me that in this captaincy women and bastards who are not of *coito danado*, and transversals and ascendants shall succeed in the way that has already been set out.

I also desire and it pleases me that at no time can the captaincy and governorship, and all the things which by this donation I give to Paulo Dias, be divided, exchanged, or broken up or in any other way alienated either by marriage of son or daughter or by gift to another person either to ransom father or son or any other person from captivity or for any other reason, no matter how pious.[24] For my will and intention is that this captaincy and governorship, and the things given in this donation, shall always go together and shall not be divided or alienated at any time, and anyone who divides or alienates or breaks them up or gives them away in marriage or for any other purpose that leads to their being divided, even for the most pious reasons, will lose the captaincy and governorship by this act, and they will pass to whomsoever will succeed in the order set out above as if he who does not [observe these terms] were already dead.

It also pleases me that if, for any reason whatsoever, the said captain and governor commits a crime for which, according to the rights and laws of the kingdom, he deserves to lose the said captaincy and governorship, and the jurisdiction and the rents and goods belonging to it, his successor will not lose them unless he has been a traitor to the Crown of these kingdoms, and in respect of any other crime that he may commit, he will be punished as the crime deserves, but his successors will not for this reason lose the said captaincy and governorship, or its jurisdictions, revenues and goods, as has been said.

So it pleases me and I find it good that the said Paulo Dias and his successors to whom this captaincy and government will come, shall make full use of all the jurisdiction, power and authority contained in this donation in the manner set out in it, because of the confidence that I have in them that in this, they will safeguard everything that is to the service of God and myself, the good of the people and the rights of individual parties.

Also, it seems good to me that no *corregedor*[25] may enter into the said captaincy at any time to exercise any jurisdiction, in any way or through any means whatsoever. However, I shall be able, whenever it appears good to me, to order an *alçada*[26] and to take advice in any matter that appears to me to be in my service and for the benefit of justice and the good government of the land. Nor shall the said captain be suspended from the said captaincy and governorship and his jurisdiction over it, although if the said captain falls into some error or does anything that ought and deserves to be punished, I or my successors will order him to come to us to be judged, and he will be given such penalty and punishment which he rightly deserves for that matter.

I therefore desire and command that all the heirs and successors of the said Paulo Dias de Novais who inherit and succeed to the said captaincy, through whatever means, shall be called de Novais and shall bear the arms of the said family; and if any of them does not abide by this, it is my pleasure that for this he will forfeit the said captaincy and it will pass and devolve at once to whoever it ought to come to, as if he who failed in this were dead. In the same way, I grant and make donation to the said Paulo Dias for his lifetime only of the lands which extend south from the River Dande to the River Cuanza, which River Dande inland divides the kingdom of Kongo from the kingdom of Angola[27]; and during his lifetime he will have, as has been said, the third part of all the revenues and dues which belong in any way to me and to the Order of Christ by virtue of the charter which I will order to be drawn up on this matter. On the death of the said Paulo Dias, the said lands from the River Dande to the banks of the Cuanza shall be free for me and the Crown of my kingdoms to do with them whatever appears to be in my service, without any jurisdiction or authority over them or revenues from them remaining to the heirs of the said Paulo Dias. There shall only remain to the said heirs by right and heredity, in the mode of succession outlined above, the *alcaidarias-mores* of the three fortresses, which are to be built in that land, in the manner to be described below, and the appointment of the officers to the said three fortresses and settlements. Each fortress shall have boundaries of seven leagues of land around it and the waters which are found in it, which seven leagues of land each fortress will have as its dependent territory. If the said Paulo Dias dies within twenty years, the person he shall nominate to continue the settlement of the land and captaincy shall not be of lesser quality than himself, and will have and hold the said third part of the revenues and dues until the twenty years shall be completed.

If the said Paulo Dias dies, I will send a governor and justices, as seems good to me, to the lands which are between the Rivers Dande and

Cuanza, and of this captaincy and governorship, and the lands above declared, I make donation to him and grant in the manner which is contained in this charter on the condition and declaration that he, Paulo Dias, shall bring to the conquest of the said land, at his own cost and expense, a galleon and two caravels and five brigantines of different sizes and build and three fishing boats[28] to explore the rivers and ports which are on this coast as far as the Cape of Good Hope, which boats shall be well provided with sails, awnings and everything that is necessary for the said voyage and enterprise.

And with the condition that, within twenty months, which will begin from the day he leaves this kingdom, he will settle in the land four hundred men who can fight with their arms in the manner of the wars of those parts. Among those four hundred men shall come eight stonemasons, four quarrymen, six plasterers, one doctor and one barber, and he shall bring provisions for one year for all these people. Among them there shall be no New Christian, and he will strive to bring as many people and officers as he can.

And with the condition that within ten years he will build three fortresses to cover the land and that within three years he will have twenty horses there and mares as well.

And with the condition that, within ten years, he will build three fortresses of stone and lime between the Rivers Zenza[29] and Cuanza, and that one of them is built in the port where it seems likely foreign fleets may come. The walls shall not be less than forty square braças[30] and twelve palmos thick and forty high with two bastions at the two corners, which shall have two traverses along the whole wall, and after that they may be finished in whatever manner shall appear most necessary. The other two castles shall be built upstream in places wherever they appear to be necessary, and each one shall be of twenty braças square and of the same thickness and height as the other, with two bastions of the same diameter. If Paulo Dias is unable to complete the said three fortresses in ten years, in spite of showing every possible diligence, I will grant him further time as it pleases me. Meanwhile, as soon as he has disembarked, he will make in that land fortifications as may be necessary from mud and wood to secure himself against the blacks and with these he will control the land as long as the castles have not yet been built.

And with the condition that within six years, beginning from the day he leaves this kingdom, he will settle one hundred moradores[31] in the said land and captaincy with their wives and children, and among them some farmers with all the seeds and plants which they are able to bring from this kingdom and from the island of São Tomé. He will do all this at his own cost and expense without my putting any capital into it or making any loan to him of arms, ships, munitions or supplies as I am accustomed to make for voyages and enterprises of this kind.

And with the condition that he departs from this kingdom to effect this business before the current contract of the island of São Tomé shall end, in such a way that when he arrives there, the said contract will have ended. I make this grant as king and lord of these kingdoms and also as governor and perpetual administrator of the Order of Christ,[32] and by this present charter I give power and authority to the said Paulo Dias de Novais that he himself, or someone appointed by him, can and shall take control of the lands of the said captaincy and government, and of its goods and revenues and of all the other things contained in this donation, and he shall use them all as he pleases. Which donation I hold good, desire and order shall be fulfilled and adhered to in its entirety, with all the clauses, conditions and declarations contained and stated in it, without any want or weakness, and for all that is said I suspend the *lei mental* and whatever other laws, ordinances, rights, glosses and customs which might contradict it, by whatever way or means it might have, even though such shall be declared here de verbo ad verbum as necessary, and notwithstanding book II, chapter 49, where it is stated that, when such laws and rights are derogated, there shall be made express mention of them and the substance of them. And for this I promise the said Paulo Dias and his successors that never at any time shall anyone go, or consent to go, against this my donation, in part or in whole. And I request and recommend to all my successors that they fulfil it and order it to be fulfilled and kept to the entire satisfaction of the said Paulo Dias, with the conditions declared above and at the times and in the manner stated here.

I order all my judges, *corregedores*, justices and officials of my treasury and whoever else to whom cognizance of this belongs, that they carry out, keep and fulfil completely this charter of donation and what is contained in it, and that they allow him and his heirs and successors to use everything declared in it without there being any doubt, embargo or impediment, for such is my grant. And if he does not fulfil the conditions or satisfy the terms in the time and manner proscribed, this donation will not have any effect, and I will make a grant of the said captaincy and governorship and lands to whoever suits my service. To confirm all this, I order that this donation charter be given to him, signed and sealed by me with my lead seal, and that it be written on six parchment leaves, with one other which I will sign, and at the end of each page they will be signed by Martim Gonçalves de Camara, a member of my Council and my private secretary.[33]

Given in the city of Lisbon on the 19th day of the month of September. António d'Aguiar made it in the year of Our Lord Jesus Christ 1571. Written by Jorge da Costa.

The said Paulo Dias will also be obliged to bring three clerics to confess and administer the sacrament to the people of the fleet, and also everything in the way of vestments, and any altar furnishings that are necessary. The first church shall be built wholly at his cost and shall be dedicated to the blessed martyr São Sebastião [Saint Sebastian],[34] and the other churches shall also be built at his expense, or at least the body of them, as will be declared in the foral. And of the slaves that by virtue of this donation he can ransom[35] and despatch to this kingdom, he shall make the necessary justifications before they have been enslaved and embarked for this kingdom, in conformity with the regimento and order of the Mesa da Consciência, which is sent to São Tomé.

Notes

1 King of Portugal 1557–78. He came of age and officially took over the government in 1568 at the age of fourteen.

2 This was the branch of the Royal Council which dealt with the ecclesiastical affairs of the Crown and with the Military Orders.

3 He had been ambassador to the Ngola in 1560 and was detained in the country as a hostage until 1565 (see Doc. 31). In 1571, he was granted the captaincy of Angola which he took up in 1575. He died in 1591.

4 Bartolomeu Dias was sent in 1487 by Dom João II to open the route to India. He rounded the Cape of Good Hope in 1488 but, following a mutiny by his men, was forced to return to Portugal reaching Lisbon in 1489. He was a captain in Cabral's fleet that sailed for India in 1500 and was lost at sea.

5 The Portuguese word is *meirinho*.

6 The Portuguese word is *sertão*.

7 In Spain and Portugal, it was usual for the jurisdiction of a town to include as much of the surrounding countryside as was necessary to keep it provisioned.

8 *Regimentos* were the official instructions drawn up to regulate the conduct of office holders and military and naval commanders.

9 A *foral* was a formal document which set out the legal rights and privileges of a town or an institution.

10 Since 1495, the king had been head of the military Order of Christ. The tithe was, therefore, effectively a royal tax.

11 Leases made *em fatiota* were perpetual leases which could be inherited.

12 The *Lei das Sesmarias* had been promulgated in 1375. It laid down the rules whereby vacant or unused land could be leased and brought into cultivation. The law was designed to address the specific problems of a countryside depopulated by the Black Death, but it remained a central element in Portuguese land law until the nineteenth century.

13 An entailed estate.

14 *Lei das Sesmarias* – see note 12.

15 In other words, one of the trades which were a royal monopoly, such as the gold trade.

16 The Charter actually says Dange.

17 Shells used as currency. See Docs. 13, 26 and 55.

18 A 'piece' or *peça da Índia*, was the unit by which slaves were quantified. A *peça* was the equivalent of an adult male slave.

19 African boys employed as crew on board ships.

20 *Sisa* was a tax paid on the sale of a property.

21 Literally *danadus coitus* means 'forbidden intercourse'. This clearly intends to exclude the children of certain unions but it is not clear whether this refers to incestuous unions or unions which were forbidden for religious reasons.

22 Possibly 'cousins' are meant.

23 The *Lei Mental* was a decree issued by Dom Duarte to protect the Crown's rights in the case of grants of Crown lands that had been made in the previous reign. By this law such grants, including entailed estates (*morgados*) had to be confirmed at the start of each reign and would revert to the Crown in the absence of a male heir.

24 The ransoming of captives was always considered by the Church to be one of the major acts of charity.

25 A *corregedor* was a royal official who had authority to enter any town or jurisdiction on behalf of the Crown to safeguard the Crown's interests.

26 The *alçada* was a peripatetic tribunal which might be sent to administer justice in a certain region.

27 It was important that the new 'kingdom' of Angola should be established in land beyond the boundaries of the Kongo kingdom with which Portugal had a longstanding alliance. However, the Kongo king had always claimed that land beyond the Dande including Luanda was part of his kingdom.

28 *Muleta.*

29 The Bengo River.

30 A *braça* was approximately two metres.

31 *Moradores*, literally settlers. This was the term most commonly used to describe civilian subjects of the Portuguese Crown resident in the colonies.

32 Here the charter uses very abstruse terminology – *gouernador e perpetual administrador que são da ordem e Cauallarya do mestrado de nosso Senhor Jhesu Christo.*

33 *Escryuão da puridade.*

34 This dedication is, of course, to the saint whose name the king bore.

35 The Portuguese use the term *resgatar* (ransom) for the purchase of slaves. The implication is that the slave is being rescued from the state of being a heathen.

---

33   WARFARE IN THE KONGO AND ANGOLA

From Filippo Pigafetta, *Relatione del Reame di Congo et delli circonvicine contrade tratta dalli scritti and ragionamenti di Odoardo Lopez Portoghese,* Grassi (Rome, 1591).

Translation by Malyn Newitt, based on that of M. Hutchinson, trans. and ed., *A Report of the Kingdom of Congo and of the Surrounding Countries* (London, 1881), pp. 60–2; Filippo Pigafetta e Duarte Lopes, *Relação do*

Reino do Congo e das Terras Circunvizinhas, António Luís Alves Ferronha, ed. (Lisbon, 1989), pp. 54–6.

In the months following the arrival of Paulo Dias in Luanda in February, 1575, relations with the Ngola steadily deteriorated, and in 1576 a state of war already existed. The Ngola who became king in 1575 was Kilombo kia Kasenda, whose reputation for cruelty alienated many of his sobas who turned to the Portuguese for help. However, it was some years before Paulo Dias was able to mount a major attack on Ndongo, and then only with the aid of the Kongo king, his avowed objective being the discovery and conquest of the silver mines of Cambambe. The campaign described in this document marked the beginning of the wars between the Portuguese and the Ngola, the king of Ndongo, in 1580.

This passage describes the advance of the Portuguese as far as the confluence of the Lucala and the Cuanza and the founding of the fortified town of Massangano. The authors describe in great detail the dress, musical instruments and weapons of the African armies, and explain some of the realities of African warfare, which the Portuguese were now learning the hard way. Pigafetta also mentions the obsession the Portuguese had with finding the silver mines of Cambambe, although five years earlier a Portuguese army had been lost in the futile search for silver mines in the Zambesi valley. There are no silver mines in either eastern or western Africa, and the conviction of the Portuguese that 'mountains' of silver existed can only be accounted for by their knowledge of the existence of a mountain of silver at Potosí in the Spanish viceroyalty of Peru, which was just coming into full production.

... Paulo Dias[1] took up arms against the king of Angola[2] and, with the people he could assemble from amongst the Portuguese whom he found in those parts and with two small galleys and other boats which he had in the River Cuanza, he conquered the land on both sides of the river and subjugated many rulers by force of arms, who became his friends and subjects. However, when the king of Angola saw his vassals submitting themselves to Paulo Dias, and the latter gaining territory, he assembled a great army in order to destroy him. Therefore, Paulo Dias appealed to the king of Kongo for men to help him defend himself, and he [the king] sent him an army of 60,000 men, commanded by his cousin Dom Sebastião Manimbamba,[3] and also a captain with 120 Portuguese soldiers who were in the district and who he paid for this enterprise. This army arranged to join that of Paulo Dias in order that together they might attack the king of Angola, but arriving at the bank where they were to cross the River Bengo, twelve miles from Luanda, and where they expected to find many boats to carry the soldiers over, they found these boats were delayed. As much time would have been lost in conveying so many people across, the army took the road along the river upstream. As they advanced, they encountered the king of Angola's men who had been posted to prevent the men of Kongo from entering their country. The order of battle of the Mwissikongo (for so the natives of Kongo are called, as those of Spain are called Spaniards) and of the Angola people is almost the same, for they both fight on foot, dividing their army into several companies, arranging them according to the field of battle, wherever it might be, and carrying their banners and colours in the way we have already described.

The movement of their troops in battle is controlled by various sounds and noises, directed by the captain-general, who is present in the middle of the army and decides what is to be done, whether to attack or to retire, to move forward or wheel to left or right, or any other military manoeuvre. By these sounds, the orders of the general are distinctly understood, as the different sounds of the drum and trumpet are with us. They use three principal sounds in battle. One is given by large kettledrums made from a single piece of wood covered with leather, which they strike with small ivory hammers. Another sound is made by an instrument in the shape of an inverted pyramid, which is pointed at the bottom and at the top is wide like the base of a triangle in such a manner that there is an angle at the base but at the top it is flat. These instruments are made of thin plates of iron and inside they are concave and hollow like a bell turned upside down. They are struck with wooden sticks, and they are usually cracked to produce a sound that is raucous, horrible and warlike.

The third type of instrument is made from elephants' tusks, both large and small, which are hollowed out and are blown through a hole at the side like a fife, and not from the top, and they are seasoned in such a way that they sound like a trumpet, producing harmonious and agreeable music, which inspires the soldiers with courage. These three sorts of war-like instrument are both large and small, the captain-general carrying the large ones with him, so that he can give a signal to the whole army. The different corps and squadrons each have smaller ones, and the captains of the individual companies have the smallest, sounding the little drums with their hands. In this way, on hearing the sound of the big drum or the trumpet or some other instrument, every part of the army responds with the same sound to show that the commands have been understood, and the lesser captains do the same. Not only are these sounds in general use, but they are also used in combat, for during the skirmishes, brave men went in front of the soldiers, striking the bells with wooden sticks, leaping and urging them on, and also warning them of the dangers of the weapons that were being hurled at them.

The military dress of the Mwissikongo lords is as follows: On the head is a cap, crazily ornamented with the feathers of ostrichs, peacocks, cockerels and other birds, which makes the men seem taller and very frightening. Above the waist they are entirely naked, but they have iron chains with rings the size of a man's little finger, hanging down on each side to right and left, which they wear for military pomp and display. Below the waist they wear breeches of canvas or taffeta, and over them a cloth that reaches down to their feet, with the folds turned back and tucked under the belt. This belt, as we have said, is of exquisite workmanship, with bells attached to it, similar to the instruments mentioned above, so that when moving or fighting they make sounds that give them courage to wield their arms against their enemies. On their legs they wear boots similar to the laced boots of the Portuguese. We have already spoken of their weapons, which consist of bows, arrows, swords, daggers and shields; these are distributed in such a manner that one who carries a bow also carries a dagger but not a shield, these two never being carried together, but only the sword and shield.

The common soldiers wear nothing above the waist and, for the rest, have bows, arrows and daggers. These first begin the skirmish attack, advancing in dispersed formation, wounding the enemy with arrows from a distance, turning here and there and quickly jumping aside in order to avoid missiles. Some young men also, as has been said, run swiftly in front, sounding the bells as if to encourage their comrades; and when it seems to the captain-general that they are tired, he recalls them by sounding one of the instruments, and when they are ordered by these sounds to do this, they quickly turn round and withdraw. In their place, others join the fight, until such time as the armies engage in the battle with their full force. Various attacks were made by one side or the other, and in the first encounters the Kongo people were victorious; but afterwards, as both sides had suffered great loss and as the men were ill and dying from lack of provisions, the camp of the king of Kongo was broken up, and all returned home.

As Paulo Dias was not able to join his allies, he advanced and, crossing the river, entrenched himself in Lucala, a strong natural position where he could resist the king of Angola. Lucala is situated where the Rivers Cuanza and Lucala join, some 105 miles from the coast and a little above the confluence, where the two rivers come within a gunshot of each other and make a sort of island between them. A small hill rises above the confluence of the two rivers, and this was taken by Paulo Dias and fortified to make it more secure. Formerly it was not inhabited, but it has now become a small territory, peopled by Portuguese.[4]

From this place, which was occupied by Paulo Dias and which he called Lucala, the River Cuanza can be navigated in small boats down to the sea, and by land one can go the 105 miles without any danger.

Nearby there are mountains called Cambambe, which produce an infinite amount of silver and which the said Paulo Dias was always trying to conquer for himself.[5] It was these mountains that caused the quarrel between himself and the people of Angola, for the latter, knowing that the Portuguese set great value on the mountains because of their abundant silver mines, did all they could to hinder them. They also fought each other in other regions, for the Portuguese crossed to the other bank of the River Cuanza and continually made inroads into the countries subject to the king of Angola.

The weapons used by these people are bows six spans long, with strings made of the bark of trees and arrows of wood thinner than a man's little finger, also six spans in length, with iron heads made like a hook and birds' feathers on the top. They carry six or seven of these in the same hand as the bow, without any quiver. The handle of their daggers resembles that of a knife, and they carry them on the left side of the belt and use them at close range. In their military manoeuvres they are familiar with the order and stratagems of war, for when fighting against the Portuguese it was evident that they knew the advantage they had over the enemy, attacking them at night or during rainy weather, when guns and bombs could not be fired,[6] and dividing their forces into several troops. The king does not go to war in person, but sends his captains. These people flee directly they see their captain slain. No argument can stop them, and so they abandon the field. They are all infantry soldiers and have no horses. If the captains do not want to go on foot, they are carried by slaves in one of three ways, which we will describe. These people go to battle in great numbers and in great disorder; no one remains behind who is at all fit for action. They make no provision for the supplies necessary for a campaign, and those who do take any victuals have them carried on the backs of their slaves, although there are many kinds of animals that they could domesticate and that might serve them for drawing and carrying, and about which we will write in another part of this history. So it happens that they arrive at a certain place with the whole army and there consume all their provisions. Then, with nothing left to eat, and just when the need of the expedition is at its height, the army breaks up and, forced by hunger, they return to their own country.

These people are very superstitious, and if a bird flies on their left hand or cries in a certain manner which they profess to understand, it predicts misfortune or tells them they are to proceed no farther. So they turn back at once, a custom also observed by the Romans in early times and by other heathen nations today. And if it appears strange that the few Portuguese soldiers who followed Paulo Dias – with others of the same nation who traded in that kingdom, and helped him to the number of 300 men at the most, and whose total number, together with their slaves and the malcontents and fugitives who fled from Angola to join him, never exceeded 15,000 men – could possibly put up such a gallant resistance to these innumerable hosts of blacks who were subjects of the king of Angola and who amounted, it is said, to a million souls, I reply that it might easily happen, seeing that, as has been said, the blacks wore no clothing, had no defensive weapons and only bows and daggers as offensive ones. Whereas our small numbers of men were well covered with quilted jerkins lined with cotton, and firmly double-sewn, which protected their arms and reached down to the knees.[7] Their heads are covered with caps of this same material, which are proof against arrows and daggers. Besides this, they use long swords and some of their cavalry carry spears. One cavalry soldier is equal to a hundred blacks, who are greatly afraid of horsemen and, above all, of those who fire the arquebuses and artillery pieces, which cause them extreme terror. As a result, a few men, if well armed and skillfully disposed, can with inventiveness and cunning easily conquer larger hosts.

This kingdom of Angola is populated to an incredible extent, the men taking as many wives as they wish, and the people multiplying without end, which is not the case in Kongo, for there they live as Christians. As a result, as Duarte Lopes said and believed, the kingdom of Angola has a million fighting men, not only because each man, having many wives, also has many children, but because all go willingly to fight for their prince.

The country is peculiarly rich in mines of the finest silver and copper, and there is a greater abundance of various metals than in any other country in the world. It also abounds in all manner of produce and has different sorts of cattle, in particular cows. It is a fact that these people prefer dog's flesh to any other food, and for this reason they breed and fatten them, and they are cut up and sold in the public shambles. It is asserted that a very large dog, resembling a bull, is sold in exchange for twenty-two slaves, which at 10 ducats a head, would cost 220 ducats, so greatly are these animals prized. The money used in Angola differs from the *búzios* of Kongo, for they use glass beads made in Venice the size of a nut and smaller, and of various forms and colours. These are used not only as money but as ornaments, by both men and women, who wear them round their necks and on their arms. In their language they are called *anzolos*, but are known as *missanga* when they are threaded in the form of a rosary.

The king of Angola is a pagan, worshipping idols like all his people. It is true he wished to become a Christian after the example of the king of Kongo, but up to this time it has been found impossible to send priests to instruct him, and he has remained in darkness. The above-named

Duarte Lopes records that in his time, this king sent an ambassador to the king of Kongo asking for priests to instruct him in the Christian faith, but he was unable to do so, as he did not have any. These two kings have now made peace with one another and are friends, the ruler of Angola having been forgiven for the attack and carnage committed by him on the people of Kongo and on the Portuguese in Cabaça.[8]

The language of the people of Angola is the same as that of Kongo[9] because, as we have said, it is all one kingdom, the only difference being such as is frequently seen between neighbouring countries, as between Portuguese and Castilians or between Venetians and Calabrians, whose dialects are so various and twisted into such different forms (although all have the same idiom), that they only understand each other, with difficulty.

Notes

1 See Docs. 31 and 32.
2 'Ngola' was the title of the kings of Ndongo.
3 That is Sebastião, the *manimbamba*, or governor, of the province of Mbamba.
4 The Lucala is the main tributary of the Cuanza which it joins from the north. The fortified settlement built by Paulo Dias at the confluence of the two rivers became known as Massangano.
5 The Cambambe Mountains lay close to the Cuanza upstream of Massangano and were incorrectly believed by the Portuguese to contain silver mines.
6 See Doc. 49 for an example of an attempt to use this tactic during the battle of Mbwila.
7 The quilted coats described here were also found to be extremely effective by the Spaniards in their conquest of Mexico.
8 This is a reference to the massacre of the Portuguese in Kabasa, the capital of the Ngola, which led to the outbreak of the war.
9 The language is Kimbundu, which is closely related to Kikongo.

34 THE ESCAPE OF PAULO DIAS FROM ANGOLA AND THE FOUNDING OF LUANDA

António de Oliveira Cadornega, *História Geral das Guerras Angolanas*, 3 vols. (Lisbon, 1972), 1, pp. 11–21.
Translated by Malyn Newitt.

The História Geral das Guerras Angolanas *was written by António de Oliveira Cadornega between 1680 and 1684 but was not published until 1940. Cadornega went out to Angola as an ordinary soldier in 1639. He married and resided in Massangano and Luanda and was still living in 1685. His book was an attempt to make sense of nearly one hundred years of warfare between the Portuguese and various Mbundu and Imbangala chiefs. Cadornega's account of the escape of Paulo Dias, helped on his way by the love of an Mbundu princess, is certainly pure myth. More directly historical is his account of the founding of Luanda. However, even the myth is interesting, for Cadornega is constructing a narrative whose fundamental purpose is to legitimize the Portuguese wars. This can be seen also in the way he uses the term 'resgate' (ransom) for the purchases of slaves, which he justifies by claiming that, through enslavement, African prisoners were both spared being eaten by cannibals (a real possibility for those captured by the Imbangala) and were baptized into the Christian religion.*

The port of Mpinda[1] is situated to leeward of the city of São Paulo d'Assunção[2] at four degrees south, and here the name of the *padrão* placed there by its discoverer Diogo Cão is preserved to this day.[3]

Some Portuguese went through the port of Mpinda and the county of Sonyo, which belongs to the kingdom of Kongo, to help the kings in their conquests and to defend them against the armies of the Jagas, who came down from Sierra Leone to invade that kingdom.[4] Those Portuguese showed themselves determined to protect it and courageously defended the said king from such great oppression, winning many victories over the said Jagas and other heathens, who were enemies of that Crown and who, apart from being very skilled soldiers and experienced in arms, were greatly feared because of the custom they followed of eating human flesh, this being their favourite form of sustenance. This custom is still practised there in the *kilombos*[5] of Queen Nzinga[6] and of Kabuku,[7] and in the *kilombo* of Kasange,[8] a great potentate in the interior who has governed many provinces and nations of different languages from whom the Portuguese ransom slaves. This is not only useful for commerce but still more for the service of God and the good of their souls. For with this trade, they avoid having so many slaughterhouses for human flesh, and they are instructed in the faith of our Lord Jesus Christ and, baptized and catechized, they sail for Brazil or other places where the Catholic faith is practised. They are thus taken away from their heathen ways and are redeemed to live lives which serve God and are good for commerce.

The *kilombo* of Queen Nzinga, as it is now called, was in former times known as Ngola Kiluanji,[9] and, as we have said, is composed in part by those Jagas who engage in their customs and rites and other practices. Today, since the arrival of the Italian Apostolic Capucin missionaries, some people there have been baptized, as also in the *kilombo* of Kasanje.[10]

As a result of the vigour which the Portuguese had shown in defending and giving assistance to the king of Kongo, their fame spread in such a manner that when the king of Angola – who also found himself oppressed and molested by those cruel butchers, the Jagas, who descended in such numbers on his lands that they overran them completely (like the Goths when they left their homelands and made such powerful incursions into the empires of Hispania and Italia and other parts) – heard about the valour and strength that the Portuguese had displayed, he sent his ambassadors to the Kongo asking that the *mundeles*, or some of them, be sent to help him defend himself against his enemies. Having heard the ambassador, the king sent most of the Portuguese who were in his kingdom to him [the king] who had requested them. When they had arrived, they performed great and valorous deeds in defending this king of Angola from his enemies, so that with the aid of the Portuguese he won great and notable victories over all his enemies. After they had delivered him from such great difficulties, he decided to repay them for these great benefits and decided, either through jealousy of their great valour or fear at seeing the deeds which they performed in his service, to command them to be killed. In order to carry out this cursed treason, he cunningly divided them among his *sobas*[11] and vassals, so that they should neither have a place to collect together nor have knowledge [the whereabouts] of each other. Having made this division of the men and taken these precautions, he ordered some to be killed and others to be beaten so that they could not walk or control their movements. This cruelty was totally undeserved by those who had rendered him such service. It was only this barbarian who could show such gratitude, while others who are not like him merely imitate him.

The piety and affection of a princess, daughter of this king, saved five Portuguese from so great a tyranny by ordering them to hide from his wrath in the lands of a *soba*, a vassal of her father, who had his lordship and lands by the River Mucozo, the waters of which flow into that famous torrent, the Cuanza. The name of the *soba* was Quilonga Quiabungo, and today he still has the same name and inhabits the same lands in the same place. As *soba* of this place he gives his allegiance as a vassal of the prince our lord to the fort of Cambambe, which is close to the lands of Quilonga and the River Mucozo.

With the greatest secrecy, the said pious and devoted princess ordered that a canoe should be prepared, of the kind that is made from a single tree called *mufuma* and is fashioned in the most suitable manner by craftsmen with tools made specially for this purpose. Here there are canoes that can carry 500 *enzeques* of cassava flour,[12] which are 1,000 *alqueires*, and on the return journey, having been relieved of their flour, twelve pipes of wine on trestles, as well as some barrels and other victuals. The princess ordered the boat to be brought when it was ready by the River Mocoso to the Cuanza, and those Portuguese should be placed in it along with the provisions necessary for the voyage, so that in this way they might escape down this spacious river. Among these Portuguese was Paulo Dias de Novais, for whose sake the daughter of the king went to these extremes, for so great is the power of love which can be experienced even by a heathen. So much is affection able to do!

When the said Portuguese had got aboard the canoe, they navigated downstream in a state of exhaustion like men who were fleeing from death. They disembarked at the bar of that powerful River Cuanza, which was well known to all sailors and is fifty leagues or more distant from the River Mucozo from where they had departed in the canoes. This is as far as from the city of São Paulo de Loanda to the fortress of Cambambe, which is close to the Cuanza and the River Mocozo.

Thus, the brave and suffering Portuguese dared to cross the bar on which the waves were breaking and sailed out to sea in that flimsy boat, going up the coast to leeward as far as the port of Mpinda on the River Congo, called the Zaire. And our ships frequented that port since the Catholic queen, Dona Caterina,[13] grandmother of our lord king Dom Sebastião, who was governor and regent of the kingdom during the minority of the king, in her piety had made that port free for entry to the kingdom of Kongo. Here out of Christian zeal for the propagation of the Faith in that powerful kingdom, king Dom Afonso,[14] as the king who then reigned was called, had ordered many priests to cultivate God's harvest there, generously expending much of his royal treasure for the cultivation of this new religion of Christianity, which bore so much fruit in these early times and in whose favour the hand of God worked so many prodigies. As we have said, the valorous Paulo Dias de Novais found a ship in this port bound for the kingdom of Portugal, and so he embarked with his companions and arrived safely in his beloved homeland.

When he arrived he gave detailed information about the kingdom of Kongo, which he had already explored, and about the great cruelty and tyranny which this barbarous and idolatrous king had shown in gratitude for the benefits brought by the Portuguese nation, and he gave an account of his own tragedy and of the others who had died such outrageous deaths at the hands of those tyrants.

When that virtuous and Catholic king had been informed of everything, he ordered ships to be prepared, with all necessary equipment of infantry, artillery, munitions, and principally in order to take those subjects who work in the vineyard of the Lord. In that company he sent the sons, so distinguished in virtues, of the patriarch Saint Ignatius de Loyola,[15] who have demonstrated in many parts of the world the power of his holy virtue and doctrine. Also according to the elders,[16] religious of the patriarch Saint Dominic came to cultivate the harvest of God, as their chronicle relates, and also those of the Order of the Carmelites.

Leaving our kingdom they headed for the coast of Ethiopia, which the ancients thought was not inhabited, calling it the Torrid Zone, and after enduring a long voyage and the perils of the sea, Paulo Dias de Novais, with his ships and companions, made the port of São Paulo de Luanda, which he had chosen when he went along the coast in the canoe to the port of Mpinda, and which could accommodate many ships in safety from the rigours and fury of the sea and the influence of the winds. This is because in front of the mainland is a very long island, which serves as a shelter for all large ships like a wall in front of them against which the fury of the waves can break. No ship is ever lost because of a storm within the calm of this port and bay.[17]

Jumping ashore he took possession of a high hill on an arm of the sea which reached to that part and which he named the Hill of São Paulo, since this holy apostle was known as the teacher of the people because of the extent of his preaching of the faith of Our Lord Jesus Christ. And this new conquistador also bore his name and came to instruct the heathen here in the law of the Gospel. This name was appropriate for him because this was the first land which he took to bring his subjects to the service of God and for the good of the souls of the Mbundu people on whose hill he fortified himself. All this can be testified by the foundations which were discovered at this site when a ditch was opened for the defenses of Fort São Miguel, and which had been built on the Hill of São Paulo. At the foot of it was also found the *padrão* where Diogo Cão, the first discoverer of this coast, placed it.[18] It also appeared that a house of God had been erected, in which the reverend Fathers of the Company, the first workers in this evangelical field, had their first College, the remains of which bear witness to this.

After this brave conquistador had taken this place and had made a fortification in the harbour to protect the ships, leaving there a garrison of people and infantry, he turned to the conquest of the kingdom of Angola. He came here, leaving the town of Luanda, which had this name from its beginning and first foundation. Therefore, the illness, which the members of his company had suffered in their gums, was called *mal de Luanda*.[19] This port only served to protect the factory, while the governors who came out in these early times set off for the interior to conquer this kingdom, until such a time as they made a base in that town which grew to become the chief in all the kingdoms which were conquered in Ethiopia.[20]

Notes

1 Mpinda was situated in the Zaire estuary and was the port of entry for the kingdom of Kongo.

2 Luanda.

3 A *padrão* was a stone pillar erected by Portuguese navigators at prominent points along the African coast. Their positions were subsequently marked on maps and charts. Diogo Cão reached the mouth of the Zaire in 1483. The point where he erected the *padrão* was known as Cabo do Padrão, though the pillar itself had been destroyed by the time Cadornega was writing. See discussion in E. Axelson, *Congo to Cape* (London, 1973) p. 51.

4 The idea was current even in the seventeenth century that there was some connection between the Jagas and the Mane. See Docs. 19 and 40.

5 *Kilombo* was a Kimbundu word that originally described the armed camp of the Imbangala where rituals initiating new warriors were carried out. It is probable that eating human flesh formed part of the rituals that initiated warriors into the Imbangala armies. It was later applied in Brazil to communities of escaped slaves. It is used by Cadornega to indicate a fortified town belonging to the African kings who opposed the Portuguese.

6 Queen Nzinga Mbande. Cadornega calls her Ginga. She had accepted baptism as early as 1621 and had taken the name Ana de Sousa.

7 Kabuko Kandonga was an Imbangala warlord who maintained an armed camp of fighters in the interior and with whom the Portuguese allied from time to time. This camp was destroyed by the Portuguese in 1653.

8 Kasanje was another Angolan state founded by an Imbangala warlord. It later established itself as a permanent kingdom.

9 Ngola Kiluanji is called by Cadornega Angola a Quiloamgi.

10 The Capucin mission in Kongo was established in 1645.

11 *Soba* was the title given to minor Mbundu rulers.

12 The Portuguese is *farinha da guerra*.

13 The queen, Dona Caterina, was sister of Charles V and wife of Dom João III. She became regent of Portugal on the death of her husband in 1557, as the heir to the throne, Dom Sebastião, was only three years old.

14 This cannot be Mbemba Nzinga (Dom Afonso I), who ruled Congo 1506–43. It must be a mistake for Nimi Lukeni (Dom Álvaro I) who reigned 1568–87.

15 Jesuits.

16 Cadornega uses the term *Antigos*. It is not clear who these were – perhaps the older settlers.

17 Luanda was formally part of the kingdom of Kongo and was renowned for its shell fisheries. The harbour is protected on the seaward side by a long spit of land, which at one time was an island.

18 Although Cão visited Luanda in 1483 on his first voyage, he did not erect a *padrão* there.

19 Scurvy. The term *mal de Luanda* is still in use.

20 That is, sub-Saharan Africa.

8

THE SLAVE TRADE

---

35 THE ARRIVAL OF SLAVES FROM WEST AFRICA IN LAGOS, 1444

From *Crónica de Guiné* by Gomes Eanes de Zurara.

Translation by Malyn Newitt, based on C. R. Beazley and Edgar Prestage, trans. and ed., *The Chronicle of the Discovery and Conquest of Guinea*, 2 vols. (Hakluyt Society, London, 1896–9); Léon Bourdon, trans., *Chronique de Guinée (1453)* (Paris, 1994).

Zurara's description of the landing of slaves at Lagos has been much quoted by historians. Portugal had been involved in sporadic slaving in the Canaries and off the coast of Morocco throughout the fourteenth century, so slaves were not in themselves a novelty. The return of Lançarote's caravels, however, brought the first large slave consignment to reach Portugal from the Sahara and its arrival greatly stimulated interest, both among the nobility and fidalgos, and among ordinary seamen, in undertaking further voyages. Indeed, Peter Russell believed that this open display of the slaves was a deliberate public relations exercise by Prince Henry 'the Navigator' to increase support for the west African expeditions.[1] Zurara's long discussion of the moral issues involved in the slave trade is of great interest. Although he reaches the conclusion that the trade is justified because the souls of the slaves will be saved, and piously concludes that this was Prince Henry's primary concern, the passage demonstrates that the morality of the trade was being questioned and actively debated in Portugal at the time. There are few such public expressions of concern about the slave trade in any subsequent public document.

The caravels arrived at Lagos, from which they had previously set out, having excellent weather for their voyage, for Fortune was not less gracious to them in the favourable weather than it had been to them previously in the capture of their prizes. From there the news reached the

Infante,[2] who happened to have arrived there a few hours before from other parts where he had been for some days.

As you see that people desire knowledge, some tried to get near the shore, and others put themselves into boats that they found moored along the beach and went to welcome their relations and friends, so that in a short time the news of their good fortune was well known, and everyone was generally very pleased. On that day it was enough for the principal men to kiss the hand of the Infante their lord, and to give him a short account of their exploits. After this, they went to rest like men who had reached their fatherland and their own homes, where already you may guess what would be the joy of their wives and children.

Next day, Lançarote,[3] who had taken the main charge of the expedition, said to the Infante: 'My lord, Your Grace well knows that you are to receive the fifth of these Moors, and of all that we have gained in that land, to which you sent us for the service of God and yourself. Now these Moors are ill and in a sorry state because of the long time we have been at sea, as well as from the great sorrow that you must realise they have in their hearts at seeing themselves taken away from the land of their birth and placed in captivity, without having any understanding of what their fate is to be, and also because they have not been accustomed to travel in ships. For these reasons it seems to be a good idea to me that in the morning, you should order them to be taken out of the caravels and brought to the field which is outside the town gate, and there divided into five groups according to custom, and that Your Grace should come there and choose one of these groups, whichever you prefer.'[4]

The Infante said that this pleased him, and very early the next day, Lançarote ordered the masters of the caravels to bring out the captives and take them to that field, where they were to make the divisions, as he had already said. However, before they did anything else, they took as an offering the best of those Moors to the church of that place; and another little Moor, who afterwards became a friar of St Francis, they sent to [the convent of] Cape St. Vincent, where he lived ever afterwards as a Catholic Christian, without having understanding or perception of any other law than that true and holy law in which all Christians hope for their salvation. The number of Moors captured was 235.

O, Thou heavenly Father, who with Thy powerful hand, without alteration of Thy divine essence, governeth all the infinite company of Thy Holy City, and controlleth all the revolutions of higher worlds, divided into nine spheres, making the duration of ages long or short according as it pleases Thee, I pray Thee that my tears may not wrong my conscience; for it is not their religion but their humanity that makes me to weep in pity for their sufferings. If the brute animals, with their bestial feelings, understand the sufferings of their own kind through natural instinct, what wouldst Thou have my human nature to do when I see before my eyes that miserable company and remember that they too are of the generation of the sons of Adam?

On the next day, which was the eighth day of the month of August, very early in the morning because of the heat, the seamen began to get their boats ready to disembark those captives and bring them ashore, as they were commanded. When these were placed all together in that field, they were a marvelous sight, for amongst them were some quite white, fair to look upon and well proportioned, others were less white like mulattoes, others again were as black as Ethiopians[5] and so ugly, both in features and in body, as almost to appear (to those who saw them) the images of the lower hemisphere. What heart, however hard it might be, would not to be pierced with a feeling of pity to see that company? For some hung their heads with their faces bathed in tears, looking at each other. Others stood groaning sadly, looking up to the height of heaven, fixing their eyes upon it and crying loudly, as if asking help of the Father of Nature. Others struck their faces with the palms of their hands, throwing themselves at full length upon the ground. Others made their lamentations in the manner of a song after the custom of their country, and, though we could not understand the words of their language, it seemed to reflect the extent of their sorrow.

To increase their sufferings still more, there now arrived those who had charge of the division of the captives, and they began to separate one from another in order to make the shares equal. It now became necessary to separate fathers from sons, wives from husbands and brothers from brothers. No respect was shown either to friends or relations, but each fell where his fate took him.

O powerful Fortune, whose wheels turn and turn again, ordering the affairs of this world as it pleases thee! Place before the eyes of those miserable people some understanding of what is to become of them, that they may receive some consolation in the midst of their great misery. And you others, who are so busy in making that division of the captives, look with pity upon so much misery and note how they cling to one another so that you can hardly separate them!

And who could finish that division without very great effort? For as soon as they had placed them in one group, sons, seeing their fathers in another, rose with great energy and rushed over to them; mothers clasped their children in their arms and threw themselves flat on the ground with them, receiving blows with little care for their own flesh, if only they might not be torn from them. So, with a great deal of trouble, they finished the division because, quite apart from the trouble they had with the captives, the field was full of people, both from the town and from the surrounding villages and districts, who on that day had rested the hands that gave them their living for the sole purpose of seeing this novel spectacle. What they saw, namely some crying and some separating the captives, caused them to make such a tumult as greatly to confuse those who directed the division.

The Infante was there, mounted upon a powerful horse and accompanied by his retinue, distributing his favours like a man who sought only to gain a small profit from his share; for he made a very speedy distribution of the forty-six souls that constituted his fifth, for his chief riches lay in his purpose, and he reflected with great pleasure upon the salvation of those souls that otherwise would have been lost. And certainly his expectation was not in vain for, as we said before, as soon as they understood our language, little was needed for them to turn Christian. And I, who put together the history in this volume, have seen in the town of Lagos, boys and girls (the children and grandchildren of those first captives, born in this land) as good and true Christians as if they were directly descended from those who were first baptized into the law of Christ.

Notes

1   P. E. Russell, *Prince Henry 'the Navigator'. A life* (New Haven, 2000) p. 241.
2   Prince Henry 'the Navigator'.
3   This captain, sometimes called Lançarote da Ilha, was the son-in-law of the *alcaide-mor* of Lagos and was a squire in Prince Henry's household. He was appointed *almox-arife* of Lagos in 1443. He sailed with six caravels, which had been equipped at his own expense, and obtained the slaves from the coast immediately south of Arguim and Cape Blanco.
4   Henry received a 'fifth' on all slaves brought back from west Africa.
5   The words used here are *pardos* and *tiopios*. The former indicated a brown skin, the latter had no reference to the region of modern Ethiopia but was a general term used to describe black Africans.

---

36   THE SLAVE TRADE IS GOOD FOR THE KONGO

Extracts from a letter of Dom João III to the king of Kongo, 1529.
António Brásio, *Monumenta Missionaria Africana* (Lisbon, 1952), 1, pp. 521–7.
Translated by Malyn Newitt.

Since his accession to the Kongo throne in 1506, Afonso had maintained close ties with the Christian Church on which his legitimacy as ruler largely depended. He had also allowed the trade in slaves to grow as a double royal monopoly, the profits shared between himself and the king of Portugal. However, by the third decade of his reign, he was becoming deeply concerned that the growth of this trade was leading to his own subjects being sold as slaves against the custom of the country. This he feared was severely damaging social and political relations in his kingdom. The king of Portugal's response[1] showed little understanding of this concern. To him, the slave trade was just another form of commerce, while the participation of the kingdom of Kongo was only what Portugal had a right to expect after all the sacrifices that had been made in the past to help the king. Moreover, the king of Portugal pointed out that the authority of the Kongo king largely rested on the wealth he derived from trade.

... You say in your letters that you do not want there to be any slave trade in your kingdom because it is depopulating your land. I can believe that you only say this as a result of the suffering that the Portuguese cause you, because I am told of the great size of Kongo and how it is so populated that it appears that not a single slave has left it. They also tell me that you send to buy them [slaves] outside [the country] and that you marry them and make them Christian, by which means the country is well populated. All this seems good to me and so now, with this order that the people carry and which you intend to send to the fairs,[2] it appears there will be many slaves.

As for those who are sold in this city, in order to know if they are natives or come from outside, there ought to be at the fair a designated place where they are sold and where there will be two of your servants who will know if the said slaves are sold in the houses [in secret], and they shall not be sold without the said two men being present. It may be difficult to find men you wish to nominate, since they serve you in other matters of greater importance, and these two men will on one day buy for the priests, on another for the officials and on another for the schoolmasters, who will pay the price according to custom and in this way all will have a good outcome.

If I say now that I desire, as you request, that there shall not be any trade in slaves in your kingdom, I will still want to provide wheat and wine for use at Mass, and for this only one caravel a year will be necessary. If this seems good to you, it shall be so. However, it does not seem to me to be to the honour of you or your kingdom because it would be more praiseworthy to draw each year from the Kongo 10,000 slaves and 10,000 *manilhas* and as many tusks of ivory. If there is now to be no trade in the Kongo at all, and only one ship a year is to come there, this and more shall be as you desire.

You also sent to ask me for a ship, which astonishes me since all my ships are yours; and you ought to remember the ship which João de Melo lent you, who is still today owed 2,000 *reis* for the costs he incurred, and in addition to this the suffering which you experienced in this. Nor do you take into account the [cost of the] boats, ships and [other] expenditure which my predecessors and I incurred on the sea, not to gain or acquire riches but only to secure the navigation and the route for sailors who make their living this way. It is these who profit by it, not the king, and this you have experienced yourself in your kingdom.

Remember the armada which the king my father sent at your request when Gonçalo Roiz[3] came and which was lost here, and also the armada which brought Simão da Silva,[4] who died there; all these things were done for honour and not for profit. You should note that these ships, which came here to profit by the sale of people, frequently did not succeed in this. So, as for what you desire, you have my ships as if they were your own.

If you do not want anyone to bring merchandise to Kongo, this would be against the custom of every country, because [merchandise] comes to Portugal from all parts of the world to be bought and sold. In this way the land is supplied with everything, and from Portugal, goods are sent to all parts; and if a *fidalgo* of yours rebels against you and receives merchandise from Portugal, where will be your power and greatness because I well understand what constitutes your military strength and the fear that all have of you.

Notes

1   The king was Dom João III (1521–57).
2   The word used here is *pumbos* from which derived the word *pombeiro* (slave trader).
3   For Gonçalo Roiz see Doc. 30.
4   Simão da Silva was the ambassador of Dom Manuel sent to the Kongo in 1512.

---

37   THE SLAVE TRADE FROM WEST AFRICA TO THE CAPE VERDE ISLANDS IN THE SIXTEENTH CENTURY

From Anon, *Viagens de um pilôto português do século XVI à costa de África e a São Tomé*, Arlindo Manuel Caldeira, ed. (Lisbon, 2000), pp. 95–8. Translated by Malyn Newitt.

This passage from the account written by an anonymous Portuguese pilot (see Doc. 12 for details) refers to the Portuguese system of leasing out trading rights to contractors, a practice that later became much more widespread and notorious in the Estado da Índia. However, it is chiefly interesting for its reference to the slave trade. Slaves from the African mainland were first sent to Santiago, where traders from the Spanish Indies came to buy (see Doc. 38). This practice kept the Spanish from trading directly with Africa, thereby undermining the lucrative Portuguese monopoly, but it also allowed the slaves to receive some instruction in the Portuguese language and in Christianity, which enhanced their value in the American markets. It seems unlikely that the author can really have believed that African parents sold their children as slaves to give them better opportunities in life, but it provides further evidence that there was some unease in Portugal about the slave trade, so that writers felt bound to offer some 'moral' justification for slavery.

The mention of the trade in cori beads from the Kongo highlights the fact that in developing their trade in western Africa, the Portuguese were often operating as middlemen in what was an exchange of goods of African origin.

All this coast as far as the kingdom of Manikongo[1] is divided into two parts, which are rented every four or five years to whoever offers the most to go and trade in those lands and ports. Those who take this contract are called arrendadori [contractors], and no one except they or their delegates can come near or disembark on those coasts nor buy nor sell there. Large numbers of caravans of blacks come there to sell gold and slaves, some of whom are prisoners of war and some their own children, who are brought by their own fathers and mothers, who consider they are doing them the greatest favour in the world by sending them in this way to dwell in other countries where provisions abound. All of them come as naked as when they were born, both male and female, just as if they were a herd of cattle. They are exchanged for glass beads of various colours, objects made of copper or brass, different coloured cotton cloths and other similar things which they take throughout Ethiopia.

The contractors subsequently bring the slaves to the island of Santiago,[2] where ships continually arrive with merchandise from different countries and provinces, principally from the Indies discovered by the Spaniards, and there they buy slaves giving some merchandise in exchange. They always require as many males as females, for if the [female slaves] do not accompany them, those to whom they are sold will not obtain good service.[3]

When these slaves are taken by sea, the men are separated from the women, the former being made to stay below decks and the latter above, and when they are having their food the men are not allowed to see the women, because they would not do anything except stare at them. Because of these blacks, our king built a castle on that coast, called Da Mina, situated six degrees above the Equator, where only his factors can go [to trade]. At this place a large number of blacks gather at the same time to sell gold dust, which is found in the river sand and which they exchange with the said factors for various goods, in particular beads made of glass and another type of bead made of blue stone which is not lapis lazuli but some other kind of mineral. This stone is brought by our king from the land of the Manikongo, where the stone has its origin.[4] These beads are tubular in shape and are called corili. For these they give a lot of gold, for they are highly esteemed by all these blacks. They put them in the fire to see if they are false, for some that are brought are made of glass and are very similar but do not withstand the fire test.

Notes

1   The kingdom of Kongo.
2   Santiago is the largest of the Cape Verde Islands.
3   Contrary to what is said here, the ratio of male to female slaves in the Atlantic slave trade is usually thought to have been two to one. The unit of account employed in the Portuguese slave trade was the *peça da Índia*, which was the equivalent of one adult male slave.
4   These are *cori* beads, widely used in west African trade. Their blue colour derives from the copper content.

38   THE SLAVE TRADE IN THE CAPE VERDE ISLANDS, 1594

Francesco Carletti, *Ragionamenti del mio viaggio intorno al mondo*, ed., G.Cardona et Bertolucci (Rome, 1992)[1]

Original manuscript is in the Biblioteca Angelica, Rome, Codice 1331 (T.3.22).

Translated by Malyn Newitt.

Francesco Carletti was born in Florence about 1573 and set off on a slaving voyage to Cape Verde and the Spanish Indies in 1594. He continued by stages around the world, visiting Japan and India before returning to Florence in 1606. His account of his travels was addressed to the grand duke of Tuscany, Ferdinando dei Medici. Carletti was one of the first merchants to complete a voyage around the world, and he gives a wealth of curious details about the social and sexual customs of the countries he visited. This account of the slave trade shows something of the confusion of thought with which Europeans contemplated this form of commerce. On the one hand, Carletti's conscience tells him that slaves are human and that the trade cannot be reconciled with religious duty, while on the other, he views slaves, in some respects, as animals who are unaware of the need to disguise their nakedness.

Yesterday, Serene Prince, I promised Your Serene Highness to recount to you the manner in which we traded in the island of Cape Verde.[2] Once we had landed, we rented a house and began to let it be known that we wanted to buy slaves. Then the Portuguese, who keep [the slaves] in their villas in the country in herds like cattle, ordered that they be brought to the town to be shown to us. After having seen some of them and asked their price, we found that the profit would be less than we had calculated on paper in Spain. This arose because they were asking much more than was usual due to the large number of ships which had called there and which all wanted to take slaves on board for the Indies. This provoked a rise in the price so that, where it had been customary to sell a slave for 50 scudi[3] or at the most 60, it was now necessary to pay 100 scudi for each one, and those who could get them at that price were very happy because they had no other choice than to drink or drown.

At this price we bought seventy-five slaves, two-thirds men and one-third women, both young and old, large and small. All were mixed together according to the custom of the country and in a flock, just as in our country we would buy sheep, having first taken all the necessary precautions to make sure that they were in good health, had good constitutions and had no bodily defects. Each owner then marks them, or to say it more appropriately, brands them with his own brand mark. This is made of silver and is heated in the flame of a candle made of tallow with which the burn is then anointed. The mark is made on the breast, or the arm or the back so that they can be recognized.

When I recall that I did this on the orders of the person under whose command I was, it does not fail to cause me sadness and trouble in my conscience, because, in truth Serene Lord, this traffic always appears to me to be inhumane and unworthy of the faith and piety of a Christian. Without any doubt this is a form of commerce in human beings or, to put it in words that are more appropriate, in human flesh and blood. It is all the more shameful for one who has been baptized because, although they differ in colour and in their fortune in life, they have nevertheless a soul that was formed by the same Creator who formed our own. I repent of this before His Divine Majesty, although I know very well that this is not necessary since he knows that in my mind I always found this business repugnant. However, so that no one should be in any doubt and so that Your Highness can be assured of it, [I say] that this business never pleased me. However that may be, we did take part in it, as I said, and perhaps this is the reason why we all had to do penance for it as will be seen at the end of the second discourse on these voyages and adventures in which I will give an account to Your Highness of what happened to us.

To return to the trade in slaves, after having bought the said seventy-five male and female moors[4] at an initial price of 100 scudi each, they came in the end with all the expenses to cost us 170 scudi, namely 25 for the royal licence and 16 for the right to leave the island of Cape Verde, and 21 more for the cost of food and other expenses in transporting them to Cartagena de Indias.[5] Meanwhile, those that died increased the overall cost still further.

I had to look after the aforementioned slaves, so I selected one moor to be in charge of each group of ten men, choosing the one who seemed to me to be most high spirited and alert, so that he could organize what I provided to meet their needs, in particular respecting the food, which was given to them twice a day and which consisted of a variety of large bean which grows there and which is cooked simply in water and then seasoned with a little oil and salt.

Until the moment we embarked, they were held separately in two rooms, men in one and women in another. They were naked, with no other clothing except that given them by nature with which they were content, only hiding with a fragment of cotton cloth or piece of leather or skin or a rag or leaves from a tree that part of the body, which original sin has made appear more shameful than any other. Most of the men, however, and the women in particular, either through necessity or through innocence or stupidity, scarcely bother with this and remain just as nature had made them without recognising that it is only decent to cover these parts and that that is the reason that others do so. Many display a certain gallantry in their own manner and attach a ribbon or threads made of grass to their member and tie it back between their thighs, hiding it in such a manner that it becomes impossible to tell if they are male or female. Others decorate it with the horn of some animal or with seashells. Others cover it and conceal it entirely with little rings made of bone or even woven grass, while others paint it or rather dye it red, yellow or green with some mixture. In these and other ways they try to conceal those parts which others among them without further ceremony leave uncovered.

.....

The slaves were embarked in the ship we had hired, the men below decks pressed and squeezed together one against the other in such a way that they had great difficulty in turning from one side to the other when they wanted to. The women were lodged after their own fashion on deck wherever they could find room in the ship. Once a day they were given to eat as much as they wanted of a kind of millet cooked in water and seasoned with oil and salt. In the morning each one was given a handful of grain as hard as aniseed but tasting different. At noon, after they had eaten, they were given something to drink, each one plunging his head into a bucket and drinking as much as he could in one go without returning a second time. Then in the evening if anything remained, he would eat it with his comrades, that is to say with the ten slaves in his group.

Notes

1 The original manuscript of Carletti's *Ragionamenti* is lost. An edited version was published in 1701, but there is a manuscript version in Biblioteca Angelica, Rome, Codice 1331 (T.3.22), which is thought to be closer to the original.

2 There are twelve islands in the Cape Verde archipelago. Here the reference is to Santiago, the largest of them.

3 Around 1600 the Florentine *scudo d'oro* was worth 1.26 Venetian ducats.

4 The term Moor was used at the time as a general term for Muslim. Here it may mean just 'blacks' or 'dark-skinned' people.

5 Cartagena on the coast of modern Colombia had been founded in 1533 and was one of the principal ports of Spanish America.

9

CONFLICT IN THE KINGDOM OF KONGO IN THE 1560s

---

39 CHRISTIANITY AND A DISPUTED SUCCESSION IN THE KINGDOM OF KONGO

From Filippo Pigafetta, *Relatione del Reame di Congo et delli circonvicine contrade tratta dalli scritti & ragionamenti di Odoardo Lopez Portoghese*, Grassi (Rome, 1591).

Translation by Malyn Newitt, based on M. Hutchinson, trans. and ed., *A Report of the Kingdom of Congo and of the Surrounding Countries* (London, 1881), pp. 92–5; Filippo Pigafetta and Duarte Lopes, *Relação do Reino do Congo e das Terras Circunvizinhas*, António Luís Alves Ferronha, ed., (Lisbon, 1989), pp. 81–3.

This account of the succession dispute that followed the death of the Kongo king, Dom Diogo, in 1561 shows how the Portuguese and the Christian faction in the capital sought to control the succession. The Portuguese priests had tried to insist that the kings observe monogamy and that the succession should be by primogeniture. This aroused the hostility of clans who would find themselves excluded from the succession if primogeniture were established. These naturally found themselves in opposition to the Christian religion and in support of the traditional pattern of multiple marriages (see Doc. 29). The fact that the Kongo Church remained subordinate to the bishop of São Tomé meant that the development of a truly indigenous church was blocked. The struggle to secure the supremacy of the Christian cult was thus inextricably caught up with the struggles of the Kongo ruling lineages over the succession.[1]

In the reign of this king, the third bishop of São Tomé and Kongo[2] came from Portugal and was received with all the usual ceremonies on the way and at the Court of São Salvador.[3] Now the devil, the enemy of the Christian faith, feeling the happy progress of the Catholic religion weighing on him, began to sow dissension between the friars and priests and their bishop, which arose from the liberty they had enjoyed for so many years without the supervision of a pastor. For each one considered himself not only as good as the bishop, but even better, and would not obey his prelate, so that great dissension arose among them, causing serious scandal and a bad example. However, the king,[4] as a faithful Catholic, always took the part of the bishop and, to make an end of these disturbances, sent some of the priests prisoners to Portugal and others to São Tomé. Some also left taking their possessions with them, so that instead of the Christian doctrine growing, it rather diminished, and this was their fault.

Nor did the adversary stop here, for he also spread discord among the rulers and their subjects and, after the death of the king, three princes claimed the succession at the same time. The first was the king's own son, who was not supported by many of the people, as they wished for another.[5] He was therefore soon killed. There remained two others of royal blood,[6] one of whom was made king by his followers, with the support of the greater part of the people and against the will of the Portuguese and certain lords, who aimed at placing the other on the throne. Whereupon, the above-mentioned lords, together with the Portuguese, went to the church to kill the newly elected king, thinking that if they killed him, the other must of necessity become king. At the same time the opposite party killed the king chosen by the Portuguese, persuading themselves that, if he were dead, there would be no difficulty in obtaining the kingdom for their king, because there was no one else left who was eligible to hold the royal sceptre. So, at the very same hour, but in different places, both these kings were murdered. In the midst of these conspiracies and killings, the people, seeing that there were no longer any legitimate successors to the royal crown, and blaming the Portuguese for all these evils, turned against them and slew as many as they found there [in São Salvador]. However, they did not touch the priests or those who lived in other places.

There being no one else of royal blood upon whom to bestow the government, Dom Henrique,[7] a brother of the late king, Dom Diogo, was chosen. He went to war against the Anzika[8] and left behind as governor, with the title of king, Dom Álvaro,[9] a young man of twenty-five, who was the son of his wife[10] by a former husband. This same Dom Henrique died shortly after the war was ended, and the aforesaid Dom Álvaro was by common consent chosen king of Kongo and was obeyed by all. With the death of Dom Henrique, the royal line of the ancient kings of Kongo became extinct.

Dom Álvaro was a just and wise ruler and a peacemaker who brought to an end the tumults in the kingdom. He gathered together all the Portuguese who had been scattered throughout the neighbouring provinces during the recent wars, both priests and laity, excusing them and explaining that they had not been the cause of the recent troubles as everyone maintained. Having also determined to write a full account of all that had happened both to the king of Portugal and to the bishop of São Tomé, he dispatched certain people with these letters. On hearing this news, the bishop, who had been afraid to go to the kingdom of Kongo during the late rebellion, set out at once for the Kongo. There he used his authority to calm the dissension and bring order to the affairs relating to divine service and the office of the priests. Soon after this, he returned to São Tomé where he became ill and died. This was the third time that these parts were left without a bishop.

Because of the lack of a bishop, the Christian religion began to weaken in the king and in the lords and the people, all of whom indulged in the things of the flesh. The king in particular was led to this by some young men of his own age with whom he was intimately associated and especially by one of the nobles, who was a relation of his, called Dom Francisco Bullamatare, which means to 'seize a stone'.[11] This man, who took great liberties because he was an important noble, and who for some time had kept aloof from Christian instruction, gave out in public that it was a foolish thing for men to have only one wife, and that it was better to return to their former customs. And so the devil, by means of this man, opened the door for the destruction of the temple of Christianity in that kingdom, which had been established previously at the cost of so much labour. All these young men strayed so far from the path of truth that, going on from sin to sin, they almost entirely abandoned the true Faith.

Meanwhile, the aforesaid Dom Francisco died and was buried, like a nobleman, in the Church of the Holy Cross, although he was clearly suspected of, and was marked by, false religion. And it came to pass (marvellous to relate, and as a sign to confirm the righteous in their holy faith, but to confound the wicked) that at night, evil spirits took off part of the roof from the Church of the Holy Cross where this man was buried, and with horrible sounds, which were heard throughout the whole city, dragged his body from the grave and carried it away. In the morning the gates of the church were found shut, but the roof was broken open, and the body of that man was no longer in the tomb.

Notes

1 There are discussions of this succession dispute in Hilton, *Kingdom of Kongo*, pp. 68, 71, and in John Thornton, 'Elite Women in the kingdom of Kongo: Historical Perspectives on Women's Political Power', *Journal of Africa History*, 47 (2006) pp. 446–7.

2 Gaspar Cão OSA, appointed 6 July 1554 and died 17 February 1572.

3 This was the name given by the Portuguese to Mbanza Kongo, the capital of the Kongo kingdom.

4 Dom Diogo I (1545–61).

5 Called Dom Afonso.

6 These were grandsons of Dom Afonso I and were known as Dom Rodrigo and Dom Pedro.

7 Dom Henrique ruled 1567–8.

8 These people are better known as the Teke and inhabited the north bank of the Zaire River.

9 Dom Álvaro I (Nimi Lukeni) ruled 1568–87.

10 Her name was Izabel lua Lukeni.

11 Bulamatari was the nickname that was given by the Congolese to H. M. Stanley and is usually thought to have meant 'breaker of stones'.

40 THE JAGA INVASIONS

From Filippo Pigafetta, *Relatione del Reame di Congo et delli circonvicine contrade tratta dalli scritti & ragionamenti di Odoardo Lopez Portoghese*, Grassi (Rome, 1591).

Translation by Malyn Newitt, based on M. Hutchinson, trans. and ed. *A Report of the Kingdom of Congo and of the Surrounding Countries* (London, 1881), pp. 96–101; Filippo Pigafetta and Duarte Lopes, *Relação do Reino do Congo e das TerrasCircunvizinhas*, António Luís Alves Ferronha, ed., (Lisbon, 1989), pp. 84–8.

Pigafetta's narrative is the only surviving contemporary account of the Jaga invasions of the 1560s, which have been seen as a decisive event in the history of west central Africa. According to one theory, the Jaga were the ancestors of the Muyaka and were people dislocated by the slave trade. They invaded the eastern province of Mbata because it was rich in food supplies. The inability of the Kongo king to resist this invasion was the result of the bitter succession dispute described in Doc. 39. Another interpretation sees the Jaga as people displaced by the rise of the Luba kingdom. After their defeat by the Portuguese, they settled in the Kwango valley and merged with the Muyaka. They may also have formed part of the Imbangala armies that began to appear in Angola in the early seventeenth century and that contemporary Portuguese documents also refer to as Jaga. The Portuguese also sometimes used the term Jaga to describe the black mercenaries they recruited into their armies in the seventeenth century. The cannibalism of the Jaga was probably part of the war rituals sometimes practised by fighters in nomadic warbands. It is likely that the term 'Jaga' was loosely applied to any nomadic warband that appeared to prey on the settled population.[1] *Cadornega, writing in the 1680s, believed that the Jaga originated in Sierra Leone (see Doc. 34), as many Portuguese believed that all nomadic warbands which practised ritual cannibalism were somehow connected.*

Pigafetta's reference to the widespread belief in Portugal that there were silver mines, the whereabouts of which were being hidden by the king, was matched by the similar belief that there were silver mines in eastern Africa. Gouveia's military expedition to help the Kongo king was exactly contemporaneous with the expedition of Francisco Barreto to find the gold and silver mines in eastern Africa.

Meanwhile certain people, who lived like Arabs or the nomads of old, came to plunder the kingdom of Kongo. They were called Jagas and inhabited the country near the first lake of the River Nile, in a province of the empire of Monemugi.[2] They are a cruel and murderous people, of great stature and horrible appearance, and they eat human flesh, but they fight in a brave and ferocious manner. Their weapons are shields, spears and daggers, and they go naked. In their customs and everyday life they are very savage and wild. These people have no king and live in huts in the forest after the manner of shepherds. When they appeared, they destroyed and put everything to fire and sword, robbing every part of the country through which they passed, until they reached [the kingdom of] Kongo, which they entered through the province of Mbata.[3] They attacked those who were the first to resist them and then went on to the capital, where the king lost heart because of the victory gained by his enemies in Mbata. Nevertheless, the king went with his people to meet his enemies on the very same plain where, in former years, Mpanzu had fought with king Dom Afonso.[4] There he gave battle, but the royal troops were defeated and the king, now a broken man, retreated again to his capital. However, he did not consider himself to be safe there and thought he had been abandoned by God on account of his sins, for he lacked the same faith in Him that Dom Afonso had shown. So he abandoned the city and escaped to a certain island in the River Zaire, called the Island of Horses, together with the Portuguese priests and other leading men from the kingdom.[5]

The Jagas were thus left in possession of the royal city and indeed of the whole kingdom, while the inhabitants fled for safety to the mountains and desert places. Meanwhile the enemy set fire to the city and the churches, destroying everything and not sparing the life of anyone. In this way they went from province to province subjugating the whole kingdom and dividing it between their armies.

In this persecution everyone in the kingdom suffered – the king, the people, the Portuguese and their priests – each according to his degree, for people wandered about the country and died from lack of food and all other necessities. The king and his followers had escaped and taken refuge in the aforesaid island and, because it was small and the people were many, all suffered so terribly from lack of provisions that most of them died of famine and pestilence. The price of a small quantity of food, for example, rose to that paid for a slave, which was bought for at least ten scudi.

Thus, forced by necessity, fathers sold their sons, and brothers their brothers, everyone resorting to the most horrible crimes in order to obtain food. The people who sold themselves through hunger were bought by various Portuguese merchants, who came from São Tomé with provisions; the sellers told them that others were slaves and these others confirmed this in order to escape the torments of hunger. In this manner, great numbers of slaves who were natives of Kongo went to São Tomé and Portugal, amongst them some of royal blood and others of chiefly families, who were all sold out of necessity. From all this, the king clearly understood that it was on account of his misdeeds that so much misery had come upon them and, although because he was king he had not suffered hunger, yet he did not escape the terrible malady of dropsy, his legs swelling enormously. This disease was caused by the bad air and food, and the dampness of the island, and the infirmity remained with him until his death. Sick from these calamities, the king was converted to God, asking pardon for his offences and doing penance for his sins. On the advice of the Portuguese he sent ambassadors to ask for help from the king of Portugal and to relate to him all these recent misfortunes.

This happened at the beginning of the reign of king Dom Sebastião, who, out of love for him, immediately sent help through a captain called Francisco de Gouveia,[6] who had had experience in various wars in India and Africa and who was accompanied by 600 soldiers and a great number of gentlemen adventurers. He brought with him orders [from the king] that the island of São Tomé should provide him with ships, supplies and everything necessary for this enterprise. Eventually he arrived with those provisions at the Island of Horses, where the king still was. The Portuguese took the king with them and, gathering together all the armed people in the country, they marched as quickly as possible against the enemy. After fighting with them many times in the field, at the end of a year and a half, the king was restored to his throne, triumphing more by the noise and power of his guns, than by numbers, because the Jagas were greatly terrified by those engines.

In this way the Jagas were expelled from the kingdom of Kongo, and few returned to their homes. The Portuguese captain, after remaining four years to see the king restored to his kingdom, returned to Portugal, bearing letters from the king of Kongo asking for priests to be sent to maintain the Christian religion. Several Portuguese who had accompanied the captain to these parts remained behind, where today they have great wealth and possessions.

Once restored to his kingdom and to his former dignity, the king remained a good Christian and married Dona Caterina, who is still alive and by whom he had four daughters. By his slaves, he had two sons and a daughter and because females cannot succeed to the throne in those countries, the eldest son, who was also called Dom Álvaro, inherited, and he reigns to this day.[7]

Whilst the aforesaid captain was in Kongo, king Dom Sebastião, hearing that there were mines of gold, silver and other metals in that kingdom, sent two skilled miners, who had been employed by the Castilians in the West,[8] to search for these mines and make some profit out of them. However, a Portuguese called Francisco Barbudo, the intimate confessor of the king of Kongo, persuaded him not to allow these mines to be discovered, leading him to believe that, if this happened, by degrees he would lose his independence in the kingdom. The king, therefore, directed the miners to be taken by routes where he knew they would find no mines.[9] As the king would not permit the discovery and working of metals, which were so highly prized in Europe, large-scale trade ceased to be carried on in the kingdom of Kongo, and Portuguese merchants were no longer interested in sailing there, and consequently few priests went either. ...

The king of Kongo sent another ambassador, a relation of his own, called Dom Sebastião Álvares, together with a Portuguese, to ask for priests, and also to ransom the slaves who were natives of that country and who were resident in São Tomé and Portugal and had been sold out of necessity. Some of these remained in slavery of their own free will, but a great number were ransomed and brought to their own country, and with the help of the many lords and nobles found amongst them, the king was enabled to reestablish the Christian religion, which had suffered great loss, and also to employ them as valued counsellors and ministers in his kingdom, their long captivity having given them much experience in the world.

Notes

1   The most comprehensive recent discussion of the Jaga is Paulo Jorge de Sousa Pinto, 'Em torno de um problema de identidade os "Jagas" na História do Congo e Angola', *Mare Liberum* 18–19 (1999–2000), pp. 193–243.
2   See Doc. 28.

3   See Doc. 28.
4   See Doc. 29.
5   The 'horses' were, of course, hippopotamuses. A Portuguese trading port, called Santo António, was established there.
6   Francisco de Gouveia Sottomaior was a former governor of São Tomé. He reached the Kongo with his army in 1571 and remained until 1576 when he returned to Portugal. He died in 1577, aged seventy.
7   Dom Álvaro II (Mpanzu Nimi) reigned 1587–1614.
8   By 'West' should be understood 'America'.
9   See Doc. 49.

10

CHRISTIANITY IN THE KONGO

---

41 SUPPORT SOUGHT FROM PORTUGAL TO MAINTAIN THE TRUE FAITH

Extract from a letter of king Dom Afonso I of Kongo to Dom João III, 25 August 1526.

António Brásio, *Monumenta Missionaria Africana* (Lisbon, 1952), 1, pp. 479–81.

Original letter is in Arquivo Nacional de Torre de Tombo, Corpo Cronológico, 34–127.

Translated by Malyn Newitt.

This is typical of the rather plaintive letters written by Dom Afonso of Kongo to the kings of Portugal. Afonso felt increasingly isolated in his attempt to impose the Christian cult in Kongo and became ever more reliant on the support of the Portuguese Crown – support which was dependent on the continuation of the slave trade (see Doc. 36). The letter refers to the building of the church of Nossa Senhora da Vitória (so named to commemorate Afonso's victory over his rivals) on the site of the royal graves. This involved destroying the grove of trees that had previously protected the burial ground and had been the focus of the cult of the royal ancestors in the previous reign. The building of this church was an important step in consolidating Christianity as a royal burial cult. It seems that Afonso was making some attempt to apply diplomatic pressure by hinting that approaches might be made to the kings of Castile and France, although it is unlikely that he seriously considered seeking support from any quarter other than Portugal.

... All of which, Senhor, will not happen if Your Highness is willing to help and favour us in the same manner as your father[1] with spiritual remedies which we cannot obtain without many priests. [In this way] the sacraments, preaching, doctrine and penance can be spread through all the parts of our large and populous kingdom, by the orders that will be given by myself and the bishop our son.[2] In such a manner the word of God may be sown in the hearts of the people, where it will remain embedded and, although they have been given diabolical poison to damn them, the virtue of this remedy will cure them.

This, Senhor, will be a good way to stop the purveyors of bad goods and false merchandise,[3] who impede the salvation of the soul and damage the good fruit which has been grown here. For the *grumetes*,[4] mulattos and Benins[5] of which our kingdom is full, without bearing any fruit or performing any service to God, will do nothing except to teach what they practise, namely vileness and bad living, and we are not able to expel them from our kingdoms.

In addition, Senhor, we have need of three or four good masters of grammar, to support those of our people who have begun [to learn] it; [although] we have many people here, both your subjects and ours, who know how to teach reading and writing, it is very necessary to [have people] to demonstrate and describe the items of the holy faith and to explain difficult matters, which these other people generally do not know.

In addition, Senhor [we need], a number of carpenters and masons to finish work on the churches, principally that of Nossa Senhora da Vitória, which we have begun to build to the service and praise of Our Lord God, in a very dense forest where previously the kings were buried according to the old heathen rites. We have cut down and destroyed all this [forest], which was a very difficult thing to do, both because of the ruggedness of the place and because we doubted whether the nobles of our kingdom would consent to it. However, they were so much in agreement that with their own hands they cut down the great, thick trees and carried the stones for this work on their own backs, which appeared to be by divine grace. And so we gave much praise to the Lord God for such a miracle and for the consent in their hearts, for we have no need of lime kilns or men to make lime, because in our kingdoms we have many of our subjects who well know how to do this.

For all these reasons we ask Your Highness, for the love of Jesus Christ, to help and show favour to us in everything that we have said and asked for on many occasions, since it is so great a service to God and to yourself and is a burden on your conscience; and because we only have the power to accomplish what we strive for and do through you. What falls to us to remedy we have carried out and performed without any other assistance, but this thing we are not able to do without the help and favour of Your Highness, and for this we seek a remedy as is our right. We have not requested this from the king of Castile or the king of France or any other Christian king, principally because this responsibility does not belong to them in view of the small part they play in this kingdom. We are loyal to Portugal and to your service, firstly because Your Highness has a right to expect this, and secondly because there is no place for ingratitude in our heart and we acknowledge the many spiritual and corporal benefits we have received....

Notes

1 Dom Manuel I (1495–1521).
2 Dom Henrique, who was consecrated bishop in Rome by Pope Leo X.
3 The Portuguese is *maãos tratos, e fallsas mercadorias*. This should probably be understood metaphorically, as well as being a direct reference to commercial malpractice.
4 These were African sailors from the *lançado* settlements in upper Guinea.
5 Africans from Benin in Nigeria. The use of the term indicates that Portuguese maritime trade had created commercial links between Kongo and Benin. See Doc. 23.

---

42 NOBLE KONGOLESE YOUTHS ARE SENT TO PORTUGAL AND ROME TO BE EDUCATED, 1539

Letter of Dom Afonso I, king of Kongo to Dom João III, 25 March 1539.

António Brásio, *Monumenta Missionaria Africana* (Lisbon, 1952), 2, pp. 73–5.

Original letter in Arquivo Nacional de Torre de Tombo, Corpo Cronológico I-64–71.

Translated by Malyn Newitt.

Afonso, who became king of Kongo in 1506, routinely sent his relatives to Rome and Lisbon to receive an education, and in some cases to take holy orders. This policy was designed to produce an educated class of Christian Kongolese who could supplement and ultimately replace the priests who arrived from Portugal. In 1506 the king sent his son Henrique who took holy orders and became the bishop of Utica in partibus infidelium *and returned to the Kongo in 1521. The king's brother was sent in 1511 and between 1512 and 1516, at least forty young men were sent to Portugal. One of these, whom Dom Afonso described as a nephew of the king, settled in Lisbon and became a teacher. However, this policy had its problems. Once again, Afonso's letters show how unsatisfactory relations with the Portuguese had become, and he refers to the miserable fate of a previous batch of young Kongolese nobles who had been sent to Portugal. The 'nephews' who were sent were both from elite Mwissikongo families and from the Nsaku Lau, and some of them were probably Afonso's own sons. As a result*

*of this policy, an indigenous Kongolese church with its own distinctive character
had emerged by the end of his reign in 1543.*

Six of our relatives go in the company of Dom Manuel, our brother
whom we now send to Rome to offer our obedience (as we have written
to Your Highness through him). Because Your Highness knows their
rank, we write to you so that in this way they may be shown favour
and orders be given for their maintenance. [They are] Dom Manuel
our grandson, son of our daughter, a nobleman with lands and vassals and of the twelve of our Court[1]; and Dom Pedro de Castro[2] who
is our nephew on both sides [of the family], son of a cousin and cousin
of a sister, a person who has already been to that kingdom with the
bishop, Dom Henrique, our son, who is in holy glory. These two men
go in order to remain in the kingdom, where they will learn to read
and write and [to understand] things [necessary] for God's service.
Dom Mateus and Dom Henrique are also our nephews. These two
are ordered to accompany our said brother and ambassador on the
journey to Rome, so that they can bear witness to the good and holy
things which they will see there; and they will learn about them and
speak of them to those who have not seen them. Dom Gonçalo and
Dom Francisco de Meneses,[3] also our nephews and intimates, who
from their extreme youth have been brought up in the church and in
our chapel, go to receive minor orders, and they will learn and in due
time be able to teach others.

We request Your Highness's favour to order them to be made welcome, provided for and treated as our relatives and members of our
lineage, which they are. And we remind you of this and request your
favour for them, so that they can fulfil the orders with which we have
sent them from this kingdom. For during the lifetime of the king, your
father (whom God has in his glory), and at his orders, we sent from this
kingdom to Portugal, through a certain António Vieira, twenty or more
boys, grandsons, nephews and relatives of ours, who were among the
most intelligent, to learn about the service of God, for such was the said
king's intention and desire. António Vieira left some of the said boys in
the land of Pangu a Lungu,[4] our enemy, and these we were later only
able to recover with much difficulty. Others whom he left in the island
of São Tomé came back to us. He took only ten boys to that kingdom [of
Portugal], and to this day we do not know whether they are alive or dead,
or what has become of them or what explanation to give to their parents. We presume that, as it was not known that they were our relatives,
and no one reminded Your Highness of them, they perished and died in
destitution. However, we are hopeful that for these youths there will be
a different remedy, and favour will be shown [to them] by the grace of

Your Highness, whose life and royal estate the Lord God has always in his keeping and whom he preserves for His holy service.

Notes

1   This is probably a reference to the twelve *kanda*, which were matrilineal descent groups, twelve of which constituted the Mwissikongo 'aristocracy' from whom the kings were selected. However, it could just be a reference to another group of twelve that formed the close circle of the king's councellors.
2   The family name of Castro was taken by one branch of the Mwissikongo aristocracy at the time of their original conversion.
3   The name of Meneses was taken by another branch of the Mwissikongo aristocracy at the time of their original conversion.
4   The king calls them 'Pamzuanlumbo'. They occupied the north bank of the Zaire and were not yet incorporated into the Kongo kingdom.

---

43   REPORT OF THE VISIT *AD LIMINA* OF FRANCISCO DE VILLANOVA, BISHOP OF SÃO TOMÉ, 1597

J. Cuvelier and L. Jadin, eds., *L'Ancien Congo d'aprés les archives romaines*, Mémoire de l'Académie des Sciences Coloniales (Brussels, 1954), pp. 473–4. Original Latin manuscript in Archivo Vaticano, Congregationis Concilii, Visitationes, Relationes Sancti Thomae, fls. 236–45.

Translated by Malyn Newitt.

In 1585, Pope Sixtus V laid down the rules to be followed by all bishops when making visits 'ad limina' to Rome to report on the state of their dioceses. The visits were to be preceded by a detailed questionnaire. A separate diocese of São Salvador do Congo had been established in 1596, so this was the last report by a bishop of São Tomé on his undivided diocese, which had been established in 1534 and which stretched from Elmina to the Cape of Good Hope. The state of the Church could hardly be described as thriving and the bishop emphasizes in particular the problem of ill health faced by European priests coming to Africa and the lack of funds to support parishes. This report should be read in conjunction with Doc. 55.

Lisbon, 24 October 1597

…..

34. What is the length and breadth of the diocese and how many benefices does it have?

The island of São Tomé is situated in an African gulf. By the Bull, which established the diocese, all the islands and continental lands from the Cape, called das Palmas 300 leagues distant from the island of São Tomé, were attached to it.[1] It is there that the diocese begins that extends to the Cape of Good Hope. At about 200 leagues or more is to be found the kingdom of Kongo, whose king embraced the Christian faith many years ago. In all this kingdom there are still no more than six parishes,[2] and these are provided by the bishop with priests who can only be removed at his will because without this there would not be any way of governing and administering them.

The principal church is in the town of São Salvador, also called Outeiro, where the king has his royal palace and where he usually resides.[3] This church is served by six or seven priests, who can all be removed. For their subsistence they receive certain grants called tithes, which are paid irregularly and which the king himself allows them. A third of this [income] comes to the bishop, the other two-thirds go to the said ministers. Episcopal jurisdiction is here exercised by a vicar, appointed by the bishop of São Tomé. The king does not submit to the authority and jurisdiction of the ecclesiastics as the law demands. Every time that the said vicar, in accordance with his charge, takes some measure which displeases him, the king at once thinks of sending him into exile, allowing himself to be guided by his tyrannical nature. Before accommodating myself to these barbarous customs, I have been obliged in the space of three years, to remove three vicars without reason and to substitute others in order to prevent the insolences of this uncontrollable man becoming excessive.[4]

I have not yet visited the kingdom in person because the serious illnesses that occur at a time when the journey is possible have prevented me. Instead, many persons worthy of trust, who know the king well, have given me a faithful report and have explained the situation to me. It is such that I cannot make this visit without it compromising my authority and dignity. However, personally I would not have been afraid to carry out my episcopal duty if only my health had permitted it.

I do not give a more detailed description of the kingdom of Kongo because I am assured that a diocese is to be established there for a new bishop

The kingdom of Kongo is bounded by the kingdom of Angola, which is being conquered by our armies at the moment. Two parish churches have already been established there. One of these, served by a removable priest, is located in a little island called by the natives Luanda. The other is situated on the mainland of this kingdom in a place surrounded by the waters of a great river. This place is called Massangano.[5] It is served by a priest who can also be removed. In this island of Luanda there is also a College of the Society of Jesus.

There is no commerce with the inhabitants of the continent anywhere from the kingdom of Luanda to the Cape of Good Hope.

On the mainland near the island of São Tomé, from the Cape das Palmas to the great river called the Zaire, which flows around the greater part of the Kongo, one does not find any Christians except those who live in that place where the fortress of the gold mines of St. George is located. Although this fortress is included within the diocese of São Tomé, it is exempt from its jurisdiction by apostolic concession and is served by priests appointed or sent by the king of Portugal.

In the kingdom of Oeri[6] or Rio dos Forçados, there is no parish church, although the king and a great part of his people are Christian. This arises from the fact that this kingdom is very poor and that ecclesiastics would not be able to subsist there with any convenience and that, in addition, their health and their very lives would be exposed to certain danger because of the great unhealthiness of the climate. At present I am in discussion with His Catholic Majesty to ensure that those who farm the revenues of São Tomé and who travel every year to these parts in pursuit of their commercial interests are obliged to take a suitably paid priest on board their boats to administer the sacraments to those from this kingdom.

The whole continent from the Cape das Palmas to the River Zaire is peopled by the heathen subjects of many black kings with whom our Portuguese compatriots trade with the consent and on the orders of the kings of Portugal.

After my arrival in São Tomé, I sent seven friars of the Order of Saint Francis, whom I had brought out at my expense, to convert them. All my attempts failed. First because the demons who opposed them showed themselves in a visible form and forbade the blacks to answer the missionaries, to speak with them in a familiar way or to follow their salutary advice, even threatening them with punishment if they obeyed them. For their parts, the kings themselves opposed them and did not allow the pagan rites to be abandoned. This conversion failed because of the incapacity of these barbarous natives, who do not know how to read or to be convinced by the arguments of reason. However, this opposition would not succeed in stopping the preaching of the word of God if the present kings of Portugal were as zealous, as formerly their predecessors were, in the pursuit of their principal objective, and particularly if they had been willing to give themselves as much trouble over spiritual conquests, and to pay for them, as is everywhere given for temporal gain.[7]

Christ is only venerated in two of the neighbouring islands, which depend on the diocese of São Tomé. The first is the island called Príncipe, which is situated to the northeast of São Tomé at a distance of twenty-five leagues. There is a town there with a parochial church, which is served by a priest and a coadjutor paid by the king. The second is the island called Annobón, which is in a direct line below São Tomé and distant only four leagues.[8] In that island there is a single Portuguese charged with administering it in the name of the island's proprietor. He has under his orders a hundred black slaves, who are all Christian. Each year a priest, paid for by the proprietor, goes to the island to hear confessions and administer the sacraments. This minister says that in the islands of São Tomé, Príncipe and Annobón, there are no heathen to be found because all those who are brought there are captives who are baptized after their arrival.

Notes

1 The diocese had been established in 1534.
2 A subsequent report in 1600 states that there were 13 parishes. See Heywood and Thornton, *Central Africans, Atlantic Creoles, and the Foundation of the Americas, 1585–1660*, p. 65
3 See Doc. 52.
4 From the beginning, the kings of Kongo had been determined to exercise direct control over the church. Disputes with the bishops were the inevitable result of this. See Doc. 39.
5 Luanda and Massangano had been made parishes in 1590.
6 This was the Itsekiri kingdom, sometimes known as Warri. The ruler was a convert to Christianity, largely to secure his trade with the Portuguese.
7 Under the terms of the papal Bulls, which had established the *padroado real*, the king of Portugal was responsible for the financing of missionary activity in Africa.
8 The actual distance is 110 miles.

---

44 *MALEFICIUM* AND ITS FORMS

Manuel Álvares S. J., *Etiópia Menor e Descrição Geográfica da Província da Serra Leoa*, A. Teixeira da Mota and Luís de Matos, eds., chap. 24.

The original manuscript is located in the Biblioteca da Sociedade de Geografia de Lisboa.[1]

Translation by P. E. H. Hair; revised by Malyn Newitt.

In trying to understand African religion and magical beliefs, Father Álvares, like other missionaries of the time, equated them with European notions of witchcraft. In his eyes, such beliefs and practices were living proof of the work of the devil. This extract shows the Jesuit trying to interpret the different manifestations of maleficium, *as it was understood and even practised in Portugal, and the way it was embedded in African and Cape Verdian society. If African religious beliefs are so distorted as to be barely recognizable in his description, he does clearly point to the importance of sexual initiation in traditional religion. His highly coloured account of these practices in Cape Verde shows, among other things, the extent to which the slaves taken to Santiago had brought with them from the mainland religious practices which, in Álvares's eyes, undermined the orthodoxy of what was supposed to be a Christian society. The Jesuit's misogyny shows through in every sentence of his account, and in particular in the way he interprets the sexual attraction of women as a form of witchcraft. What appears to be the recruitment of young girls into prostitution becomes for him another manifestation of African maleficium.*

Maleficium is the art of doing ill to others by the power of the devil. The ways in which the ill is done are called *maleficium*. They can be divided into two types. The first is *amatório*. It is employed in order to generate sensual feeling in individuals, so that they will wish to perform the sexual act with certain partners and will refuse to do so with others. This gives rise to strife between married couples. This art is widely employed among the heathen of the Serra [Leoa] by means of love potions, and they are skilful at it. They concoct potions from different herbs, and it is sufficient for them to carry these around with them to be loved, not only by women who lack self-control, but by those who normally possess it very strongly. The second type of *maleficium* is *venefacio* or poisoning. This always results in evil. When it is applied to anyone, it kills him or makes him very ill. How frequent this is in Ethiopia! How many deaths result! How many incurable illnesses develop sooner or later, bringing poor pilgrims to their deaths! I have known one man, who, although he was young and strong and of a healthy appearance, was so damaged by the cursed poison that, as well as turning him into a cripple, it forced his mouth to make certain contortions and grimaces that it was astonishing to witness. Today in Guinea there are districts and villages where this vicious and diabolical art reigns, and in which reside those who are suspected of practising it....

Let us continue our list of physical ills. *Maleficium* also causes sexual sterility, as stated in the canonist's chapter 'Concerning Frigidity and *Maleficium*'. As far as *maleficium amatório* is concerned, it must be noted that devils cannot control man's will. The imagination and fancies of man can only be aroused by feeling, which is controlled by the will. Beauty makes the partner appear more lovable and also excites the sexual appetite. But the will always remains free, so that the devil can only persuade and cannot constrain. 'He can bark but not bite', as St. Augustine put it. *Maleficium* does not work by itself. Evil spirits do it all, introducing men to poison or working at their plea or request, but with God's permission.

The other sort of *venefacio*, which harms things, destroying vines and trees, tearing down houses in storms and killing animals, is completely the work of evil spirits, working on the demand of the poisoners. These wretches are such miserable beings that, even when they want to do evil, they cannot do it without the help of their masters. They pay dearly for that service, in that when they make images of wood or other material and beat them or stick pins or needles into them so that the poor wretch feels the blow or the torture in those parts of his body where the image is ill-treated, the feeling of pain does not come from the image which the witch so treats, but from the devil, who by imitating the action, subtly carries out the same on the human body. The truth is that the devil deceives the poisoners themselves.

...

In one of the Cape Verde Islands there were two women skilled in the diabolic art. The devil never tires and is always finding new ways in which he can be worshipped. So it was in the house of the Jolofa[2] woman. In the apartment properly dedicated to rest and repose at night, she entertained him, the enemy of all peace, seated on his throne in fine robes. In this place she kept a large bowl of water, around which a number of candles were kept burning on special days. This wicked woman began to organize a novitiate of poor girls, all of whom she consecrated to the devil. When those girls that seemed to her most suitable passed by her door, she asked them to have a word with her. This they did in innocence. She went on to ask them about their lives and what comforts they enjoyed, although their form of dress showed how very poor they were, and with various yarns she persuaded them, telling them that her only aim was to bring them respect, and that they would lack nothing if they agreed to conform to her principles. What individual would not poverty bring down and reduce to idolatry? The Jolof woman so harried the poor girls that she obtained their consent, and thus their souls and bodies for the evil spirit. She acquired so many followers this way that the devil saw himself well repaid by his devotees. As each girl submitted and joined the group, the first thing the woman did was to order the novice to enter immediately into the infernal room, and then one after the other they came to recognize the devil in this form and to reverence him. After coming into her power these 'nuns' lacked nothing, for she dressed them like the finest women in the island, who now accepted them, although hitherto, they had not noticed them because of their poverty. This wicked woman once pressed one of these innocents whom she thought less drawn to this religion, pointing to the example of those who had already professed it: 'Daughter, have you not seen how Sebastiana has prospered, how she is admired by Mr So-and-so'?

Gain or the hope of gain concludes everything. The poor girl did not resist further but went upstairs and entered the room. There the Lord permitted the novice to see the foot of the abominable host. She invoked the most holy name of Jesus and the enemy disappeared. The Jolof woman was greatly upset, 'Daughter, you have driven away my master'! The girl replied, 'A master who has feet so ugly that his toes are the claws of animals cannot be a good master. For my part I am not willing to serve him'. As the diabolical sorceress was losing the initiative, she praised the enemy and tried to make the girl love the infernal spirit. She reiterated the status of her nuns and the happiness they enjoyed: 'Do you know Miss X? Who do you think arranged her friendship with Canon you-know-who? Or fixed up this girl or that girl with Francisco Y? Or that other girl with Father Z? And those of them who today are decently married, how do you think this was done, if not by the guest of my soul? These daughters of mine keep me alive'. What could the innocent novice do? On feast days, the entire scum of the island danced around the dish and its burning candles, worshipping the enemy of the Lord. When the feast was finished they all left, after each woman had gone alone to speak to this master of filth, and during this time what went on was nothing other than abominable vice between the nuns and the guardian of hell.

This was on regular days, Tuesdays and Fridays. All the 'nuns' wore a sash of woven cords, which was small and tight, the size of a hair shirt. This business continued for seven years. The girls were able not only to appear very beautiful but to obtain from their [earthly] masters whatever they wanted, since they occupied the best apartments in their houses and were mistresses of their hearts.

There was another diabolical woman who did great evil in this island, a renowned sorceress, who by the proper means was recognized and arrested. She was burned, and when the fire was consuming her whole body, this creature of the Lord made haste to touch her secret parts, which caused great astonishment, since even animals are loathe to touch the abominable parts. Enough has been said about this final daughter of superstition.

Notes

1   P. E. H. Hair's translation of Álvares's manuscript was never published because of the death of the editor, Teixeira da Mota (see Doc. 19).
2   More often written as Wolof.

11

THE ANGOLAN WARS

---

45 CONFLICT BETWEEN THE PORTUGUESE AND KONGO IN THE EARLY SEVENTEENTH CENTURY

Summary of a Letter from Dom Pedro,[1] King of Kongo, to Monsignor João Baptista Vivès, São Salvador, 23 November 1623.[2]

J. Cuvelier and L. Jadin, eds., *L'Ancien Congo d'aprés les archives romaines*, Mémoire de l'Académie des Sciences Coloniales (Brussels, 1954), pp. 453–6.

Original in Biblioteca Vaticana, Vat. Lat. 12516, fol 93.

Translated by Malyn Newitt.

This letter (which should be read in conjunction with Doc. 46) from the Kongo king to his ambassador in Rome, reflects a very disturbed period of Kongo – Portuguese relations and also growing conflict within the Portuguese community itself. After years of unsuccessful campaigning on the Cuanza River, the Portuguese had made an alliance with the Imbangala chiefs (the 'Jaga') and, with their support, had begun the conquest not only of territory of the Ngola a Kiluanje, but of the hinterland of Luanda itself. The main objectives of these wars was to destabilize the African kingdoms and obtain captives to send as slaves to Brazil. The governor, João Correia de Sousa, successfully defeated the Mani Kasanze, a tributary of Kongo, executed the chief and exiled his elders to Brazil. When Dom Pedro succeeded to the throne of Kongo in 1622, he was not recognized by the Portuguese, who took the opportunity to invade the kingdom. The Portuguese and Imbangala army overran Mbamba, and won a major victory in which the Manimbamba and ninety of the Mwissikongo aristocracy were killed, although they were subsequently defeated with the arrival of the main Kongolese forces. Following this defeat, a number of the Portuguese in Kongo were massacred and urgent petitions were sent by the rest to Luanda for the governor to halt his campaign. What was virtually an insurrection then broke out in Luanda, and on the return of the governor's army, the rebels took refuge with the Jesuits who protested strongly against the conduct of the governor. This protest led to their imprisonment and exile to Brazil, though two of them escaped to Kongo. As a consequence of these events the governor was forced to relinquish his office and leave the country.[3] As a result of this war, Dom Pedro made diplomatic overtures to the Dutch.

The founding of the see of the Kongo in 1596 had not helped Portuguese–Kongo relations as the bishops usually resided at Luanda and challenged the Kongo king's control of the church in his kingdom and even the control of his private chapel. The Kongo king wanted to have the final say in the appointment of the bishops and tried to negotiate directly with Rome behind the backs of the Portuguese. He eventually succeeded in having his private chapel recognized as an institution separate from the chapter of the Cathedral of São Salvador. The two Jesuits remained in Kongo, and in 1625 founded a Jesuit College there, providing the king with independent access to Rome and Madrid.

He [Dom Pedro] mentions letters written and orders given immediately after his accession.

He offers obedience to His Holiness.[4] He says that he has taken steps to obtain all the favours that his predecessor Dom Álvaro III had asked for.[5] By letters sent by two different routes, he has given an account of his chapel, asking for exemption from the jurisdiction of the Ordinary and all the privileges which royal chapels and their ecclesiastics usually obtain. He is surprised not to have received any replies.

At the end of last July [1623], two Fathers of the Company of Jesus,[6] who had fled from Luanda because of the persecution of the governor of the conquest of Angola, João Correia de Sousa, reached him.[7] He had had the rector and other Fathers of the College of this port of Luanda imprisoned and subsequently had them put on board a ship, on the pretext that in their sermons they had reproved the governor for the tyrannies and scandals he had committed in this Christian kingdom of Kongo, which he had invaded with an army of more than two hundred thousand Jagas who fed on human flesh. There was, in addition, the Portuguese army which was in Angola. During a period of … ,[8] he had ravaged and destroyed a number of provinces where an infinite number of Christians had been killed and eaten. In addition many had been reduced to slavery. Moreover, this governor with his army of Jagas and Portuguese had attacked the duke of Mbamba who was accompanied by the marquis of Mpemba and other *fidalgos*. All were killed and eaten. After this event, the king set out with his army putting all the Christians at risk.

The above-mentioned Fathers of the Company reached the king of Kongo and delivered to him a little box of the Agnus Dei sent by the pope to his predecessor.[9]

He acknowledges the receipt of a brief written to his predecessor, but he has had no letters from Vivès, which astonished him. He thinks they must have been intercepted, as happened the previous year with the briefs of Paul V[10] granting indulgences to his royal chapel. These briefs were opened by the governor João Correia, who read them out in public. After this, he fabricated criminal proceedings against the king's confessor Bras Correia, on the pretext that he had persuaded the said king to write to the pope and to have direct relations with him, saying that that was to the discredit of His Catholic Majesty.[11] [One wonders] How can these relations be reprehensible, since they are religious, Catholic and very old,[12] having begun with the first establishment of Christianity in this country and continued with the sending of ambassadors and private letters.

The collector of Portugal should be notified that he should take precautions to send letters by the route and by the means indicated to Monsignor Coramboni, the previous collector, and as the above-mentioned confessor has specified.

He is making a report to His Holiness of all these events and of the human greed [behind them]; and that he considers that the interventions of His Holiness with His Catholic Majesty, of which Vivès has made mention, has produced little effect for this kingdom, since the governors of Angola, together with these barbarians, do nothing less than destroy Christianity.

The king has decided to send an ambassador to the pope and to the Catholic king.

Frightened by the indignation of the people, the governor took ship and abandoned the government of Angola.

Shortly afterwards, Dom Frei Simon Mascarenhas, the new bishop of Kongo, arrived and accepted the secular governorship of Angola.[13] He accepted this post without going to visit this capital and without residing there, although his pontifical see was there. One might imagine that he would have helped us, etc. ... but he became the governor and chaplain to a whole army of Jaga barbarians, heathens who, united with the Portuguese, do nothing but destroy everything they meet.

That Vivès should act in such a way that what has been asked for should be obtained. It is now many years since there has been a bishop. However, Vivès had written to his predecessor that all had been arranged. One can see from the letters of the collector, Antonio Albergati,[14] that the matter has deviated a long way from the direction outlined in the negotiations with Vivès.

The king recommends to Vivès all that his predecessor had instructed. He ratifies and confirms everything.

On his part, he kisses the feet of His Holiness and asks for his blessing. He excuses himself for not having written to His Holiness, as he has been overwhelmed with his afflictions. He hopes to be able to do this by special messengers, which he soon intends to send to Spain.

Written in Kongo, 28 November 1623.

King Dom Pedro

Notes

1 Dom Pedro (Nkanga Mpemba) ruled 1622–4.
2 Vivès is described as 'apostolic protonotary' and the king's 'ambassador in Rome'. The letter was received in Rome September of 1624.
3 The most detailed account of these events is given in Louis Jadin, *Relations sur le Congo et l'Angola tirées des archives de la Compagnie de Jésus, 1621–1631*, Academia Belgica (Rome, 1968) extract from *Bulletin de l'Institut historique belge de Rome* 39 (1968) pp. 338–349.
4 In 1623 the Pope was Gregory XV (1621–3).
5 Dom Álvaro III (Nimi Mpanzu) ruled 1615–22.
6 Father Duarte Vaz and Brother Gaspar Álvares.
7 Governor of Angola 1621–3.
8 Left blank in the original.
9 Possibly a portable altar with an image of the Lamb of God.
10 Paul V was pope 1605–21.
11 Brás Correia was a Spanish priest who had gone to Kongo in 1606. He held various ecclesiastical appointments and rose to become head of the king's Council and of the king's private chapel. Expelled from the Kongo in 1625, he entered the Society of Jesus and offered his services to the king of Spain to plan the conquest of the mines in the Kongo kingdom. He died in 1632. For details of his biography see Beatrix Heintze, *Fontes para a História de Angola do século XVII*, Franz Steiner Verlag (Suttgart, 1985) pp. 83–4.
12 In other words 'long-established'.
13 He was appointed bishop of Angola and Congo in 1621, was ordained 1623 and arrived in Luanda in August. He died October of 1624.
14 Probably the Bishop of Bisceglie who became Papal Nuncio in Germany and Madrid.

---

46 THE LIFE OF DOM PEDRO II AFONSO

Letter of Cordeiro, Canon of Kongo, to Father Manuel Rodrigues of the Luanda College, 1624.

J. Cuvelier and L. Jadin, eds., *L'Ancien Congo d'aprés les archives romaines*, Mémoire de l'Académie des Sciences Coloniales (Brussels, 1954), pp. 473–4.

Original in Biblioteca de Évora, Codice CXVI 2–15, no. 7.

Translated by Malyn Newitt.

This letter, which should be read in conjunction with Doc. 45, gives a good idea of the struggle between the rival patrilineages for control of the Kongo kingdom. This political instability was being ruthlessly exploited by the Luanda Portuguese, who were steadily annexing territory on the southern borders of Kongo. The Kongo kingdom, however, still maintained the trappings of Portuguese Christian culture, which dated back to the end of the fifteenth century. The leading aristocracy bore Portuguese names and titles, and the institutions of the church still provided a focus for power. Habits of the Order of Christ were even sought by the Kongo aristocracy, and later in the century a specifically Kongolese Order of Christ came into existence as a religious congregation reserved for the aristocracy.

[Dom Pedro II Afonso] was the legitimate son of the duke of Nsundi, Dom Afonso Mbika a Ntumba, and of Dona Cristina of the very noble house of Sonyo, grand-daughter of the counts of that country.[1] He was grandson of Dona Anna Ntumba Mbemba, daughter of king Afonso I, who was the mother of Dom Afonso Mbika Ntumba, duke of Nsundi.

He was always a strong Christian, God-fearing, humble and pious. However, he was persecuted, above all by the duke of Mbamba, António da Silva,[2] who wished him dead and tried to kill him, levelling accusations against him in order to make him hated by the king. He was twice banished and twice had everything taken from him. He was often imprisoned and was once publicly humiliated in the main square of Kongo.

He bore everything with a Christian spirit, which made him so dear to the king that, as a consequence, he received honours from him. He was made marquis of Wembo and knight of the Order of Christ, and given one of the habits which the king of Portugal had sent. He was named duke of Mbamba.[3] False accusations were again brought against him, so that the king was on the point of removing his dukedom from him. The governor João Correia de Sousa tried to discredit him so that he would not become king.[4]

However, to the great happiness of all, he was elected king on 26 May 1622, the feast of Corpus Christi. He had his tribulations. In August of the same year, João, the duke of Mbata, was killed along with his *fidalgos*, and the king of Okanga, who was his vassal, was conquered by one of his own men who revolted. The governor, João Correia de Sousa, claimed the copper mines in all the kingdom, and all the land from the Dande to Luanda was recognized as his, and also the island of Luanda. The Portuguese, aided by the Jaga, destroyed the district of Nambu a Ngongo, his vassal.[5]

On the 18th of December, the same governor sent his troops to Bumbe where the duke, Dom Paulo Afonso, was killed, along with the marquis of Mpemba, Dom Cosme, and many other *fidalgos*. All these were buried in the bellies of those barbarous Jagas. There followed a massacre of the Portuguese who lived in Bembe, and the king had great difficulty in saving those who were in his kingdom.

In public he was called the king of the Portuguese. For three months he went to fight the Portuguese and Jagas who had invaded his kingdom. He rejoiced very much at the arrival of the Jesuits, whose superior was Father Duarte Vaz.[6] Captain Sylvestre Soares destroyed Ngombe and Cabenda with an army of Jagas. The kingdom of Vungu was destroyed.[7] He gave a great celebration to mark the arrival of Bishop Mascarenhas.[8]

He fell ill on Easter Saturday and on the Tuesday after Easter was confessed. He died on Saturday, 13 April, age 49. He reigned in all two years less forty-two days and was buried in the church of Saint Anthony on the south side of the altar.

Notes

1   On his mother's side, he was descended from the important Silva patrilineage, which had ruled in Sonyo. The name Afonso after his title indicated his father's patrilineage. He was the grandson of a daughter of Afonso I. For personal details see Adriano Parreira, *Dicionário de Biografias Angolanas séculos XV-XVII* (Luanda, 2003) pp. 182–3.
2   Head of the Silva patrilineage. He had secured the throne for Álvaro III in 1615 and, although he led an unsuccessful rebellion the next year, the king eventually made peace and married his daughter.
3   Mbamba and Wembo were the two southernmost provinces of the kingdom and were directly contiguous to the Portuguese governorship of Luanda.
4   See Doc. 45.
5   This war and the Jesuit protest are described in Doc. 45. It represented a major assault by the Luanda Portuguese on the southern marches of the Kongo kingdom.
6   See Doc. 45.
7   Vungu was located on the River Zaire.
8   Dom Frei Simon Mascarenhas (see Doc. 45).

47   AN ESSEX MAN IN THE ANGOLAN WARS

From E. G. Ravenstein, ed., *The Strange Adventures of Andrew Battell of Leigh* (London, Hakluyt Society, 1901), pp. 36–9.

The story of Andrew Battell's eighteen years spent as a soldier in Angola was first published in 1625 in Purchas His Pilgrimes. *Battell was an English sailor*

*who was taken prisoner by the Portuguese. He was a captive of the Imbangala
in 1600–01 and witnessed their cannibalism. He also served as a soldier in the
Portuguese army during the governorship of João Rodrigues Coutinho and
spent some time trading on the Loango coast. His account is that very rare
thing, a narrative by an ordinary soldier and sailor. In this extract he describes
the Portuguese campaigns that eventually led to the conquest of the Kisama
salt mines and the legendary mountain of Cambambe. This was the first major
victory for the Portuguese in the wars that had been continuing already for
nearly twenty-five years. He refers to the fact that Coutinho combined the position of governor with the contract to supply slaves to Brazil, and shows how the
Portuguese operated through attracting African volunteers to their armies and
winning over the chiefs of the Cuanza region to their cause.*

*Battell's account of his trading expedition to Loango graphically describes the
position of European traders, valued 'guests' while they were active and alive,
but a serious threat to the welfare of the people if their dead bodies remained in
the land.*

Being departed from the Gagas,[1] I came to Masangano, where
the Portugals have a town of garrison. There was at that time a new
Governor, which was called Sienor Iuan Coutinho,[2] who brought authority to conquer the mines or mountains of Cambamba; and to perform
that service, the King of Spain had given him seven years' custom of all
the slaves and goods that were carried thence to the West Indies, Brazil,
or whithersoever, with condition that he should build three castles, one
in Demba,[3] which are the salt mines, the other in Cambamba, which
are the silver mines, and the other in Bahia das Vaccas, or the Bay of
Cows.[4]

This gentleman was so bountiful at his coming that his fame was
spread through all Congo, and many mulatoes and negroes came
voluntarily to serve him. And being some six months in the city, he
marched to the Outaba of Tombe, and there shipped his soldiers in
pinnaces, and went up the river Consa or Coanza and landed at the
Outaba of Songo sixty miles from the sea. This lord Songo is next to
Demba, where the salt mines be. In this place there is such store of salt,
that most part of the country are perfect clear salt, without any earth
or filth in it, and it is some three feet under the earth as [if] it were ice;
and they cut it out in stones of a yard long, and it is carried up into the
country, and is the best commodity that a man can carry to buy anything whatsoever.

Here the Governor staid ten days, and sent a pinnace to Masangano
for all the best soldiers that were there. So the captain of the castle sent
me down among a hundred soldiers, and I was very well used by the
Governor; and he made me a sergeant of a Portugal company, and then

he marched to Machimba,[5] from thence to Cauo, and then to Malombe, a great lord. Here we were four days, and many lords came and obeyed us. From thence we marched to a mighty lord called Angoykayongo,[6] who stood in the defence of his country with more than sixty thousand men. So we met with him, and had the victory, and made a great slaughter among them. We took captives all his women and children, and settled ourselves in his town, because it was a very pleasant place, and full of cattle and victuals. And being eight days in this town, the Governor sickened and died, and left a captain in his room to perform the service.

[*Manuel Cerveira Pereira Who Was Governor 1603–07, Carries on the War*]

After we had been two months in the country of Angoykayongo we marched towards Cambambe, which was but three days' journey, and came right against the Serras da Prata, and passed the river Coanza, and presently overran the country, and built a fort hard by the riverside. Here I served two years.

They opened the silver mines, but the Portugals did not like of them as yet, because they yielded small share of silver.

This new up-start governor was very cruel to his soldiers, so that all his voluntary men left him; and by this means he could go no further.

At this time, there came news by the Jesuits that the Queen of England was dead, and that King James had made peace with Spain.[7] Then I made a petition to the Governor, who granted me licence to go into my country; and so I departed with the Governor and his train to the city of St Paul.[8] But he left five hundred soldiers in the fort of Cambambe, which they hold still.

[*A Trading Trip to Congo*]

Then I went with a Portugal merchant to the province of Bamba, and from thence to Outeiro, or city standing upon a mountain of Congo,[9] from thence to Gongon and Batta,[10] and there we sold our commodities and returned in six months to the city again.

. . . .

[*The Royal Tombs*]

There is a place two leagues from the town of Longo,[11] called Longeri,[12] where all their kings be buried, and it is compassed round about with elephant's teeth pitched in the ground, as it were a Pale, and it is ten roods in compass

[*Europeans Committed to the Sea*]

These people will suffer no white man to be buried in their land, and if any stranger or Portugal come thither to trade, and chance to die, he is carried in a boat two miles from the shore, and cast into the sea. There was once a Portugal gentleman, that came to trade with them, and had his house on shore. This gentleman died, and was buried some four months. That year it did not rain so soon as it was wont, which beginneth about December, so that they lacked rain for some two months. Then their *mokisso* told them that the Christian, which was buried, must be taken out of the earth, and cast into the sea; and within three days it rained, which made them have a great belief in the devil.

Notes

1 Imbangala.
2 João Rodrigues Coutinho was governor 1601–3.
3 The Kisama salt mines.
4 Benguela.
5 Possibly Muxima, where the Portuguese had a fort.
6 Agoacaiongo, a Christian chief.
7 The peace with Spain was signed 19 August 1604.
8 Luanda.
9 São Salvador, the capital of Kongo (see Doc. 51).
10 Ngongo and Mbata.
11 Loango.
12 Loangele was still a royal burial ground in the nineteenth century.

---

48 WAR IN THE REED BEDS – ANGOLA AFTER THE EXPULSION OF THE DUTCH

From António de Oliveira Cadornega, *História Geral das Guerras Angolanas*, 3 vols. (Lisbon, 1972), 2, pp. 24–30.
Translated by Malyn Newitt.

The Dutch West India Company had seized control of Luanda in 1641 to use it as a base to provide slaves for its colony in northern Brazil. Many African rulers took the opportunity of allying with the Dutch to free themselves from

Portuguese control. After Salvador Correa de Sá e Benevides had achieved the expulsion of the Dutch from Luanda in August of 1648, the Portuguese set about settling scores with the rulers who had sided with the Dutch. Cadornega describes how a Portuguese army was made up at that time: professional soldiers, local backwoodsmen and settlers with their slaves, friendly sobas and the guerra preta – the black mercenaries that made up the core of the Portuguese armed forces in west Africa. The campaign that is described is surely one of the most bizarre in the long history of the Angolan wars, but it illustrates how difficult the conquest of Angola was proving to be. Cadornega loved to enrich his narrative with references to medieval and classical history, about which he had somehow managed to learn while serving in Angola. In doing so, he was equating the wars in Africa with earlier struggles which formed part of the epic of Portuguese history. However, his prose style is far from classical and the translator often has to be content with worrying out the author's meaning rather than giving an exact rendering of his language.

Seeing that there was a need to punish the insults of the heathen, a majority of whom had sided with the Dutch in their hatred of the Portuguese nation, advice was taken and it was decided to go to war. To organize and carry it out, Vicente Pegado da Ponte, a person of valour and experience from among the original conquistadors of these kingdoms, was appointed *capitão-mor* and Diogo Gomes de Sampayo was appointed *sargento-mor* of this enterprise, a person of experience in the wars of the interior. He was given backwoodsmen as his captains, with infantry and settlers skilled and experienced in the wars of conquest of this kingdom, together with artillery, arms and the necessary munitions. The *tandala* of the kingdom[1] and the *capitão-mor* of the *guerra preta*, who at this time was Diogo Dias Mendes, went with his weapons of war, together with the Kilambas and the *kabuko* Jaga[2] and slaves of the Portuguese. With this army the *capitão-mor*, who had been elected by the city, set out. After only a few leagues he went in search of a powerful *soba* who had a valiant reputation, called Pangi a Ndona, whose lands were situated on the Nsaka de Kasanze, which had been conquered by the governor João Correia de Sousa as we mentioned in the first volume. He was the descendant of the ruler who had been called Casangi and from whom the conquest had been made.[3] This powerful ruler had a large and loyal following of neighbouring *sobas* who, since they were all guilty of having acted in an evil way, wanted to unite to defend themselves in opposition to our arms.

Because of the formidable power that he had, [Pangi a Ndona] was very arrogant and boastful as he waited for our army. When they [the armies] came in sight of one another, they joined in a bloody conflict and battle, both parties fighting with valour, and with dead and wounded on each side. The enemy was in the better position to defend themselves and to attack our men with many shots from their firearms. These had been supplied to them, together with a lot of ammunition, by the Dutch out of hostility and hatred towards us, and they had taught them how to handle the firearms, not seeing or understanding that these skills might one day do them damage. The battle and combat continued with very great resistance [from the enemy], but the courage of the Portuguese prevailed, and at the end of some hours, the enemy's position was breached and the brave Pangi a Ndona was killed with many of his men, while others were taken prisoner.

This was a good beginning to the punishment which he had so much deserved. However, a large part of the baggage and the women escaped from this conflict, together with the army, which fled cross the River Bengo and reassembled near the River Dande on the *mabus* islands.[4] There they were situated on the waters of a great lake, which is made by the river making a wide bend, where some of the *sobas*, foreseeing their defeat, had already placed their baggage and their women. When the *capitão-mor* heard of the rout suffered by those who had escaped, he marched after them with his camp and all his forces, but he found himself blocked by the reeds and quagmires which nature had produced in those marshes. The islands were made of that material, connected one to the other with thickly intertwined roots which would not sink whatever weight was placed on them. Rather they continually moved on the water from one part to another according to the movement of the wind, which made the place appear enchanted or magical.

This so-called *mabus* is a kind of thick straw, which is produced by those roots through the humidity of the water and the mud in which it has its roots. It is much thicker than the sedge of Portugal from which they make mats and fishing rods. The material produced by these marshes is so thick and closely packed that it grows straight up like cane brakes, and it is so dense that in the middle of it, there are clearings where these heathen have their houses and lodgings. This sort of *mabus* is very green, and they cover their houses and make mats with it. In order to make use of it, they make large piles months before, leaving them there cut down until they are quite dry from the sun. Then they take them and bind them into bundles.

The *capitão-mor* perceived the trap into which he had driven the quarry, and to hunt it down he informed the general[5] back in the city of the difficulties he was having in getting [the people on] those extensive *mabus* to surrender. He [the general] ordered that the war should be prosecuted and that they should be besieged until they surrendered, carrying on the war in every part with all the ferocity he could. All this the *capitão-mor* did, obeying the order of the general. He ordered the whole circumference of the lake to be surrounded, thereby depriving them of the means to leave to seek what was necessary for their sustenance after they had consumed all that had been accumulated in that humid abode. The posts were divided among the people of most importance, both chiefs and captains, the *capitão-mor* taking for himself the position of greatest danger, from where he issued the necessary orders. And from all the positions they put pressure on the enemy with discharges of artillery and musketry and, as some thickets were distant from the land, our people went in canoes to seek them out. However, on reaching them we suffered many casualties in dead and wounded, especially when, with the evening breeze, the islands moved from one place to another. For when the thickets of reeds were blown along by the wind, they were blown on to our canoes and sank them because they did not have any place to which to escape.

I have already said that this appeared to be magical, because one morning all those thickets would appear to be little islands all in one place, and in the evening would be moved to another by the wind and the sea breeze getting up. We killed many of them even though they were not clearly visible to our men because they were so completely hidden by the said *mabus*. Afterwards we were able to see what our arms had achieved for, although they could see our men, we could not see them. This siege had already lasted some months, and the captain and chiefs saw that we were doing them little damage, because we did not have boats able to reach the thickets, and the artillery did not have the range to knock them down. So the *capitão-mor* informed the general of the state of this enterprise, of the unwillingness of the enemy to surrender, and of what was lacking to bring to a conclusion this so-called war of the *mabus*, which was so hotly contested. The general ordered that some boats armed with artillery of good calibre and with sufficient munitions should be sent from the city because those which had been brought by the captain had already been consumed in the many combats. When the boats arrived they entered by the bar of the River Dande and began to unload the artillery and other implements of war. A platform was built at a site that was most suitable for bombarding the whole of that distant lake and its thickets, which might well be called bastions because of the resistance that its defenders put up and not because they were made from any fixed material.

The boats were floated on the estuary which the current of the River Dande made in that lake, and armed men were embarked on them, both those who had come in them from the city and those who had taken part in the siege, bringing with them their shields so that they could move with less risk. In this way they began to put pressure on those who were surrounded and besieged in those places where they could be attacked, firing the artillery very accurately from their stations. Our fighters avoided being attacked, making use of the shields which they had brought in the boats. So these marshes came to look like an infernal lake from the confusion, smoke, fire, stench of putrefaction of the waters which were drying out, and the shouts from the people in the thickets, who seemed like demons in human flesh but who were heathen idolaters, which came to be almost the same thing. All this was a representation of hell itself. We can compare the savage confusion which reigned in those thickets and which had overtaken the green *mabus*, to that which is represented by that Comic Poet.[6] But why do we have to look for poetic fictions when we have real sights with which to compare them?

It is written in the life of our first king, Dom Afonso Henriques, that at that time there was a Portuguese vassal of great strength and valour called Giraldo the Fearless, who had fallen into disfavour with the king.[7] Many vassals in similar circumstances find themselves in a very dangerous situation. Together with other Portuguese who accompanied him, he desired to undertake some deed against the Moors worthy of his great valour, by means of which he would regain the favour of [the person] who had disgraced him. Having learned from his spies that the army of the Moors had withdrawn from the city of Évora where it had been, he decided that this would be the enterprise which he had desired so that he could carry out what had been decided by the king. Being in sight of the city, he ordered some green brushwood to be carried, among whose leaves he and his men hid themselves. A Moor who was watching from a tower above the principal gate of the city, growing tired of acting as sentry, lay down to sleep, leaving his daughter who was with him to watch while he slept. The valorous Portuguese, hidden in the branches with his companions, began to stagger towards the city with his disguise. When the daughter observed this she awoke her sleeping father saying, 'Father, the brushwood is walking'. The father came to the window or look-out point, and when the adventurer saw that it was the Moor, he stopped. Then, as the Moor did not see any branches or brushwood move, he returned to sleep. So they began once again to move forward, coming each time closer, at which the female sentry turned to awaken her father. He was angry and looked out but, as he did not see the brushwood move, he became angry with his daughter who had awakened him without his being able to see why. Then Giraldo, seeing that the Moor did not molest him but went back to watch as before, overcome once again with sleep, realized that in this way God was making it possible for Catholic people and not Arian Moors to seize and govern that noble and populous city, which formerly had been ennobled by the Romans, who had made there a colony where the brave and energetic Sertorius, who gave so much to the Romans, had lived.[8]

That prolonged and confused war of the *mabus* almost turned out the same way, and it was necessary for the captains of the boats and canoes to be very vigilant, because when the breeze blew, the thickets bore down on them with such great force that they had to take rapid evasive action. 'Captain, the thickets are coming' [was the cry] to escape the danger and not to be submerged, just as the Moorish girl said to her sentry father, 'Father, the brushwood is walking'. In the former case this favoured the Christians, and in the latter those who were not. I will not finish my history by padding out my account of the end of this enterprise. It is known by all that Giraldo the Fearless in this way captured the famous city of Évora, and in our time his picture is still displayed on the main gate of that noble and most ancient city in memory of such a great triumph.

The besieged continued to defend themselves with excessive obstinacy, eating the very roots of the *mabus* and other disgusting things, but seeing that they were already in miserable circumstances, lacking all necessities, and were now hard pressed by our men, they surrendered. Many, however, were not able to do this, as they were already dead, which we discovered after their surrender, because until then the damage had not been openly known. Many who had the strength to do so fled, for as the area was so large, it could not be surrounded to prevent their escape. Of those who remained, principally the women and children, many died after surrendering because of the great hunger they had suffered. With this ended the war and campaign of the *mabus*, which the valour of the Portuguese brought to a conclusion with so much effort and trouble, but, as the outcome was what was desired, all the fatigues afterwards appeared light.

Notes

1   The *Tendella do Reyno* was the chief interpreter. The title was used in both the kingdoms of Kongo and Ndongo for a senior official, described by Thornton as 'a sort of viceroy with authority to rule in the king's absence and to handle day-to-day business' (Heywood and Thornton, *Central Africans, Atlantic Creoles, and the Foundation of the Americas, 1585–1660*, p. 75).

2   According to Miller, the *kabuku ka ndonga*, who was an Imbangala warlord, fought for the Portuguese against the Dutch and in this war against Pangi a Ndona, and was given the title of 'Jaga' by the Portuguese. In 1652, he was exiled to Brazil by the Portuguese, who believed he had been negotiating with their enemy Queen Nzinga,

but he was recalled and served with the Portuguese in campaigns in the 1660s and in the ill-fated raid on Sonyo in 1670 (see Doc. 51).

3   This territory, called by Cadornega Ensaca de Casangi, was known as Nsaka de Kasanze. For its conquest, see Doc. 45.

4   *Mabus*, from the Mbundu *dibu*, were papyrus reeds.

5   The general was Salvador Correa de Sá e Benavides, who had commanded the armada that recaptured Luanda.

6   Cadornega uses the phrase 'Poeta Comico'. He could be referring to Dante's *Inferno* which was part of the *Divina Commedia*.

7   Giraldo sem Pavor (Giraldo the Fearless) captured Évora from the Moors in 1166.

8   Quintus Sertorius was a Republican general belonging to Marius's party. He held Hispania against Sulla and later Pompey and was eventually murdered in 72 BC.

---

49   ACCOUNT OF THE BATTLE OF MBWILA, 1665

'Relação da mais glorioza e admiravel uictoria que alcançarão as armas de ElRey D. Affonso 6° Neste Reino de Angola, contra ElRey de Congo gouernando o senhor André Vidal de Negreiros,'

António Brásio, *Monumenta Missionaria Africana* (Lisbon, 1952), 12, pp. 582–91.

Original Manuscript in British Library Add. MSS 20,953, fols. 227–229.

Translated by Malyn Newitt.

The author of this account is unknown but he appears to have been a resident of Luanda. The manuscript was originally published in 1960 by C.R.Boxer,[1] who claimed he had used the 'utmost rigour' in transcribing the text. António Brásio was very critical of this version, which he considered to be highly inaccurate. He added the following note on Boxer's version to his own transcription: 'From the notes appended to the text, the "rigour" observed in maintaining the orthography can be judged, quite apart from the other errors that we have shown, to be evidently errors of typography'.

During the early part of the seventeenth century, the relations between the Luanda Portuguese and the Kongo kingdom deteriorated as the Portuguese governors challenged the supremacy of the Kongo over the small Mbundu kingdoms to the north of Luanda, one of which was Mbwila. As the bishop of Kongo resided in Luanda, the Angolan Portuguese were also able to exert control over the Kongo Church. The Kongo king tried to open direct links with Rome, which the Portuguese chose to treat as a challenge to their authority. When the Dutch attacked Luanda in 1641, the king of Kongo sided with the invaders in the hope of expelling the Luanda Portuguese for good. There was also a suspicion that, after the revolt of Portugal against Spain, he had contacted Madrid to establish an alliance against Portugal. It is not surprising, therefore, that the Portuguese looked for an opportunity to settle scores with an erstwhile ally who now represented the main obstacle to their dominance of the region south of the Zaire river.

A casus belli was found in the alleged refusal of the king to surrender mines in his kingdom to Portugal (see Doc. 40), but the immediate occasion of the war was a disputed succession in the small kingdom of Mbwila, with rival factions appealing to Luanda and Kongo for aid. The battle of Mbwila has usually been seen as the moment when the Kongo kingdom went into terminal decline. Although the Kongolese won a notable victory over the Portuguese shortly afterwards (see Doc. 50), succession to the kingdom now became more frequently disputed and the authority of the king weakened. The Portuguese based in Luanda increasingly dominated the region and gradually reduced the remaining quasi-independent kingdoms to the position of client states supplying the Atlantic slave trade.

A striking feature of this account is the role played by Brazilians. Ever since Angola had been won back from the Dutch by Salvador de Sá, the links with Brazil had been strong. The governor, André Vidal de Negreiros and his predecessor, João Fernandes Vieira, both came from Brazil and the Portuguese forces in Angola were now regularly reinforced by Brazilian soldiers among whom were blacks and Indians. As Brazil was the destination for the lucrative Angolan slave trade, the south Atlantic was rapidly becoming a Portuguese lake.

God our Lord continued to give good fortune to André Vidal de Negreiros[2] through the intercession of the Most Holy Virgin of Nazareth, his protector. And with reason this can be called the good fortune of all good fortunes, since our kingdom of Portugal had such a great interest in it. Because, in reality, this led to the true restoration of our kingdom of Angola, since at this time all these kingdoms were being weakened by Kongo, and even those we thought of as favourable to us were plotting the total ruin of the Portuguese nation.

The senhor governor was in the fourth year of his government and was expecting his successor to come to relieve him of the labours of warfare.[3] In May 1664, His Majesty, whom God preserve, sent him aid from Lisbon, Pernambuco and Bahia, which amounted to 650 men because of the fear which the Castilian enemy had caused by announcing that he was coming to invade this kingdom,[4] and with this aid came a letter and orders from His Majesty that the gold mines should be discovered, which the king [of Kongo], Dom Álvaro, had promised to the Queen Regent, Dona Caterina of Portugal, in exchange for aid which had been sent to him against the Jaga, who had expelled him from his kingdom.[5] And with the said aid, he had recovered his kingdom. At the time nothing was done about these mines because of the death of king Dom Sebastião and because Castile had taken possession of Portugal and was concerned rather with its own affairs than with ours.

The said governor felt himself obliged to obey the orders of His Majesty and also the petitions of the Senado da Câmara[6] of this city and of its citizens, who had persuaded him to [undertake] such a discovery, because of the great benefits which they hoped to obtain from it. So he wrote to the king of Kongo, called Dom António I,[7] that he should hand over to him the mines, which he was obliged to do as his ancestors had promised, and also because of the agreements which the king of Kongo, Dom Garcia his father,[8] had made with the governor, João Fernandes Vieira.[9] To this he responded, replying through his canons[10] in a noncommittal fashion, that nothing was due from his mines and that they did not contain gold. [The governor] sent a second message that he should look to the surrender of the mines, which he was obliged to do by the treaties, and that investigation of them should be carried out so that our illusions might be removed and he might satisfy his obligations. If he would not do this, infantry would be sent to discover them. He replied twice through the said canons that the mines had some gold but only a little, and that he had considered this and they were his and he had to defend them. This reply was [considered] insolent, and it was said that he must have written to Castile to come and take this city with his help and that he had shown all the advantages which would result from this victory, and that he sought to join forces with Castile to gain that which the said governor had intended to obtain.

With the second note from the king of Kongo, news also reached the city that the Castilians had changed their intentions. So the governor took 200 soldier scouts[11] from the garrison, with a further 150 settlers from there and from Massangano and Ambaca and Cambambe,[12] who together amounted to 366 men, and from these he formed ten companies and appointed as captains Manuel Nunes Barreto, Baltasar Luís Pimentel, António Barreto, Gomes Pegado da Ponte,[13] Domingos Francisco, Fernão Pinto, Simão Francisco Frade, Leonardo Ferreira, Lourenço Martins, António d'Araújo Cabreira (who came from the garrison at Ambaca with Baltasar Luís Pimentel), Manuel Soares from the regiment[14] of Henrique Dias, who came with help from Pernambuco as *sargento-mor*,[15] Manuel Rebelo as *capitão-mor* of the *guerra preta*, Simão de Matos, who brought 3,000 archers and 100 *empacaseiros*[16] and musketeers, and as *capitão-mor* of the whole army Luís Lopes de Sequeira,[17] who commanded the army and had orders that he was to discover the gold mines and not to do any harm to the king of Kongo or to his vassals, but that if the said king came to seek them out, they should defend themselves and fight with him.

The king did not ignore the warnings that he received through messages from this city, where there were traitors everywhere. He at once sent a proclamation through his kingdom notifying all his vassals and chiefs, under grave penalties, that they should accompany him in this war which he wished to wage against the whites, and he assembled in all 100,000 men, among whom were 800 with shields and *trasados*[18] and 190 musketeers and a company of whites drawn from those present at his Court under their captain, Pedro Dias de Cabrada,[19] his captain of arms, a mulatto born in the Kongo. He brought more than 150,000 men who carried the baggage and with this great force, he came in search of our army, which awaited him in the lands of Mbwila,[20] our vassal, who had pledged his allegiance in the time of the governor, Salvador Correa de Sá. He had refused obedience to the Kongo to which he had previously owed his allegiance. [Meanwhile] our army had still not left a place called Camalemba, which was twenty leagues from this city, where it had assembled prior to marching thither.

The king of Kongo sent his ambassadors to Dona Isabel, who was the regent of Mbwila, because of the youth of her nephew, the ruler of Mbwila.[21] However, as she was openly a friend of ours, she took the ambassadors prisoner and sent them to this city to the governor, together with information about the army of the king of Kongo. She asked many times that we would help her with our army and replied to the king that she was the vassal of the [Portuguese] king, Dom Afonso,[22] and knew no other king, and that whatever the risk she must and would help the Portuguese. So, with this grievance the king of Kongo came with his army close to the principal city of her kingdom, destroying everything and bringing fire and blood to the sobas so that many submitted to him and refused obedience to Dona Isabel. Her general also did this, since his heart was still in the Kongo from where it had not been freed. When Dona Isabel saw that she was under increased pressure and without people to defend her, and that the king was approaching, she ordered all the *pombeiros*[23] of the white men to assemble in some naturally impregnable rocky places, along with all their goods, so that the king would not take them, and she placed a guard for their protection.

The said regent Dona Isabel was under extreme pressure and every day was abandoned by more and more of her people, who fled to the king of Kongo, until she was threatened with having nowhere to go. Faced with this great affliction, it pleased God to remember her loyalty and to deliver her from the hands and power of the king who had burned and laid waste her kingdom and thrown everything to the ground. At this time, our army marched as fast as it could to help her, and through interpreters[24] it became known that she was hard pressed, that the king was six leagues from the Court of Mbwila and that she was in a circle of rocks which had been strengthened by the sobas and where in one more day she would surrender. In order to bring this enterprise to a conclusion, [the king] determined to go to the place where Dona Isabel was to devastate it and throw everything to the ground.

On Thursday, the 29th of October, our force joined up with that of Dona Isabel and they perceived the stratagem of the king. On that Thursday morning our army caught sight of the king, and to prevent our succeeding in our intentions, he came at once to seek us out with great resolution. And [he advanced] so rapidly that he barely gave us the opportunity to come out of a small wood, which, because it was a very weak [position], our army was leaving to find higher ground where it was more suitable to form up. This the *sargento-mor* at once ordered to be done, forming four points of a diamond, which was carried out altogether and in good order.

The captain Manuel Nunes Barreto marched in the vanguard on the right-hand side and captain Domingos Francisco on the left. Captain Baltasar Luís Pimentel commanded the main force, with captains António Barreto and Gomes Pegado da Ponte. Each one marched in whatever form he had adopted up to that time, but those on the flanks kept parade ground order. Captain Fernão Pinto marched on the right flank and captain Simão Francisco Frade and captain António d'Araújo Cabreira on the left. Captain Lourenço Martins commanded the right flank of the rearguard and captain Leonardo Ferreira de Moura the left and the main force. Of the troops in the rearguard Captain António Ferreira Lobato commanded a company with Domingos da Frota and Manuel Lopes, who were consigned as adjutants to distribute the orders of the *sargento-mor*, the adjutant Domingos Martins, with two others in the battle.[25] The black captains Faba and Bombo reinforced the rearguard with their black musketeers, with Kilambas[26] and certain with sobas with their *guerra preta* archers. And having come to a halt everyone remained in the placed allotted to them.

The *capitão-mor* always marched in the vanguard with the reserve captains Diogo Rois Dessa, Inacio Mendes de Carvalho and Inacio Carrilho. António Trancoso was adjutant in charge of the distribution of orders. With the vanguard went two pieces of artillery together with the cavalry captain Pedro Borges, all the companies of *guerra preta* led by their captain Simão de Matos, and the company that had come from Pernambuco under captain Manuel Soares of the regiment of Henrique Dias; also captain Anjo with his company of black musketeers, which was under his command, and the Kilambas and Jagas who were the irregular fighters, which he had; and all was carried out in good order.

Having collected together the sick, who amounted to a little more than seventy, the *capitão-mor* ordered a bugle to be sounded as the enemy was advancing with a regiment dispatched by the king and commanded by his general, Dom Álvaro Penha, and the duke of Mbamba,[27] together with the marquis of Mpemba, with four thousand archers and all the musketeers and four hundred shield bearers. They all came in no sort of order, concerned only with what they could pillage and believing they had already won the battle. The *sargento-mor* ordered Captain Simão de Matos to go out with his *guerra preta*, and the enemy pursued them in such a way that it was necessary to order them to retire; and when an artillery piece was turned in that direction, so much damage was done to the enemy that three chiefs and many nobles and other people were killed, which forced the enemy to retire.

Then the king advanced in person with his vanguard, along with the rest of his men. They attacked a second time in good order, the other regiments fighting with admirable valour. He personally looked everywhere to find where he could break through to restore his reputation, and he was not at all afraid of the force of our artillery. And some of his men protested that he should abandon the battle and the campaign, and that he should seek terms and a treaty because of the damage he had received. However, he did not wish to put his life before his reputation and, advancing on all fronts against our army, he paid no heed to himself and resolved to attack us.

When the *sargento-mor* saw his intention, he ordered the captains to advance, and they attacked the enemy with such resolution and valour, and fought so fiercely that, as the enemy charged, all our *guerra preta* fled and we remained with our breast exposed. However, we did great damage to the enemy, who had relied to a great extent on the heavy rain, because it seemed to him that we would not be able to use our firearms. This was a mistake since the Portuguese produced flashes of fire from the very water itself. The king became discouraged because so many of his men had been killed and, as he had received two bullet wounds, he decided to retire. However, he was not able to do this, for his retreat was so completely cut off by Captain Manuel Soares and Captain Simão de Matos with their *guerra preta*, that they killed the king and all the nobles who tried to defend him, leaving us with the most glorious victory ever won in this kingdom. The battle lasted eight hours, and most of the enemy fled together with the duke of Bengo, who was guarding the baggage. On our side, all our *guerra preta* fled, and we lost a great prize because we could not follow them, so that those who most benefitted were the blacks of Mbwila, who Dona Isabel had placed under the command of Captain Lucas de Carvalho, consisting of four hundred archers, and they were all that we had to help us.

We found fourteen cases of the richest goods, among which were two [cloths?] of velvet and damask as well as much silk, two silver writing cases and very valuable jewellery together with a lot of bark cloth, which had been brought for the payment of the soldiers. There was also a large quantity of provisions and many cattle and sheep. [We found] the king's crown and the staff, decorated in silver, which he took with him to church, and a hat which he wore when attending festivals. The sceptre has not been found up to now, although the blacks of Mbwila looked for it. The king's crown, the staff and the hat were sent by the *capitão-mor* to this city and were dispatched by the governor to His Majesty. He ordered the head of the king to be buried with all due pomp and ceremony, and it was accompanied to the Brotherhood of the Misericórdia by the majority of the citizens with all the priests and people of the land. [The king] was buried in the chapel of Nossa Senhora da Nazaré, who was the author of this victory and in whose honour, because of the great devotion that he had for her, the governor had a church built in the city at his own cost.[28]

Fifty thousand of the enemy remained on the field, among them four hundred nobles and ninety-five title-holders, and those whose names were known are listed below.[29] There were many prisoners, and the blacks of Mbwila benefited most from this. Those who were brought to this city are named below.[30] On our part, only twelve whites were wounded without any being killed, and twenty-five of our *guerra preta* died and two hundred and fifty were wounded, among them the *capitão-mor* of our black people, Simão de Matos and captain Manuel Soares and the cavalry captain, Pedro Borges, and the soldiers who made up the twelve wounded whites.

The blacks who fled from the battle brought news to the city that our army had been defeated. It can be imagined with what feeling this sad news was received. There were great lamentations throughout the city for friends, for relatives and for the good reputation of Portuguese arms and in particular for the loss of this kingdom, since the king had sworn not to leave a single white man alive and had resolved to besiege the city after having taken the other *presídios*.[31] However, it pleased God, through the intercession of his most Holy Mother, that three days after the arrival of this sad news, the Carmelite fathers were saying a litany [in the church of] Nossa Senhora da Monte do Carmo, praying to her that she should send us better news, when the Virgin performed a miracle before their eyes, to which the said Fathers bore witness. This was that a great halo appeared around the head of Our Lady, at which the Fathers were astonished. When news of this reached the people in the city, the chief interpreter[32] went through the streets crying 'Victory, victory', and at the same time news arrived of the success mentioned above and of the grace which God had done to us.

The governor went at once to the cathedral[33] with the Senado da Câmara to give thanks for such a great blessing, and he at once ordered all the prisoners to be released who had not had any part in it. On the following day, he ordered a great celebration at [the church of] Nossa Senhora da Nazaré, the author of this miracle and of the victory, at which Frei Francisco da Trindade, a Dominican friar, preached.

This is the true account of this victory, praise and thanks be to God our Lord and to his most Holy Mother.

Notes

1 C. R. Boxer, 'Uma Relação Inédita e Contemporânea da Batalha de Ambuila em 1665', *Boletim Cultural do Museu de Angola, (Luanda)* 2, 1960, pp. 65–73.

2 He was governor from 1661 to 1666, having served in Brazil against the Dutch.

3 He had taken up his appointment in May 1661.

4 By 'this kingdom' is meant Angola.

5 See Doc. 40.

6 Town council.

7 Dom António I (Vita Nkanga), 1661–5. For personal details see Adriano Parreira, *Dicionário de Biografias Angolanas séculos XV-XVII,* (Luanda, 2003) pp. 38–9.

8 Dom Garcia II (Nkanga Lukeni) reigned 1641–61. Adriano Parreira, *Dicionário de Biografias Angolanas séculos XV-XVII,* (Luanda, 2003) pp. 86–7.

9 He was a Brazilian mulatto who had led the Pernambuco rebellion against the Dutch. He was governor of Angola from 1658 to 1661.

10 That is canons of the cathedral of São Salvador who were often employed on diplomatic missions.

11 *Baqueanos.*

12 The text renders these names 'Cambaça e Sambambe'. The spelling of all the personal names has been modernized.

13 This may have been Vicente Pegado da Ponte, who commanded in the war against Pangi a Ndona (see Doc. 48).

14 The word *terço* is used.

15 Manuel Soares was a pilot who had originally gone to Angola in 1645. He was captured by the Dutch and eventually sent to Brazil. Henrique Dias was a black soldier who distinguished himself in the wars against the Dutch in Brazil, commanding a regiment of black soldiers and Indians.

16 This term was often used by the Portuguese for professional African soldiers but Miller has shown that the term originated in a secret society formed to oppose one of the Imbangala chiefs, which took the identity of 'buffalo hunters' (Miller, 1976) p. 160.

17 One of the most successful Portuguese commanders, Sequeira commanded the army that defeated and killed Ngola Ari in 1671.

18 A kind of sword.

19 Usually written Pedro Dias de Cabra.
20 In French, and in older works, this is written as Ambuila, but Mbwila is now accepted as the more usual rendering.
21 Álvaro Afonso Mbwila-a-Samba.
22 Dom Afonso VI of Portugal reigned from 1656 to 1668, when he was deposed by his brother Dom Pedro II. He died in 1683.
23 The *Pombeiros* were traders who attended the inland fairs in the service of the Portuguese.
24 The word used is *línguas*. These were interpreters but were also employed to gather intelligence.
25 'O ajudante Domingos Martins com dous maes na batalha'. The meaning of this is obscure.
26 Kilamba was a kingdom conquered by the Imbangala in the 1620s.
27 They were both killed in the battle.
28 This church still exists in Luanda and contains a depiction of the battle made of *azulejos*.
29 The figure of 50,000 is clearly an exaggeration and may be a mistake for 5,000. Thornton estimates that the Kongo army numbered scarcely more than 20,000 in total. Thirty title-holders are listed at the end of the document. The list of the dead is headed by the king, followed by four 'dukes' and five 'marquises'.
30 Five named prisoners are listed including the king's chaplain (*capelão-mor*) Manuel Roiz de Medeiros. Two sons of the Kongo king were among the prisoners.
31 *Presídio* was the term used for any settlement where there was a garrison of soldiers.
32 *Tendela do Reyno.*
33 *Sé.*

50   PORTUGUESE DEFEAT IN SONYO IN 1670

From António de Oliveira Cadornega, *História Geral das Guerras Angolanas*, 3 vols. (Lisbon, 1972), 2, pp. 280–84.
Translated by Malyn Newitt.

After the Portuguese victory at the battle of Mbwila, the Kongo kingdom began to break up into its constituent parts and the capital city was largely abandoned as rival claimants competed for the throne. The new governor, Francisco de Tavora (1669–76) and his capitão-mor, *João Soares de Almeida, were principally concerned with warfare and collecting slaves in Ndongo, but in 1670 joined with the Kongo king to raid Sonyo. Ruled by its 'count' and controlling the port of Mpinda, the province of Sonyo had become, in effect, an independent kingdom, trading with the Dutch and maintaining close relations with the peoples on the north bank of the Zaire River. In this war the Portuguese were acting in alliance with the Kongo king who wanted to restore his authority in Sonyo. This account describes the eventual outcome of the campaign, which began well with the defeat and death of the 'count' of Sonyo. This campaign, like so many others fought by the Portuguese at this time, seems to have been largely a slave raid, and it came to grief as the Portuguese and their black troops were trapped in marshy country near the coast with their backs to the Ambriz River and the slaves they had captured earlier in the campaign broke free and joined their compatriots. Defeat in this battle, known as the battle of Kitombo, was as decisive in its way as the battle of Mbwila, for it ended any serious attempt by the Luanda Portuguese to establish their supremacy in the Kongo kingdom.*

When our Kilambas and the Jaga, *kabuko ka ndonga*,[1] saw the determination of the *capitão-mor*, they requested him and some of our captains not to move from the place and the encampment where he was, saying that they would go to attack the villages and the *mbanza*[2] of that count and his vassals, by means of which they would slow him down and would discover the present strength of his forces, and affirming that everyone would share in the booty they would win. He [the captain] was not willing to grant any of this because of the fighting mood he was in, and he gave it little consideration, as he believed that our Jaga with his own and our Kilambas, and the captains of the *guerra preta* with their *capitão-mor*, would deprive him of the sack of the count's *mbanza* and town. Although [the previous count] had been killed in battle, he was already succeeded by another one who had been elected and acclaimed in his place, without being in any way a Pythagorean spirit.[3] In this interval there had been time for the Muxilonga nation to elect a new count and lord, as has been said, and they had a large army of men paid for with their money; and on the other bank of the River Zaire, the king of Ngoyo and the kings of Kakongo and Cabinda had their lands and vassals.[4] As the kingdom of Ngoyo was situated on the bank of the river and by the seashore, this was the place from which most of the king's forces came and, as it had a good port, there were quantities of war canoes well equipped with rowers, which could move with great speed and bring men armed with missiles, spears, *trasados*, bows and arrows. They were protected by leather shields and did not lack firearms, for they had their share of those which the Northern Nations[5] had brought to their port to trade. They had supplied these to all the people of that coast, which the zeal of the Portuguese had discovered at so much labour and expense, so that they could enjoy the increase [of peaceful trade].

With this powerful support, the new count made his preparations and our *capitão-mor* resolved to go in search of the *mbanza* and other settlements. Moving from the site where he was encamped with all his forces, he began his march with his military formations in as good order as was possible in that terrain, putting in the front all the *guerra preta* with their *capitão-mor* and chiefs, and the black musketeers and gunmen, and in the rear the captain of the cavalry with his limited force, the flanks being taken by black soldiers with two companies of infantry in the centre.[6] And there were more people in the rear with the baggage, artillery and munitions.

He marched in this formation through all the cultivated lands and settlements of the enemy, when suddenly he [the enemy] appeared with a numerous army, the new count leading the vanguard, and like mad people they attacked our men with the utmost fury and resolution, caring nothing for their lives. They inflicted so much damage on our *guerra preta* and cavalry and on the infantry who were acting as escorts that they were about to break. The enemy was in the rear and was gathering on the flanks of our squadron, but they attacked the vanguard of our formation because there was marshy ground on each side so that our men did not have room to give more than one discharge of artillery and other arms. They then rushed on our *guerra preta*, and this was the cause of our total ruin, for they took no notice of our gunfire. Everything then became mixed in total confusion, and the prisoners broke free from the shackles and bonds in which they were being held and went to the aid of those of their own nation. Our Portuguese, not being able to use their firearms, performed great deeds with their swords and, as they had the leather shields which the enemy [soldiers] had lost in the first battle so that the majority of them now had none, the enemy's death toll was huge, our Portuguese selling their lives at the price of many of the enemy, who were already tired of so much fighting and killing. But the numbers of the enemy grew the whole time with the multitude of combatants they brought to conquer or die, without risking their own lives. In this situation, our brave Portuguese saw themselves growing fewer in number, and the *capitão-mor*, the principal chiefs and captains, and the horsemen with their leader were killed, having all performed valiant deeds. However, as the many hold the advantage over the few, and no one came to reinforce them, they were not able to resist any more.

Some of the infantry began to lose ground and retire, but finding the mudflats wetter than they had been when they had crossed them, because the River Ambriz had risen and overflowed its banks, our men became bogged down so that they were no longer masters of their own actions, and many were killed there. They tried to find a ford[7] or thickets [of reeds] where they might cross the River Ambriz, but not finding any they plunged into the river to swim across. And the fury and speed of its current made the waters their burial place. Others went to search farther down where its waters joined the sea and were not so deep because they were more spread out. Here some crossed to the other bank, thus escaping the current, but they could not escape the heathen who killed them there. It was said that it was the vassals of this king who preferred to do it. Everything can be believed of such heathen, for there is no such thing as a good snake, and the most active people are those that conquer.

This was related by those who escaped this rout and defeat and who brought the news, and by some who were taken prisoner and were later ransomed from the power of the Muxilonga and their allies who went to their aid, as has been said. As our *guerra preta*, are very nimble, they escaped more easily, some by swimming and others by hiding in the *mabus* thickets,[8] principally the Jagas. Moreover, it was said they brought back many of the prisoners they had taken in the first battle or else they had sent previously, which was more likely. They left dead their chief, *kabuko ka ndonga*, and many of their men, as also our Kilambas, who had died like lions alongside the Portuguese, and few saved themselves even though they could have done so. Some black slaves belonging to the settlers also returned, having left their masters dead on this campaign.

We have already said that the reason we lost this campaign was ambition, and also the fact that the *capitão-mor*, João Soares de Almeida, was a man without much knowledge of the land, who paid little attention to the opinions about conditions in the interior, expressed to him by persons of wide experience who accompanied that enterprise. However, what counts for most is that God gives success to him who serves Him best and, although on this occasion we lost [the battle], would always be regretted by that county of Sonyo and by the Muxilongo vassals and the other kings of the far bank of the Zaire, because in those two battles, whether they went for or against them, they lost such a great multitude of people, including the first count their lord and the second newly elected one, both being killed in those two battles with all the people of the greater part of that county and lordship. As a result, their celebrations were marked by lamentations for the many who died. And every time that there were discussions about this among these heathen, they decided that they would use their great numbers, in the same way as the Grand Turk, to achieve many conquests and difficult enterprises, since they did not mind losing many men because of the great number of combatants they had.

Our loss served also as gain for the [Kongo] king, Dom Raphael, who escaped from that battle, in which he had not risked much, with some of his men and went by the most direct route to reach his kingdom and his city of São Salvador. And as that county had been so destroyed by his forces and [those of] his principal *fidalgos*, there was no opposition nor anyone to oppose him. It could truly be said that we had died for him and as loyal vassals of the prince our lord, since he favoured this king, whom he called his brother, with his arms and vassals.

When the news of this rout reached the city of São Paulo da Assunção,[9] think gentle reader, that for the governor and captain-general, Francisco de Tavora,[10] there remained only the pain and emotion that he felt at seeing so disastrous an outcome to such an enterprise, which was so honourable and important for his reputation and at which he had laboured so hard, ordering everything so well to achieve success; and that having achieved success, the majority of those chiefs, who were dominated by personal ambition or private interest, allowed it to be lost and never brought what they had begun to a successful conclusion. It is true that victories and good success are given by God, as Lord of battles and armies, to him who serves Him, and that when whoever is the commander organises military affairs with skill and good disposition, it does not appear that He should have to do anything further. It is those who carry out the enterprises and campaigns who make the mistakes or fail in this or that respect by not following the orders of their generals.

Notes

1 See Doc. 48, note 2.
2 *Mbanza* is a term used for the capital of a ruler.
3 This is apparently a reference to Pythagoras's theories about metamorphosis.
4 These were states on the north bank of the Zaire which traded with Sonyo. Ngoyo was situated at the mouth of the Zaire and Kakongo on the coast to the north. Both were already in existence in the early sixteenth century.
5 The English, Dutch and French – but in this case principally the Dutch.
6 The word used here is *regaço* meaning 'lap'.
7 The word used is *ponte* meaning a bridge but in this case presumably a ford is intended.
8 *Mabus* were a variety of papyrus reeds (see Doc. 48).
9 Luanda.
10 Governor of Angola from 1669 to 1676.

12

PEOPLE AND PLACES

---

51 THE TOWN OF CACHEU IN THE EARLY
SEVENTEENTH CENTURY

Manuel Álvares SJ, *Etiópia Menor e Descrição Geografica da Provincia da Serra Leoa*, A Teixeira da Mota and Luís de Matos eds., chapter 4 (unpublished).
The manuscript is located in the Biblioteca da Sociedade de Geografia de Lisboa.
Translation by P. E. H. Hair; revised by Malyn Newitt.

This description of Cacheu, probably written sometime around 1615, provides a vivid picture of an Afro-Portuguese trading town, a number of which existed along the coast of upper Guinea. Such towns were gateways to the interior and for the Africans a port through which to access the Atlantic world.[1] Cacheu was situated on the left bank of the São Domingos River (later called the Cacheu River) in the Papel state of Cacanda. The name first occurs early in the sixteenth century, but the Portuguese town appears only to have come into existence after about 1560. The settlement was raided by John Hawkins in 1567 and, as French interlopers became increasingly active along the coast, the Portuguese sought permission to fortify their town. Once inside their fortifications, the Portuguese began to assert their independence from the Papel and it was this that led to the attack on the settlement in 1590, which is described in such triumphal terms by Álvares.

Early in the seventeenth century, it was made the 'capital' of the Guinea settlements. The Portuguese population was largely made up of people of mixed race and settlers who came over from Cape Verde, along with their clients and slaves. There was also a large population of Sape refugees from the Mane who had adopted Christianity. Father Álvares gives a description of a creole society, rendered all the more vivid by the strong language in which he expresses his prejudices. He emphasizes the wealth and luxury of the richest families but dismisses most of the population with the opprobrious terms of lançados *and* tangomaos. *The hostility between a priest such as Álvares and the* lançados *is to be accounted for by the latter's religious practices, which incorporated many African beliefs and customs, and by the fact that they traded not only with Africans but also with other European interlopers in contravention of Portuguese monopoly rules.*

Álvares was describing Cacheu at the height of its prosperity, for it was superceded later in the century by Bissau, which had better access for ocean-going shipping.

The settlement has two older names or titles. The first, Cacheu, was given to it by the natives and its etymology is not known to us. It may derive from the name of some king, just as the town on the [Windward] coast is called Porto de Ale after the name of the king who used to live there, Ale.[2] But if not, it will be no easy task to discover why it bears this first name. Its second name, Rio de S. Domingos, which although it does not really describe a place on land, is more interesting, and of more profit to the land since it is, of course, the name of the patriarch of the holy and religious Order of Preachers.[3] The third name is incomparably and altogether superior to the others, to as great an extent as the Queen of Angels is to all created things. This name was given to the town by the captains and soldiers living there, in gratitude for the signal victory they won over the neighbouring heathen, when the Sacred Virgin fought here in the midst of her soldiers. The successful outcome being hers, inasmuch as she was mistress in the field of both armies, her name was taken [for the town] in the form Our Lady of Victory, and this is the correct explanation of the third name of this port.[4]

The whole site of the settlement is flat. It is rendered agreeable by the variety of trees surrounding it, large cotton trees, palm trees, and a similar sort of tree which bears an even greater resemblance to the coconut because its fruit, though smaller, is somewhat like a coconut – such trees are called *cibes*.[5] But the spot is made less healthy by the lack of springs and streams, and the nearest water supply is insalubrious, causing much sickness and being very inconvenient for the whole population. In extent it is about two musket-shots in length and includes the district of St. Anthony, a finer name for it and a very suitable one because of the variety of the inhabitants and their devotion to the great Portuguese saint. A finer name, did I say? If its other name of Vila Quente[6] refers to the ardent charity of its inhabitants, then it is in no respect inferior to finer names, for anyone with that virtue is so incomparably of the first rank that the rest of us can only follow after.

Let us leave it as Vila Quente district. It is not fair to deprive it of its heat since we have found no one who can explain the true derivation of this name while, since the popular explanation is in bad taste, it is better to be evasive and remain silent about it than to offend by discussing it. As I have said, its full length is about two musket-shots; its width is only that of its houses. Most of these belong to Portuguese and are square shaped, large and well placed, some having an upper floor. The walls are of burnt brick and are roofed over with *cibe* leaves, which are very large and therefore very suitable, although they have to be renewed annually, on account of the heat which damages them in summer. Inside they have *cobetes*,[7] which are square, with walls like those of the house, but whose roofs are first covered with closely-set timber and then with earth. This design is most praiseworthy. Those who live in these parts should thank the man who first thought of it, for because of him the frequent loss of goods, which on land is caused annually by fires, is greatly reduced. Similarly (by equal forethought) they could avoid many great losses at sea, especially on this coast, if the contractors did not so notably neglect to provide vessels for it in compliance with a specific decree of His Majesty: Their lack of compliance, which is as culpable as it is deliberate, deprives them of the right to large grants of compensation. In this district, the houses are almost all round, although of the same material as was mentioned. Here a number of Portuguese and other whites also live as guests, but others have their own houses in which tenants also live. This is the district principally inhabited by common people and persons in employment, all of them free persons, who maintain themselves by their daily work and wages, being carpenters, sailors and men in other sea-going trades.[8]

Having discussed the sort of persons who live in Vila Quente, now let us discuss those who live in Vila Fria,[9] so that there can be no discrimination to which the envious can point. Cacheu has all that is needed for a well-organized community. On the spiritual side it is in the hands of pastors of outstanding and superior wisdom; on the temporal side, in all those respects relating to the preservation of life and to good conduct, it has no need to envy Europe. Since those who make their homes there have large houses and varied lines of commerce, which they conduct in the interior as well as by the sea, they are in the main very well off, but they all follow a very glittering life-style.

They are not sparing in their generosity, as can be seen from the way they treat themselves to clothes. They cut up silks to provide costly garments, or some use less expensive materials for their clothes, material such as damask from the Indies or China of different qualities, this material being more suitable for a land where English cloths and such like are intolerable. If they are particular in this matter of dress, they are no less so in equipping themselves with means of defence and attack, [with] such apparel as breastplates and so forth, and daggers, shields, swords and other weapons. When the countryside permits the use of horses, there is no lack of enthusiasm for this exercise.

....

Father Delgado[10] said with reason: 'Gentlemen, it does not seem to me that all this forms the portrait of the little Babylon I was told about'. I consider that Father's experience and his conclusion can still stand today in refutation of those who, carried away more by passion than concern, or to express it better, drawing their information more from the shadows than from the light, apply to all the settlers in Guinea the infamous names of *lançados* and *tangomaos*. These names properly only apply to those who, not content with cooperating with the idolatrous heathen in the practices and sacrifices of their false religion, erect huts and build pedestals for their infernal idols. The *lançados* are truly 'run-aways', and not only from the Lord's grace, a precious jewel their souls are as far from as they are close to divine justice. These are truly *tangomaos*, for at the repast of guilt they not only snatch the dish but fill themselves like starving dogs, yet they remain famished for the word of God. They are pursued by guilt and fear of punishment, since they are not content merely to repeat falls from grace; instead, and for the worse, they persist in sinning, so that by the bad example of their lives they discredit the preaching of the Faith of the Gospel in the eyes of the heathen. I can say more about them. They are evil itself, they are idolaters, perpetrators of homicides, libertines, thieves who steal reputation, credit and good names from innocents as well as property, and also traitors – for they run away to help pirates, leading their ships to those places where our vessels are in the habit of anchoring and trading. They are people without understanding of right and wrong, without respect for anything other than their own appetites, and are the very spawn of hell. When the epithet 'infamous' is heard in this midden of the world, for a midden undoubtedly exists in this Ethiopia of ours, it is as appropriate for these people as it is far-fetched, even at the most malicious, for the noble Christian spirit of the worthy and most devoted soldiers of Our Lady of Victory, her sons, a spirit which is the glory of the Court of the Queen of Angels. This will suffice to indicate the character of the vassals of Mary, Our Lady.

Now let us discuss the size of the population. The settlement shelters some 1,500 persons counting together Portuguese and natives of Santiago island, of whom about 500 or so are fighting men. Some of these persons have truly deserved well from the point of view of this river, but no less do they deserve well from the royal munificence, because of the services which in peace and war they have performed, for God and His Majesty, in company with the slaves each possesses and with their various other retainers, including certain natives who put more trust in us than in their own parents and relatives. Out of self-interest – the abominable idol of Ethiopia – these natives are so greatly attached to us that at every opportunity they extend help and loyalty in such a natural fashion that it is astonishing.

Notes

1 See also Doc. 19.
2 Porto deAle is situated on the coast of Senegal just south of the Cape Verde.
3 Saint Dominic.
4 The name Porto de Nossa Senhora do Vencimento was adopted after the successful battle fought in 1590 when the image of Our Lady had been brandished at the attackers. George E. Brooks, *Eurafricans in Western Africa* (Oxford, 2003) p. 72.
5 This is the fan palm (*Borassus Aethiopum*).
6 Hot Town.
7 More usually written *cumbetes*, these are storehouses for trade goods with earthen roofs made to resist fire. See Peter Mark, *"Portuguese" Style and Luso-African Identity. Precolonial Senegambia, Sixteenth-Nineteenth Centuries* (Bloomington, 2002) p. 47. In his study of 'Portuguese' architecture in Guinea, Mark appears not have made any use of Álvares's account.
8 This may refer either to the *grumetes*, the African members of the Christian Portuguese community or to the Sape refugees who had settled along the Cacheu River, or to the local Papel population.
9 Cold Town.
10 This is the Jesuit Father João Delgado, a colleague of Álvares's who had been sent to found a mission at Ziguinchor and who died in 1609.

52 SÃO SALVADOR, CAPITAL OF THE KINGDOM OF KONGO

From Filippo Pigafetta, *Relatione del Reame di Congo et delli circonvicine contrade tratta dalli scritti & ragionamenti di Odoardo Lopez Portoghese*, Grassi (Rome, 1591).

Translation by Malyn Newitt based on M. Hutchinson, trans. and ed., *A Report of the Kingdom of Congo and of the Surrounding Countries* (London, 1881), pp. 65–7; Filippo Pigafetta e Duarte Lopes, *Relação do Reino do Congo e das Terras Circunvizinhas*, António Luís Alves Ferronha, ed. (Lisbon, 1989), pp. 59–61.

This description of São Salvador places the Portuguese encounter with the Kongo kingdom in its physical environment. During the sixteenth century the Portuguese became an influential faction in Kongo society, providing priests for the royal Christian cult, military aid, prestigious imports, literacy and a range of cultural symbols including exotic dress and European names and titles. However, valuable as they were as allies for successive Kongo kings, they remained a deeply unpopular minority group. In the capital, they lived in their own walled enclosure, almost a city in its own right, which constituted a symbolic separation between themselves and the country in which they were settled. Pigafetta's description was based on information he was given, not on first-hand knowledge. What he does not make clear is that the houses of the Kongolese, including that of the king, were for the most part of traditional African construction and were situated within their own enclosures.[1]

Although the capital of the kingdom of Kongo is, to some extent, included in the region of Mpemba, since its government and that of its surrounding territory, which extends for about twenty miles, belongs to the king himself, let us treat it separately.

This city is called São Salvador, and was formerly known as Mbanza in the language of the country, which generally means the Court where the king or governor resides. It is situated 150 miles from the sea, on a large and high mountain, almost entirely of rock with seams of ironstone, out of which the houses are built. This mountain has on its summit a plateau, which is all cultivated and has houses and villages extending for about ten miles around, where more than 100,000 people live. The land is fruitful and the air healthy, fresh and pure, and there are springs of water good to drink which never at any time harm the body. Here also are many animals of every description. The summit of the mountain is separate and distinct from everything around it, and for this reason the Portuguese call it Outeiro, that is to say the look-out point.[2] It is particularly high, and the whole country round about can be seen from it. It is true that only towards the east and the river it is steep and very craggy.

The first lords of the country placed this town on this summit for two reasons: First, because it lies almost in the very middle of the kingdom, so that help can quickly be sent to every part; and, next, because the natural elevation of the site gives it good air and a secure position which cannot be taken by force. By the royal road which comes from the direction of the sea, which is 150 miles away, as has been said, the summit is reached by a walk of five miles along a winding, broad and well-made path. On the east side a river runs along the base of the mountain, to which women descend by a path a mile long to wash their clothes.

In some parts there are valleys which are planted and cultivated, nor is any region left uncultivated, as this is the country where the Court resides.

The city is placed in a corner or angle on the south side of the summit of that mountain, and was enclosed with walls by Dom Afonso, the first Christian king, who gave the Portuguese their own separate part, shut off with a wall. A large space was left between these two enclosures, where the principal church was built, in front of which was a square, and the gates of the houses of the nobles and of the Portuguese were built so as to face the said church. At the entrance to the square live certain great nobles of the Court, and behind the church the square ends in a narrow street, which has its own gate, outside which are several houses facing to the east. Beyond these walls, in which the royal residences and the city of the Portuguese are enclosed, there are several buildings belonging to different nobles, each one occupying in a disorderly fashion the site most agreeable to him in order to be near the Court. It is impossible to determine the size of this city, since the whole country beyond the boundaries of the two walls is covered with country houses and palaces, and each noble has his houses and lands enclosed like a town. The wall around the Portuguese settlement is nearly a mile long, and the palaces of the king as much again. The walls are of great thickness, but the gates are not shut at night, and are not even guarded. There is no lack of abundant water on this high plain, but the Court and the Portuguese drink from a spring that rises on the north side and flows continuously. To this they have to descend a musket-shot distance down the hill and then carry the water into the city on the backs of slaves in vessels of wood and clay, and also in gourds.

Notes

1   See discussion in Georges Balandier, *Daily Life in the Kingdom of Congo* (London, 1968) pp. 146–52.
2   See Doc. 43. The Portuguese word *outeiro* usually just means 'hill'.

---

53   THE COURT OF THE KINGS OF KONGO

From Filippo Pigafetta, *Relatione del Reame di Congo et delli circonvicine contrade tratta dalli scritti & ragionamenti di Odoardo Lopez Portoghese*, Grassi (Rome, 1591).

Translation by Malyn Newitt based on that of M. Hutchinson, ed., *A Report of the Kingdom of Congo and of the Surrounding Countries*, (London, 1881), pp. 108–13; Filippo Pigafetta e Duarte Lopes, *Relação do Reino do Congo e das Terras Circunvizinhas*, António Luís Alves Ferronha, ed. (Lisbon, 1989), pp. 93–5.

Duarte Lopes's description of life at the Kongo Court dates from the late sixteenth century when Portuguese relations with the Kongo were relatively close and friendly. With the rise of Luanda as an independent Portuguese state in western Africa, rivalry with the Kongo grew and resulted in a series of destructive wars (see Docs. 48, 49 and 50). The position of the Portuguese as honoured strangers or guests in the kingdom is well described in this extract. The Kongolese elite had adopted many features of Portuguese culture along with Christianity, but these were superimposed on traditional customs and practices. Lopes measures quite judiciously the limited extent to which the Kongo had been Europeanized.

In former times the king and his courtiers used to wear palm cloth, with which they covered themselves from the waist down, and which was fastened with belts of the same material of beautiful workmanship. In front, as an ornament, they hung beautiful and delicate skins such as those of small jaguars, civet cats, sables,[1] martens and similar animals, leaving the shape of their heads to provide greater pomp. Next to their skin was a circular garment, somewhat like a rochet,[2] which they called *incuto*, reaching to below the knees and made like a net from the threads of fine palm-tree cloths, with tassels hanging elegantly from the meshes. These rochets they threw back over the right shoulder, so as to leave the hand free, and on the same shoulder they carried a zebra's tail fastened to a handle, according to the ancient custom in those parts. They wore small yellow and red caps on their heads, square at the top, which covered the top of the head, and were used more for show than as a protection against the sun or the air. For the most part, the people went barefoot, but the king and some of his nobles wore sandals of an antique design, like those seen on Roman statues, and these were also made from the palm tree. The poorer sort and common people wore the same kind of garments, from the waist downwards, but of a coarser cloth, with the rest of the body being naked. The women wear three kinds of garment below the waist; one long, reaching from the waist to the feet, the second shorter and the third shorter still, each one having a fringe round it. Another garment is like a doublet and reaches to the waist. Each one is tied from one side to the other and is left open in front. From the breasts down they wear a sort of doublet which reaches to the waist and on their shoulders a cape of the same material, all these garments being made of cloth from the palm tree. The women go about with the face uncovered and wear the same kind of caps as the men. The common people also dress in this way, but using much coarser materials. Slaves and the lowest people only wear garments from the waist down, the rest of the body being left entirely naked.

However, after the kingdom became Christian, the nobles of the Court began to dress in the Portuguese fashion, wearing cloaks, capes, scarlet tabards and silk robes, every man according to his means. On their heads they wear hats and caps and on their feet velvet or leather slippers, and buskins in the Portuguese manner, with broad swords at their sides. The ordinary people, who cannot afford Portuguese clothes, retain their former dress. The women also have adopted the Portuguese fashions although they do not wear a cloak. Over their heads they wear veils, and above these black velvet caps, ornamented with jewels, and necklaces of gold round their necks. However, the poor continue to dress in the old fashion, and only the ladies of the Court adorn themselves in the above-mentioned manner.

After the king's conversion to Christianity, his Court was also reformed to some extent in imitation of that of the king of Portugal, and especially with regard to the service at his table. When the king eats in public, a dais with three steps is set up, covered with Indian carpets, and on this is placed a table with a chair of crimson velvet, studded with golden nails. He always eats alone; no one ever sits at table with him, and the princes stand around with heads covered. For eating and drinking he possesses a service with a salver made of gold and silver.

He maintains a guard of the Anzichi[3] and other tribes, who remain near his palace, armed with the weapons already mentioned; and when he goes abroad, they beat the drums so that they can be heard five or six miles off, so making it known that the king has set out. All his lords accompany him, and also the Portuguese, in whom he puts great deal of trust, but he seldom quits his palace. He gives an audience in public twice a week, and then he only speaks with his nobles and, as no one owns their own estates or lands but everything belongs to the Crown, they have no disputes beyond a few minor matters. They have no writing in the Kongo tongue. Criminal cases are treated lightly, and seldom is anyone condemned to death. The excesses committed by the Mwissikongo (for so the people of Kongo are called in their own tongue) against the Portuguese are judged in accordance with Portuguese law. If any of them commits a very grave crime, the king punishes the malefactor with exile to some desert island, as he considers it to be a greater punishment to exile a man from his fellows so that he can do penance for his sins than to execute him at once. And if it happens that someone who is punished in this way lives for ten or twelve years, the king usually pardons him if he is worthy of it, and even employs him in the service of the state as someone who has been tamed and been made used to suffering.

In civil disagreements it is arranged that, if a Portuguese has any dispute with a Mwissikongo, it must be referred to a Kongo judge, but if a Mwissikongo has a suit against a Portuguese, the matter is brought before the Portuguese consul and judge, for the king has granted this post in that country to one of their own nation.[4] No writing or legal instruments are used in transactions, either between these people themselves or with the Portuguese, but all matters are transacted by word of mouth and in front of witnesses. They preserve no history of their ancient kings, nor any memorial of past centuries.[5] As they do not know how to write, they usually measure the seasons by the moons, being ignorant of the hours of the day and night, and accustomed to say that in the time of such and such a person, a certain thing happened.

Notes

1   The word used is 'zibelino'.
2   A rochet is a white vestment similar to a surplice gathered at the sleeve and worn especially by bishops.
3   Teke people.
4   At exactly the same time, the Portuguese resident in the kingdom of Monomotapa in eastern Africa was also accorded jurisdiction within the trading fairs.
5   This was not, of course, true as many narratives of origins and traditions linked to the past kings were remembered and transmitted orally. See discussion in John Thornton, 'The origins and Early History of the Kingdom of Kongo', *The International Journal of African Historical Studies*, 34 (2001), pp. 89–120, and more recently in António Custódio Gonçalves, *A História Revisitada do Kongo e de Angola* (Lisbon, 2005).

54   LOSSES SUFFERED BY WHITE TRADERS

From Manuel Álvares SJ, *Etiópia Menor e Descripção Géografica da Província da Serra Leoa*, chap. 3.

A. Teixeira da Mota and Luís de Matos, eds., (unpublished).

The manuscript is located in the Biblioteca da Sociedade de Geografia de Lisboa.

Translation by P. E. H. Hair, revised by Malyn Newitt.

Álvares's account of the peoples of the Gambia and Casamance regions in the early seventeenth century reveals more about his attitude towards the African

peoples of the region (see Doc. 51). The Cape Verde Islands were frequently dev-
astated by drought, and the islanders had to resort to the Guinea mainland to
obtain food. From there traditional African religious practices found their way
into the islands (see Doc. 44), and particular reference is made to the amulets
brought back from Muslim regions by Mandinga traders. Álvares was deeply
prejudiced against most of the African groups, of which he had knowledge and
which he dismisses as 'heathen'. Although these attitudes are by no means typi-
cal of the Portuguese at this period, they do represent one extreme of European
reaction to the cultures of Africa. However, behind Álvares's characterization of
the different ethnic groups lies his attitude towards the Portuguese traders. The
Portuguese were finding life increasingly dangerous, as European pirates lay in
wait for them in the coastal rivers, and they were also attacked by some African
groups who found plunder more profitable than trade. Of particular interest is
his account of the way captured Portuguese risked being themselves be sold as
slaves.

Because the land is rich it has trade. Ships, sloops and launches come
here from various parts. The normal trade is in slaves, cotton and cotton
cloth, hides, ivory and wax.[1] The land has great swarms of bees, which
the natives ingeniously keep in hives of woven straw hung on trees. Some
gold is traded, which comes from the hinterland at the direction of the
Mande merchants who make their way to the coast from the provinces
and lands of their supreme emperor Mande Mansa.[2] The fruitfulness of
the land we are discussing was revealed to Santiago Island in 1609 in
its time of great need, when the land came to its aid by providing foodstuffs. These commodities are obtained from the country in exchange
for illegal cloth, different sorts of precious stones from the East Indies,
beads, wine and cola – the last so much valued that throughout Ethiopia
it is reckoned a gift from heaven, and Mande merchants carry it to all
parts of Barbary and, in powdered form, as far as Mecca; there they are
created superior *bexerins*[3] and they return with the normal reward of
nominas,[4] which they offer around through all these provinces. The fame
of the great trade in this river has served the Portuguese captains ill, for
at times pirates come here on the special advice of those heathen who
know the coast well, and so not only the captains but also His Majesty's
revenues suffer great losses and other damage.

While nature has shown itself generous to the country, endowing
it with an abundance and variety of things, it has been correspondingly mean with the country's sons, giving all of them a character so
base that they seem more a product of error than of nature. 'Sons' I call
them [in the plural] because the people to whom the land belongs, the
Sonequei,[5] are today so mixed and coupled with the Mandingas that
the land is called after the latter. To be specific, the Gambia River and

that hinterland commonly called the Mandingas, really belong to the Sonequei, an idolatrous heathen people, while the Mandingas originate from Mande Mansa, as stated in the second part of this treatise – a fact which confirms the natural tendency of character to which the savage is always prone. As the blood of those who people this river is thus united, so also are their characters and inclinations; and even worse, the Sonequei inheritance dilutes that from the Mandingas. In the latter, covetousness ameliorates their natural character, for they practice the trade of merchant in which it is so important to gain respect and be scrupulous, because on such conduct depends the growth of profits. The nature of these people is so depraved, so dishonest and so double-dealing that the saying of the Prophet applies *'Iniquitatem in corde et corde locuti sunt'*.[6]

They have two hearts, one in the mouth and the other in the normal place. They are malicious, greedy and treacherous. Although living in their own country, they have today become *lascarins*.[7] Whatever their evil spirit tells them, they carry out totally, as far as is possible. It is very necessary to be on guard in their ports, and failure to do this has often caused great disasters, when launches laden with goods have been lost. The much prized joy of life itself has also been lost, as happened to Diogo da Costa, from the Algarve, who was most cruelly killed by a Jalofo *jagara*,[8] a native of Manigar, in the land of the Grand Borcalo,[9] a land also peopled by Mandingas of this union.

Now let us say something about the Cassangas[10].... This empire acquired a king called Masssatamba,[11] who was the family head and progenitor of the rulers who reign today. Massatamba was the best friend the Portuguese nation has had in these parts. If he took a boat full of goods, he was most strict in paying the owners. Because he was so attached to us, he was greatly pleased when he was called the brother-in-arms of the king of Portugal. Further along the seaboard is the coast of the Banhu heathen,[12] which stretches as far as a creek from which Cacheu can be reached on a single tide.

From Cape St. Mary the coast runs south to Cabo Roxo, another lair and coastal strongpoint of pirates. There they lie in wait for ships of all kinds, whether from Iberia or from the rivers, in order to attack them and seize their loot. One cannot fail to note the laxity in this matter on the part of the contractors for these rivers. So many thousands of *cruzados* are received by them from His Majesty, or are kept back from him instead of being spent on building the coastal patrol ships for which the money is intended. Large losses regularly result from this, losses greater than need be, and affecting not only those involved but also the Crown revenues. Experts assert that these losses could be easily avoided if the lapse was corrected or if in the public interest the contractors proposed [other measures] to His Majesty, as they should. ...

All the heathen here (whom I shall not discuss as they have little trade with our people, such having been the case up to the present day on the part of Felupos[13] and Arriatas) are mortal enemies of all kinds of white men. If our ships touch their shores, they plunder the goods and take the white crew their prisoners, and they sell them in those places where they normally trade for cows, goats, dogs, iron bars and various cloths. The only thing these braves will have nothing to do with is wine from Portugal, which they believe is the blood of their own people and which therefore they will not drink.

It is pitiful to relate what white men suffer when they are captured by these savages. They immediately strip them, leaving only the meanest garments on their bodies. Although the captives are given plenty to eat by their masters, this is because of the profit the latter hope to make by selling them, a gain which, however slight, will repay the host for his food. They are treated by the heathen as if they were lunatics, and a couple of hundred children follow them around. This happened to a Benedictine monk who, together with a captain, fell into their hands. The savages took his robe and thus made it difficult for him to work in Cacheu. The fertility of their lands and the industry of the people, which result in their being no lack of the various foodstuffs found in Guinea, are the reasons for this hostility. They have rice, *funde*,[14] *milho*[15] and root crops, and they raise large quantities of cows and goats and consequently have much milk and butter.

All of them are skilled at fishing and at wine-tapping, there being plenty of palm trees on which to exercise their skill. They are notable farmers, so successful that the abundance of products has corrupted their natural ambition. For only the person who does not live among a sufficiency of what is needful for him learns to seek out the Good, or at least what he thinks to be good. This can be seen with regard to many of the heathen in this Ethiopia, who without doubt were greater tyrants than the Felupos and Arriatas when they lived in the same fortunate state. I could demonstrate this by various examples relating to many different peoples who, if they wish to cultivate our friendship, do so only out of self-interest, because in this way they can obtain a supply of whatever goods they lack. Because all these goods abound with the Felupos, the Lord has worked well on them so that their cruel nature is tempered in such a way that they serve as agents of divine justice in relation to those who, by his secret judgments, fall into his hands. Their lives are always spared, since he does not choose to pass over the reins of life to these savages to the point where they might tighten them with their own hands, a decision he reserves for himself. We see this daily, so that however rough and uncouth the heathen are, they never do harm [to this extent] to any captive in their power. If sometimes on the contrary it does happen [that whites are killed by blacks], this occurs at sea. There, in order to safeguard themselves when seizing goods, the heathen first kill those who are least on their guard, as happened in 1612.

Notes

1 Beeswax was a commodity which had been little valued prior to the arrival of European traders, but it had acquired great value in the European market and constituted an important export from upper Guinea.
2 The ruler of Mali.
3 Elsewhere Álvares explains that they are what the 'Moors of Barbary call cacizes and the Moorsof Guinea bexerins'. See Doc. 18, note 9.
4 Amulets.
5 Soninke.
6 This appears to be an inaccurate reference to Psalm 11, verse 2, which says 'Vana locuti sunt unusquisque ad proximum suum; labia dolosa in corde et corde locuti sunt': 'They have said vain words one to another with deceitful lips and with double heart have they spoken'.
7 Here the word is used in the sense of 'sailors'.
8 Jagra was a small kingdom on the south bank of the Gambia.
9 The *Bor Salum* was the king of Salum on the Delta du Saloum south of Cape Verde.
10 The name of the people living along the Casamance river.
11 Massatamba is first mentioned in 1582.
12 The Banhuns of the south bank of the Casamance river.
13 Felupes.
14 *Funde* is *digitaria exilis*, sometimes called 'hungry rice'.
15 *Milho* is a general term used for a variety of grains. In upper Guinea, the term is used to apply to sorghum or pennisetum.

55 THE KINGDOM OF KONGO IN 1595

Report Sent by Frei Martinho de Ulhoa, Bishop of São Tomé, to Fabio Biondi in Rome

From J. Cuvelier and L. Jadin, eds., *L'Ancien Congo d'aprés les archives romaines*, Mémoire de l'Académie des Sciences Coloniales (Brussels, 1954), pp. 194–207.

The Latin text entitled *De Statu Regni Congi* is printed in António Brásio, *Monumenta Missionaria Africana*, (Lisbon,1952), 3, pp. 505–10.

See also António Brásio, *Portugal em Africa*, May–June, 1951, pp. 142–5.

Two copies of this document exist in Archivo Vaticano. Fondo Borghese, Series IV, vol. 54, fls. 181–5, and in Biblioteca da Ajuda, *Rerum Lusitanicarum*, vol. XXV, fls. 261–74.

Translated by Malyn Newitt.

The occasion for the writing of this report was to provide information to the Holy See before a decision was reached whether to create a diocese of Kongo. It should be read in conjunction with Doc. 43. The see of Kongo was duly established in 1596. The information was gathered in Rome directly from the king of Kongo's ambassador and other witnesses. The object of this memorandum was to present Christianity in the Kongo in a favourable light and, although this aspect is clearly exaggerated, it still presents a great deal of detail about the way the kingdom was organized and operated as an African Christian state. The list of six provinces which were ruled over by 'dukes' was a list of the most important provinces within the kingdom at the time, but is not a complete list as at least three provinces ruled over by 'counts' were omitted from the list. The adoption of the European titles suggests that the Kongolese recognized a hierarchy among the provincial rulers.

The kingdom of Angola is situated in lower Ethiopia. The town of Angola is situated on the seacoast in that part of Africa called Guinea. The slave trade is carried on there. This town borrows its name from the kingdom of Angola, although its territory actually belongs to the king of Kongo.[1] In the island of Luanda, which is near the town, the Fathers of the Society of Jesus have a residence. There they cultivate the tender plants of Christ with the health-giving waters of doctrine and win many souls.

For some years the Portuguese who live there have undertaken expeditions against their enemies. By the help of God alone, they have killed a great number and have won an unexpected victory against the army of the pagan king of Angola, so that a third of the chief men of Angola have submitted to the power of the Portuguese.[2]

The kingdom of Kongo is the neighbour of [the kingdom] of Angola. Its extent is very great and it has a circumference of about three hundred Spanish leagues. It is situated about seven degrees below the equator and its limits are to the west the ocean, to the east the kingdom of Matamba,[3] to the north the kingdom of Loango and to the south that of Angola. This kingdom is great in the extent of its territory and in the multitude of its inhabitants. However, what makes it still greater is to have Álvaro as king, whom the inhabitants call the 'most Christian'.[4] The other kings are all heathen (we make an exception of Prester John, who is little known).

Three kings pay tribute to him, although they do not share his religion. They are [the kings] of Matamba, of Ocanga[5] and of the Mbundu.[6]

The king of Angola recognizes him as his superior, but unlike the others is not obliged to pay any tribute. There are also six Christian dukes, who could be described as petty kings, and who also submit to the king – those of Mbata,[7] Mbamba, Nsundi, Wembo, Wando and Mbala.[8] There are also counts and marquises, all of them Catholic, who obey the orders of the king with the greatest possible submission. If they do not carry out their functions well, they are dismissed by the king and replaced by others. The governors of the provinces reside in large centres called *mbanzas*, which are like towns. There are other localities of less importance.

The capital of the kingdom is called São Salvador and is where the king resides. In this town the climate is very temperate and healthy. When it is summer, because of the different condensation in the air, it can be as cold as in winter. However, nowhere is the cold excessive. When it is winter the rains are very frequent. The land has plenty of water from fountains and springs; these feed the rivers, which are full of fish.

The most famous river is the Zaire, which is the largest of them all and whose source is unknown. It flows past the kingdoms of Kongo and Angola and at its mouth is 36,000 paces wide.[9] Along the banks there is a numerous population who live in towns. The river discharges into the sea with such velocity that it forces its way through the salt waves of the sea and, for a distance, maintains its own current of fresh water, which one can draw up as far as 80,000 paces from the mouth.

The kingdom itself is extremely rich and, thanks to its fertility, is able to furnish in abundance the principal products necessary for the subsistence of its inhabitants. Whatever is sown germinates in a short time, but the ground is not suitable for wheat, which will not form ears. Millet, which among the people replaces wheat, is very abundant. It is found in different colours: white, black, red and blue; however, the flour is entirely white. European flour and wine from the vine, which are needed for the Holy Mass, are imported from Portugal. There is also a great quantity and diversity of fruit and vegetables which are different from ours. There is reason to believe that the seeds of European fruits will grow in these regions. Grapes are only served as a dessert, and the inhabitants make their wine from the palm and make drinks from other fruit. Sugar cane yields well, but they do not know how to make sugar from it. Apart from this, they have a considerable taste for sweetmeats.

They possess an immense quantity of sheep and cattle and other domestic animals of this kind, and also birds of different varieties. The horses and donkeys found there come from Portugal. There are many elephants and 'gonnos' or 'gongos', which are animals peculiar to this kingdom and from which their name derives. They are like horses with two horns and are black and white in colour. They differ little from the 'palanga' in number and size, but they have straight horns.[10] There are also lizards which live in the rivers like crocodiles, and hippopotamuses, or river horses, as big as elephants and sometimes bigger, and which are dangerous on land or in the river.

The black population eat pork throughout the year and also goat meat, which they think has the most agreeable taste. The Kongo people do not know how to milk or how to make butter or cheese. Their sheep do not produce any wool.

The king can mobilize an army of 100,000 Christian men, who offer their services for love of him and from goodwill, without receiving any pay. They maintain themselves at their own expense or at that of their enemies. The king never declares war unless he is first assured that it is just. In this case, after having invoked the Holy Virgin Mary and other saints, he takes up arms, which consist of shields, swords and bows. The king has a guard commanded by four of the principal nobles of the kingdom. Each one of them has under his command four or five thousand men following military discipline.[11] He is never short of soldiers for garrison duty or to go abroad.

At court there are two persons, who are like dukes and occupy the first rank. They are called Mani Vunda and Mani Lau.[12]

The royal revenues consist of slaves, raffia cloth woven with admirable skill, ivory and different skins (which are the principal items of commerce in this region) and of a kind of money particular to this kingdom. The people of Kongo have neither gold nor silver but only copper, deposits of which were discovered in 1594. In the region of Cambambe, in the interior of Angola, it is said there are mountains very rich in silver.

The people of Kongo have no gold or silver money except for pieces that come from Portugal for the purchase of slaves. For a long time they have used as money certain snails or, if one prefers, small shells which are called búzio. Only the inhabitants of the kingdom, and in particular women, are allowed to fish for them along the seashore in accordance with certain regulations.[13] Gold and silver have an inestimable value for them, like a treasure. They are used to make necklaces, rings and other things. They hold frequent markets where there is a brisk trade in the things we have mentioned.

Royal power is bestowed on the son of the king best endowed with judgement and virtue, above all the most pious and most influenced by Christian precepts without any account being taken of whether or not he is the eldest. According to the law of the country, daughters are excluded from the succession. If the king does not leave any son, then the closest [male] relative succeeds. The wife of the king occupies an elevated rank.

According to a very ancient custom, the king only takes as wife a daughter of the duke of Mbata, who according to tradition has the power of confirming the royal power.[14]

There exist neither chronicles nor annals which preserve the memory of past kings. However, certain laws and public ordinances are observed which contribute to the good government of the country.[15] Debts left by the dead are reviewed without any procedure but, after men worthy of trust have given evidence, they are immediately paid. If the dead man has not left anything with which to liquidate his debts, the king himself will indemnify the creditors. In all the territories of his kingdom, the king appoints judges to hear cases according to their mode of procedure and to pronounce judgement according to the inclination of the inhabitants of each region. The inheritance of parents is divided among children in equal portions. The children of the great nobles of the kingdom are educated at Court, which helps to maintain bonds of friendship with their parents.[16]

The king often changes his dress either to show off his wealth or to enhance his royal authority. Sometimes he is seen clothed in the Portuguese manner; at others he has his chest uncovered and is clothed in the manner of the country.

The character of the people is such that violent controversies and altercations are avoided and they love peace and are easily enflamed with the love of God. In the year 1491, in the reign of Dom João II of Portugal, the faith and religion of Christ was brought by the Portuguese to the inhabitants of this kingdom. There is a great lack of evangelical workers in this kingdom and in all the localities in this country, which number about thirty thousand; there are only twenty or thirty priests. As a result there is a very great ignorance of divine matters. Questioned on religion and the faith, the people only reply one thing: 'We have eaten the salt' because, according to the ritual of the Roman Church, one puts a little salt in the mouth of those who are going to be baptized.

These people, otherwise uncivilized, were easily converted to the Catholic faith as soon as it was presented to them. The then king received the name of João, which was that of the king of Portugal.[17] Instructed in the precepts of Christianity, he was baptized after only a short time. He conformed very courageously to Christian law. Afonso I followed in his father's footsteps[18]; Pedro I succeeded him.[19] The fourth king was Diogo[20]; the fifth was Afonso II, to whom succeeded Bernardo I and Álvaro I.[21] At present Álvaro II, the eighth king, is reigning.[22] All the kings have been baptized according to the Catholic rite and, up to the present, have kept the faith and the Christian religion.

Álvaro II has no other matter in his heart but to win others for the Church and to promote the Catholic Church, as is expressed in his titles. He is called Álvaro II 'by the grace of God, promoter of conversion to the faith of Jesus Christ, defender of that faith in the land of Ethiopia, king of the kingdom of Kongo, Angola, Matamba, Ocanga and of the Mbundu and other kingdoms and lordships which have submitted to me on this side and beyond the Zaire'. For this reason the king has issued a severe decree that prohibits the pagans from establishing themselves in his kingdom and has ordered that they remain at a distance of one hundred leagues from the capital of São Salvador.

As the king himself lives according to Christian law, he tries as far as he can to lead his subjects to do the same. When he nominates or appoints any duke or governor, he first orders him to construct a chapel, then to choose a place where the people can receive lessons in the catechism and where children can be initiated into the elements of Christian knowledge. To attain this end, in his own capital of São Salvador he set aside one of the four palaces in his enclosure to instruct and educate the children, intending to establish a kind of seminary there. There books are expounded which treat of pious subjects, notably instruction in Christian doctrine, the Holy Bible, the lives of the saints and other books of this kind translated into Kongolese. However, he could not realize this pious work because of the lack of evangelical workers. The same happened with the Dominican convent which King Diogo had begun, but which he was not able to complete because the absence of the bishop of São Tomé meant that [membership of the] Order could not be conferred on the religious who had been admitted. The king himself had erected various churches, which he had endowed with many gifts and had provided with necessary objects. For their part, the inhabitants had contributed to decorating them.

In São Salvador, for a population of about 10,000 families, there are six or seven churches, of which two are parish churches.[23] The church of the Holy Saviour, built of stone and lime, is quite large. Although the other buildings, except those of the king, are built of straw, they have an elegant appearance. The church which will be the cathedral needs enlarging and repairs.[24] The priest who has the charge of souls there also exercises the office of vicar-general for the bishop of São Tomé. The priests who live there are either blacks or Portuguese, and are all removable at the discretion of the bishop.

The sacristy is sufficiently provided with sacred ornaments and silver vessels for the Mass, which is sometimes sung to the accompaniment of music according to the possibilities that exist in that country. However, there are no organs.

The king assiduously frequents the churches which he has erected and enriched with many gifts. The people who have provided them with furnishing also flock there. They go there in a crowd, and the Holy Offices are celebrated according to the precepts of the Church with as much pomp as is possible. At the times prescribed by the Church, a prescription which the king confirms, everyone goes to confession and receives the Holy Eucharist. They observe the Easter fast very strictly and they fast even before Advent. In this the women are exemplary for, with God's grace, they try to bring them up in piety and prudence.

Money is collected for the needs of the sick, and each one tries to help the poor churches according to his means and to give what can be useful to them. Large gifts and offerings are made on the day of the commemoration of the dead and also on the occasion of the solemnities of Holy Week. They then erect a sepulchre in the church. The Blessed Sacrament is exposed on a large altar surrounded by numerous lights and receives the prayers and adoration of the faithful.

The emoluments received by the priests are quite large. Each year the king collects a tithe for them in the country and himself makes gifts from his personal revenues. The king gives one of the nobles the job of looking after the construction, maintenance and ornamentation of the churches. Each noble has his own oratory, sufficiently decorated and, as a result, in each town and city there are many oratories dedicated to God. Public prayers take place according to the season of the year or for particular reasons.

Marriages are conducted according to our custom, publicly before the door of the church with the word, as one says, de praesenti.[25] Men give a dowry[26] to their wives, and when the king gives one of his daughters in marriage to a son of one of the chief nobles who have submitted to him, he endows them richly. It is not allowed among them to marry women of the same blood.

The king himself has had his name inscribed [as a member of] the most pious confraternities, and each year he is elected president of one of them. He personally carries out certain acts of piety as if he were an ordinary person. There are six confraternities, namely the Holy Sacrament, Misericórdia, the Immaculate Conception, the Rosary, the Holy Spirit and Saint Anthony of Padua.

This very Christian king does not seek the friendship of any heathen monarch but greatly desires the friendship of all Christian kings.

The Kongolese have a great devotion for the holy city of Rome, where are the tombs of the holy apostles Peter and Paul and where the Supreme Pontiff, the head of the Christian world, resides, and equally for the holy places of Jerusalem, out of love for Christ Our Lord, who lived and died there.

Following the example of the king, those who have embraced the Christian religion have discarded their old customs and live in a manner which the Portuguese greatly admire.

Here, Your Eminence, you will find what I have learned about the kingdom of Kongo for its recently nominated bishop. I have received this information from the ambassador of the king and other witnesses worthy of trust. It only remains for God to grant this very Christian king of Kongo and all his kingdom, increase in their faith and to bring to the new prelate, prosperity and the strength to spread the seed of the word of God, and to safeguard his health and his life.

Notes

1   At this stage, the king of Kongo still claimed sovereignty over Luanda Island and all the provinces to the north.
2   This probably refers to the victories won by Paulo Dias de Novais over the Ngola in 1585 and 1586.
3   The kingdom of Matamba was in the region known as the Baixa de Cassanje and in the sixteenth century was briefly made tributary to the kingdom of Kongo.
4   Dom Álvaro II (Mpanzu Nimi), who reigned from 1587 to 1614.
5   Okanga was a state on the northeast borders of Kongo beyond the Cuango River.
6   Sometimes written Ambundos, this was the Dembos mountain region of modern Angola, immediately to the south of the core provinces of Kongo.
7   See Doc. 28. Usually only the first three of these were described as duchies.
8   This list of provinces is problematic. It does not, for example, include the provinces of Sonyo, Mpangu and Mpemba – probably because they were ruled over by 'counts', not 'dukes'.
9   The width of the Zaire at its mouth is 9.8 kilometres.
10 The *palanca negra* was the name used to describe the Giant Sable antelope. The *gongos* were presumably the ordinary sable.
11 The core of Kongo armies consisted of a relatively small body of well-armed and well-trained soldiers, who would be supplemented by much larger number of provincial levies.
12 The Mani Lau was the ruler of Mbata – the Nsaku Lau was the ruling dynasty of Mbata (see Doc. 28). There is some dispute whether the Nsaka ne Vunda or Mani Vunda was the *kitome* (head of the territorial cult) of Mbanza Kongo or merely an official of the Court appointed by the Manikongo. He was one of the nobles who traditionally selected the new Manikongo and personally installed the newly elected monarch. The Mani Vunda at the end of the fifteenth century had been sent to Portugal as an ambassador.
13 Luanda was one of the most important fisheries and it control was therefore much contested between the Portuguese and the king of Kongo. See also Docs. 13, 26 and 32.
14 See Doc. 28.
15 Compare Doc. 53.

16 European-style schools had been established by Afonso I, and literacy in the Portuguese language and knowledge of Christian doctrine were important components of the education provided.
17 João I (Nzinga Nkuwu), d. 1506.
18 Afonso I (Mbemba Nzinga), 1506–43.
19 Pedro I (Nkanga Mbembe, 1543–4.
20 Diogo I, 1545–61.
21 Bernardo I, 1561–7; Álvaro I (Nimi Lukeni), 1568–87. The author has omitted Henrique I, who ruled from 1567 to 1568 (see Doc. 38).
22 Álvaro II (Mpanzu Nimi), 1587–1614.
23 According to the *ad limina* visitation of 1640, there were eight churches dedicated as follows: Santiago Maior, Nossa Senhora do Rosário, Conceição, Santa Cruz, São João Batista, São Miguel, Santa Isabel (the Misericórdia church) and Nossa Senhora da Vitória.
24 The Cathedral was served by twelve canons.
25 A marriage contracted *per verba de praesenti* was a verbal contract of marriage considered binding in law.
26 In Africa this should be understood as bride price.

---

56 THE LAWS AND CUSTOMS OF THE WOLOFS

From André Donelha, *Descrição da Serra Leoa e dos Rios de Guiné do Cabo Verde*, A.Teixeira da Mota and P. E. H. Hair, eds. (Lisbon, 1977), pp. 128–30.
Translated by Malyn Newitt.

Donelha's account of the Wolof kingdom of the Senegal region refers to the presence of European traders, who by this time included French as well as Portuguese. He mentions the New Christian (Jewish) community of traders, which is well attested from other sources, and he also refers to the religious co-existence characteristic of the trading communities and which, he says, was insisted upon by the king. He also describes the situation that prevailed when one of the European traders died. As 'strangers' in the land their property belonged to the ruler, and so the custom arose of hiding some of the valuables so that they would not be seized. For another account of the problems that ensued on the death of a European, see Doc. 47.

The Wolof[1] kingdom is large and powerful. The king's title is the Grand Jalofo.[2] The people are very warlike and are brave horsemen and very skilful riders. His army is made up of both horsemen and foot soldiers. Their defensive armour is made of very long lengths of cotton cloth, twisted as much as possible, which they employ only for this purpose. They wrap these around them from the waist to below the arm, so that they protect the belly, chest and back, and they are so tough that no arrow or spear can pierce them. They wear cotton shirts with wide necks on top of this armour, and they carry shields of buffalo hide, which are so tough that neither arrows nor spears can penetrate them. Their trousers are made of many lengths of cloth which are short and do not come below the knees but are folded at the waist with many pleats. For offensive weapons, the horsemen carry seven small barbed spears and a large spear like a short lance called a *tala*. After throwing the little spears, which they call *chemcherem*, they keep the *tala* in their hand, like a lance, and with this they fight to the death. The foot soldiers carry spears, shields and arrows.

Those Wolofs were formerly heathens but adopted the law of Mohammed[3] less than eighty years ago. Portuguese Jews[4] and Christians, who go there as adventurers to trade, live in his kingdom, as well as Frenchmen, but the king will not permit them to argue about whose laws[5] are the best. He declares that each person must please himself and live according to the law he accepts. If there is any quarrelling in his kingdom they will be punished. Whenever a Christian adventurer, a Jew, or a Frenchman dies, the king is his heir. So, when one of them falls seriously ill, the governor,[6] who is called *falfa*, immediately has his house surrounded and places a guard on it, so that nothing can be taken. The houses of both the whites and the blacks who live in these ports are built on the sand and [are constructed] of wood and are covered inside with hides. The tangomaos bury all their property, including wine and other goods, in the sand because of the greed of the blacks.

The principal trade consists of hides, wax, ivory and some gold, but if a ship went there from this island with a cargo of horses, as formerly four or five ships used to go, slaves and other goods could be loaded there. Both men and women wear Moorish shoes and go about well dressed.

Here the nephew, who is the son of the sister and not of the brother, inherits and the sister must be sister through the mother, not through the father.

Notes

1   Donelha calls them Jalofos.
2   At the time that Donelha was writing (1625), there were two Wolof kingdoms. This reference to a single kingdom reflects a situation that may have existed in the sixteenth century. See Docs. 7, 10 and 19.
3   It appears that some of the Wolofs were already Muslim in the fifteenth century.

4   Hair (p. 283, note 212) suggests that this is a specific reference to the New Christian trading community at Porto de Ale and Rufisque. For the Jewish community of this region, see Richard L. Kagan and Philip D. Morgan, *Atlantic Diasporas* (Baltimore, 2009) pp. 172–8.
5   The word used is *lei* but this should be understood as law in the sense of religious law.
6   Donelha uses the Portuguese term *alcaide*.

57   BLACK ANTS, TANGOMAOS AND THE BAGAS

From André Donelha, *Descrição da Serra Leoa e dos Rios de Guiné do Cabo Verde*, A. Teixeira da Mota and P. E. H. Hair, eds. (Lisbon, 1977), pp. 96–8. Translated by Malyn Newitt.

Donelha's account dramatizes the barbarity which a 'civilized' Cape Verdian attributed to the Africans of the Guinea coast. The Baga people lived along the coast of modern Guinea and Guinea–Bissau, and were active in the seaborne trade of the region. The juxtaposition of the account of the bagabagas *and Bagas may not have been merely incidental – the former being a metaphor for human social interaction, as well as a description of the insect world.*

There are two kinds of ants – black ones which live in holes under the ground and in the trunks of trees, and red ones called *bagabagas*.[1] Their houses are made of earth all mixed together, which rise ten or fifteen hand breadths above the ground. In some parts there are so many of these mounds that, from the sea, those who have not been to Guinea easily mistake them for groups of houses or villages. The ants live inside these mounds. In the middle there is a large chamber for their king who never leaves it. The blacks are said to eat the king of these ants, which is as long as a thumb. The rest of them are all the same and they are larger than the black ants. There is constant warfare and in the open the black ones have the advantage and usually emerge victorious, but the *bagabagas* are able to put up a good defence in and around their houses. If the ants manage to get into a food store they fill it up with earth in half an hour, ruining most of it and carrying the rest to their houses. In this way they can ruin many measures so that the tangomaos place charcoal under any room or store containing food to prevent the ants from getting in. One of the greatest punishments that kings inflict on witches or robbers is to place them alive, bound hand and foot, in one of the *bagabaga* mounds and within an hour their flesh will be consumed and only cleaned bones will be left.

. . . .

Cape Verga is low-lying and extends some way out into the sea. The Bagas,[2] who are ill clothed, are to be found near there. The land is flat and marshy and they make salt by boiling [sea water] on a fire. Ships are loaded with dyestuffs, which are the main item of trade and are taken to the São Domingos river. There is also some commerce in slaves, rice, wax, ivory, cola and some gold, which comes from the Sosos.[3] Their weapons are spears and shields, but they are a cowardly, treacherous people. They are not cannibals but they drink wine out of a human skull, and they cut off heads and remove them to make drinking vessels. If the head is that of a white man or a Christian black or some nobleman or lord of the land who they killed, such drinking vessels are more valued and they are displayed at public feasts. The man most honoured is the one with most drinking vessels and if their treachery is successful and they kill someone from behind in an ambush along the road or from behind a tree or in front if there are many of them, they immediately cut off the head and then strut around like a gentleman and afterwards are more honoured and respected.[4] They eat rice, *funde*,[5] mangroves[6] – which they cure like lupines under the mud in rivers – fish, oysters, palm wine and large quantities of other fruits and vegetables.

Notes

1   This is the standard Crioulo term for termites. The different colours describe the different soils in which they build their nests.
2   People speaking the Baga language still inhabit this area.
3   The Soso were the people who lived inland to the south of the Bagas.
4   Hair refers to this as the 'skull dance' of the Bagas (Donelha, p. 243, note 122).
5   *Funde* is Digitaria Exilis 'hungry rice'.
6   Apparently a reference to *tarrafe*, a sort of tamarisk which grows in salt water.

GLOSSARY

alçada: ambulatory tribunal which might be sent to do justice in a certain region.

alcaide-mor: governor of a town or fortress.

almadia: canoe.

arrátel: unit of weight equivalent to about 1 pound.

arrematadores: contractors for the Guinea slave trade.

arroba: unit of weight equivalent to 15 kilograms.

asiento: the contract to supply slaves to Spanish America.

azulejos: glazed wall tiles.

bambalou: a kind of drum used by look outs in the trees to sound the alarm at the approach of raiders.

bexerins: also *bixerim* and *bicherin* from Arabic el-Mubecherin. Itinerant preachers, 'Moors of Barbary call cacizes' (Álvares).

braça: unit of length of approximately 2 metres.

búzio (casis tuberosa): species of cowry found in west Africa and used as currency.

cabeça: literally 'head', but used for a ruler or chief minister.

cabondos: women who assumed the role of temporary wives for traders and other 'strangers' in west African society.

cantara: the same as an **alqueire** or 13.8 litres.

capellão-mor: principal chaplain of the king of Kongo.

capitão-mor: captain-major; title of Portuguese military commanders.

cavaco: more commonly **cavaquinho**, a small stringed instrument with four strings.

cobetes (cumbetes): storehouses for trade goods with earthen roofs made to resist fire.

cori: beads made of a blue-coloured stone, manufactured in the Kongo region and used in west African trade.

corregedor: royal official who had authority to enter any town or jurisdiction to safeguard the Crown's interests.

cristãos novos: New Christians; used for Jews who converted to Christianity.

dobra: gold coins minted in Morocco and Castile. Monetary reform in Portugal led to the minting of *escudos* in 1435–6 with a parity with the **dobra**.

Dom: lord; title of all noblemen and of the kings of Portugal and Kongo.

em fatiota: leases which could be inherited.

empacaseiro (Kimbundu: mpakasa): buffalo hunter; used for light troops in the Angolan wars.

escrivão da puridade: the king's private secretary.

Espanha: Spain; this term was frequently used for the whole Iberian peninsula including Portugal.

Estado da Índia: the name given to the Portuguese empire east of the Cape of Good Hope.

Feitiço: 'sorcery' literally 'magic' or 'sorcery'' in Portuguese, describes a wide range of traditional African religious objects and practices equated with sorcery or witchcraft. English 'fetish' derives from it.

fidalgo (filho de algo): gentleman or member of the lesser nobility.

foral: formal document which sets out the legal rights and privileges of a town or an institution.

funde (digitaria exilis): a species of rice known as 'hungry rice'.

grumetes: servants of the Afro-Portuguese traders in Guinea; often used for sailors.

guerra preta: black soldiers in Portuguese service.

Infante: title of Portuguese princes.

kanda: matrilineal descent groups in the kingdom of Kongo.

kilombo: see **quilombo**.

kitome: head of a territorial-based cult in Kongo and Ndongo.

lançado: Portuguese living among Africans.

lascar: sailors usually of Indian origin (Persian: *lashkar*).

Lei Mental: decree of Dom Duarte by which grants of Crown lands had to be confirmed at the start of each reign and would revert to the Crown in the absence of a male heir.

língua: interpreter.

mabus (Kimbundu: dibu): papyrus reeds.

maleficium: witchcraft or black magic.

manilha: copper or brass rings, like bracelets or anklets, used as trade currency in western Africa.

mbanza: principal town of a Kongo ruler.

meirinho: bailiff.

Mesa da Consciência: branch of the Royal Council which dealt with the ecclesiastical affairs of the Crown and with the Military Orders.

milho: a general term used for 'grain'.

milho zaburro: sorghum.

mocambo: community of escaped slaves in São Tomé.

morador: settler; used usually for Portuguese who had the status of *casado* or married man.

morgado: entailed estate.

Mouros de paz: Moors who had submitted peacefully to Portuguese overlordship.

nau: carrack; large multidecked Portuguese ship used on the *carreira da Índia*.

nkisi: used in Kongo for images or objects (sometimes people) which were possessed of spiritual power.

nominas: amulets.

nzimbu: currency shells.

outeiro: hill; name given by the Portuguese to the city of São Salvador.

ouvidor: judge.

padrão: stone pillar surmounted by a cross and the arms of Portugal placed on prominent sites on the African coast to aid navigation and establish Portuguese sovereignty.

padroado real: the Portuguese Crown's right of patronage over the church.

peça da Índia: units of account in the slave trade, equivalent of one adult male slave.

planalto: plateau; especially the Angolan plateau in the hinterland of Benguela.

pombeiro: African trader frequenting the fairs in the interior of Angola.

praça: garrisoned stronghold.

presídio: name given to any Portuguese settlement where there was a garrison of soldiers.

privado: royal secretary.

quilombo (Umbundu: ocilombo): fortified camp where war rituals initiating warriors were carried out. In Brazil, used for settlements of escaped slaves. Also written **kilombo**.

quinta: country farm or estate.

real (reis): Portuguese coin and unit of currency. One **cruzado** was 400 **reis**.

Reconquista: the reconquest of the Iberian peninsular from the Moors.

regimento: official instructions drawn up to govern the conduct of office holders and military and naval commanders.

reino: kingdom; applied to Angola, which was declared a separate 'kingdom' of the Crown of Portugal.

resgatar: to ransom or redeem. Term often used for the purchase of slaves.

scudo d'oro: Florentine coin worth 1.26 ducats.

Senado da Câmara: town council.

sertão: interior or backlands.

sesmaria: waste land. Land which could be leased for cultivation under the terms of the *Lei das Sesmarias*.

sisa: sales tax.

soba: title used to designate minor African rulers in Angola.

sotaalmirante: a subaltern admiral; might be translated as vice-admiral.

stara: or *setier* as a measure of wheat was the equivalent of 152 litres.

tangomao: Portuguese-speaking adventurers and merchants, who resided in Guinea, against the orders of the crown, and who established families there.

tendella do Reyno: official interpreter in Angola.

terço: regiment.

trasado: a kind of African sword.

urca: medieval cargo ships.

BIBLIOGRAPHY

Abulafia, David, *The Discovery of Mankind* (New Haven and London, 2008).
Albuquerque, Luís de, *Introdução à História dos Descobrimentos Portugueses* (Lisbon, 1980).
Dúvidas e Certezas na História dos Descobrimentos Portugueses (Lisbon, 1990).
Andrade, Elisa Silva, *Les Îles du Cap Vert de la Découverte à l'Indépendance Nationale (1460–1975)* (Paris, 1996).
Anon [um pilôto Português], *Viagem de Lisboa a Ilha de S. Tomé*, Augusto Reis Machado, ed. (Lisbon, 1960).
Balandier, Georges, *Daily Life in the Kingdom of Congo* (London, 1968).
Ballong-Wen-Mewuda, J. Bato'ora, *São Jorge da Mina 1482–1637* (Lisbon/Paris, 1993).
Barradas de Carvalho, Joaquim, *Á la Recherche de la Spécificité de la Renaissance Portugaise*, 2 vols. (Paris, 1983).
Bentley Duncan, T., *Atlantic Islands* (Chicago, 1972).
Bethencourt, Francisco, and Kirti, Chaudhuri eds., *História da Expansão Portuguesa*, 5 vols. (Lisbon, 1998).
Birmingham, David, *Trade and Conflict in Angola* (Oxford, 1966).
'Central Africa from Cameroun to the Zambesi', in *Cambridge History of Africa*, vol. IV (Cambridge, 1975), pp. 325–83.
Blackburn, Robin, *The Making of New World Slavery* (London, 1997).
Blake, J. W., ed., *Europeans in West Africa*, 2 vols. (London, Hakluyt Society, 1942).
Bovill, E. W., *The Golden Trade of the Moors*, 2nd edition (Oxford, 1968).
Boxer, C. R., *Salvador da Sá and the Struggle for Brazil and Angola, 1602–1686* (London, 1952).
Boxer, C. R., 'Uma Relação Inédita e Contemporânea da Batalha de Ambuila em 1665', in *Boletim Cultural do Museu de Angola* (Luanda), 2 (1960), pp. 65–73.
Brooks, George E., *Eurafricans in Western Africa* (Oxford, 2003).
Carletti, Francesco, *Voyage autour du monde*, F. Verrier, trans. (Paris, 1999).
My Voyage Around the World, H. Weinstock, ed. (London, 1965).
Cook, Weston F., *The Hundred Years War for Morocco* (Boulder, 1994).
Crone, G. R., ed., *The Voyages of Cadamosto* (London, Hakluyt Society, 1937).
Curtin, Philip, *The Atlantic Slave Trade: A Census* (Madison, 1969).
Diffie, Bailey W., and George D. Winius, *Foundations of the Portuguese Empire 1415–1580* (Oxford, 1977).
Garfield, Robert, *A History of São Tomé Island 1470–1655* (San Francisco, 1992).
Godinho, Vitorino de Magalhães, *A Economia dos Descobrimentos Henriquinos* (Lisbon, 1962).
Gonçalves, António Custódio, *A História Revisitada do Kongo e de Angola* (Lisbon, 2005).
Hair, P. E. H., 'Discovery and Discoveries: the Portuguese in Guinea 1444–1650', *Bulletin of Hispanic Studies*, 69 (1992), pp. 11–28.
The Founding of the Castello de São Jorge da Mina: and Analysis of the Sources (Madison, 1994).

Havik, Philip J., *Silences and soundbytes: the gendered dynamics of trade and brokerage in the pre-colonial Guinea Bissau region* (Münster, 2004).

Havik, Philip and Newitt, Malyn, eds., *Creole Societies in the Portuguese Colonial Empire* (Bristol, 2007).

Heintze, Beatrix, *Fontes para a História de Angola do século XVII* (Stuttgart, 1985).

Heywood, Linda, and John Thornton, *Central Africans, Atlantic Creoles, and the Foundation of the Americas, 1585–1660* (Cambridge, 2007).

Hilton, Anne, *The Kingdom of Kongo* (Oxford: Clarendon Press, 1985).

Jadin, Louis, *Relations sur le Congo et l'Angola tirées des archives de la Compagnie de Jésus, 1621–1631*, Academia Belgica (Rome, 1968) extract from *Bulletin d e l'Institut historique belge de Rome*, 39 (1968), pp. 333–54.

Kagan, Richard L., and Philip D. Morgan, *Atlantic Diasporas* (Baltimore, 2009).

Letts, Malcolm, ed. and trans., *The Diary of Jörg von Ehingen* (London, 1929).

Lomax, D., and R. J. Oakley, eds., *The English in Portugal 1367–87* (Warminster, 1988).

Lopes, David, *A Expansão em Marrocos* (Lisbon, n.d.).

Mark, Peter, *'Portuguese' Style and Luso-African Identity. Precolonial Senegambia, Sixteenth-Nineteenth Centuries* (Bloomington, 2002).

Martyn, J. R. C., *The Siege of Mazagão* (New York, 1994).

Massing, Andreas, 'The Mane, the decline of Mali and Mandinka expansion towards the South Windward Coast', *Cahiers d'Etudes Afriaines*, 25 (1985), pp. 21–55.

Miller, Joseph, *Kings and Kinsmen: Early Mbundu States in Angola* (Oxford: Clarendon Press, 1976).

Monteiro, João Gouveia, *A Guerra em Portugal nos Finais da Idade Média* (Lisbon, 1998).

Nafafé, José Lingna, *Colonial Encounters: Issues of Cuture, Hybridity and Creolisation*, (Frankfurt am Main, 2007).

Newitt, Malyn, 'Prince Henry and the Origins of Portuguese Expansion', in M. Newitt, ed., *The First Portuguese Colonial Empire* (Exeter, 1986), pp. 9–36.

'Formal and Informal Empire in the History of Portuguese Expansion', *Portuguese Studies*, 17 (2001), pp. 2–21.

A History of Portuguese Overseas Expansion 1400–1668 (London, 2005).

Nowell, Charles E., 'The Treaty of Tordesillas and the Diplomatic Background of American History', in *Greater America: Essays in Honour of Herbert Eugene Bolton* (Berkeley, 1945), pp. 1–18.

'Prince Henry the Navigator and his Brother Dom Pedro', *Hispanic American Historical Review*, 28 (1948), pp. 62–7.

Oliveira e Costa, João Paulo, 'D.Afonso V e o Atlântico a base do projecto expansionista de D.João II', *Mare Liberum*, 17 (1999), pp. 39–71.

Oliveira Marques, A. H. de, *History of Portugal*, 2 vols. (New York, 1972).

A Expansão Quatrocentista, vol. II of *Nova História da Expansão Portuguesa* (Lisbon,1998).

Parreira, Adriano , *Dicionário de Biografias Angolanas séculos XV-XVII* (Luanda, 2003)

Pereira, Duarte Pacheco, *Esmeraldo de Situ Orbis*, G. T. Kimble, ed., (London, Hakluyt Society, 1937).

Penrose, Boies, *Travel and Discovery in the Renaissance* (Harvard University Press, 1952).

Phillips, J. R. S., *The Medieval Expansion of Europe* (Oxford, 1988).

Pimentel, Maria do Rosário, 'O escravo negro na sociedade portuguesa até meados do século XVI', in *Congresso Internacional Bartolomeu Dias e a sua Época*, vol. IV (Porto, 1989), pp. 165–77.

Radulet, Carmen M., *O Crónista Rui de Pina e a 'Relação do Reino do Congo'*, Mare Liberum (Lisbon, 1992).

'Os Italianos nas rotas do comércio oriental (1500–1580)', in Arturo Teodoro de Matos and Luís Filipe Thomaz, eds., 'A Carreira da Índia e as Rotas dos Estreitos', *Actas do VIII Seminário Internacional de História Indo-Portuguesa* (Angra do Heroísmo, 1998), pp. 257–2.

Rodney, Walter, *A History of the Upper Guinea Coast, 1545–1800* (Oxford: Clarendon Press, 1970).

Rodrigues, Vitor Luís Pinto Gaspar da Conceição, 'A Guiné nas cartas de perdão (1463–1500), *Congresso Internacional Bartolomeu Dias e a sua Época*, vol. IV (Porto, 1989), pp. 397–412.

Russell, P. E., *English Intervention in Spain and Portugal in the Time of Edward III and Richard II* (Oxford: Clarendon Press, 1955).

'Prince Henry the Navigator', *Diamante*, XI, (1960).

'Castilian documentary Sources for the History of the Portuguese Expansion in Guinea in the last years of the Reign of Dom Afonso V', in P. E. Russell, *Portugal, Spain and the African Atlantic 1343–1490* (Aldershot, 1995).

Prince Henry' the Navigator'. A Life (New Haven, 2000).

Ryder, Alan, *Benin and the Europeans* (Harlow, 1969).

Sanceau, Elaine, *The Perfect Prince* (Porto, 1959).

Sansi-Roca, Roger, 'The Fetish in the Lusophone Atlantic', in Nancy Naro, Roger Sansi-Roca and David Treece, eds., *Cultures of the Lusophone Black Atlantic* (Basingstoke, 2007), pp. 19–39.

Saunders, A. C. de C. M., *A Social History of Black Slaves and Freedmen in Portugal 1441–1555* (Cambridge, 1982).

Scammell, G. V., *The World Encompassed* (London, 1981).

Seibert, Gerhard, *Comrades, Clients and Cousins. Colonialism, Socialism and Democratizaion in São Tomé and Príncipe* (Leiden, 1999).

'Castaways, Autochthons, or Maroons? The debate on the Angolares of São Tomé Island', in Philip J. Havik and Malyn Newitt, eds., *Creole Societies in the Portuguese Colonial Empire* (Bristol, 2007), pp. 103–26.

Sousa Pinto, Paulo Jorge de, 'Em torno de um problema de identidade os "Jagas" na História do Congo e Angola', *Mare Liberum*, 18–19 (1999–2000), pp. 193–243.

Thomas, Hugh, *The Slave Trade* (London, 1997).

Thornton, John, *Africa and Africans in the Making of the Atlantic World, 1400–1800* (Cambridge, 1992).

Warfare in Atlantic Africa 1500–1800 (London, 1999).

'The Origins and Early History of the Kingdom of Kongo', *The International Journal of African Historical Studies*, 34 (2001), pp. 89–120.

'Elite Women in the kingdom of Kongo: Historical Perspectives on Women's Political Power', *Journal of Africa History*, 47 (2006), pp. 437–60.

Sources from which the Texts Are Taken

Álvares, Manuel S. J. *Etiópia Menor e Descripção Géografica da Província da Serra Leoa*, A.Teixeira da Mota and Luís de Matos, eds., and P. E. H. Hair, trans. (unpublished; copy in SOAS Library).

Azurara, Gomes Eannes de, *The Chronicle of the Discovery and Conquest of Guinea*, Beazley, C. R ., and E. Prestage, eds., 2 vols. (London, Hakluyt Society, 1896).

Azurara, Gomes Eannes de, and José, de Bragança eds., *Crónica de Guiné* (Lisbon, 1937).

Azurara, Gomes Eannes de , *Crónica da Tomada de Ceuta* (Lisbon, 1992).

Azurara, Gomes Eannes de, Léon Bourdon, trans., *Chronique de Guinée (1453)* (Paris, 1994).

Brásio, António , *Monumenta Missionaria Africana*, vols. I and II (Lisbon, 1952).

Cadornega, António de Oliveira, *História Geral das Guerras Angolanas*, 3 vols. (Lisbon, 1972).

Caldeira, Arlindo Manuel, ed., *Viagens de um pilôto português do século XVI à costa de África e a São Tomé* (Lisbon, 2000).

Caddeo, Rinaldo, ed., *Le Navigazioni Atlantiche di Alvise da Cá da Mosto* (Milan, 1929), in *Viagens de Luís de Cadamosto e de Pedro de Sintra, Academia Portuguesa de História* (Lisbon, 1948).

Carletti, Francesco, *Ragionamenti del mio viaggio intorno al mondo*, ed., G. Cardona et Bertolucci (Rome, 1992).

Cenival, Pierre de, ed., *Les Sources Inédites de l'Histoire du Maroc: Archives et Bibliothèques de Portugal, Tome I (1486–1516)* (Paris, 1934).

Cuvelier, J., and Jadin, L., eds., *L'Ancien Congo d'aprés les archives romaines* (Brussels, 1954).

Donelha, André, *Descrição da Serra Leoa e dos Rios de Guiné do Cabo Verde*, A. Teixeira da Mota and P. E. H. Hair, eds. (Lisbon, 1977).

Ehingen, Georg von, *Reisen nach der Ritterschaft*, Gabriele Ehrmann, ed. (Göppingen, 1979).

Fernandes, Valentim, *Description de la Côte Occidentale d'Afrique (Sénégal au Cap de Monte, Archipels)*, Th. Monod, A. Teixeira da Mota and R. Mauny, eds. and trans. (Bissau: Centro de Estudos da Guiné Portuguesa, 1951).

Hutchinson, M., ed., *A Report of the Kingdom of Congo and of the Surrounding Countries* (London, 1881).

Pereira, Duarte Pacheco, *Esmeraldo de Situ Orbis*, Damião Peres, ed. (Lisbon, 1988).

Pigafetta, Filippo, *Relatione del Reame di Congo et delli circonvicine contrade tratta dalli scritti & ragionamenti di Odoardo Lopez Portoghese*, Grassi (Rome, 1591).

Pigafetta, Filippo and Lopes, Duarte, *Relação do Reino do Congo e das Terras Circunvizinhas* (Lisbon, 1989).

Pina, Rui de, *Crónica de El-Rey D. João II*, edited by Alberto Martins de Carvalho, Atlântida (Coimbra, 1950).

Ravenstein, E. G., ed., *The Strange Adventures of Andrew Battell of Leigh* (London, Hakluyt Society, 1901).

INDEX